The Next Religious
Establishment

American Intellectual Culture

Series Editors: Jean Bethke Elshtain, University of Chicago,
Ted V. McAllister, Pepperdine University, Wilfred M. McClay,
University of Tennessee at Chattanooga

The books in the American Intellectual Culture series examine the place, identity, and public role of intellectuals and cultural elites in the United States, past, present, and future. Written by prominent historians, philosophers, and political theorists, these books will examine the influence of intellectuals on American political, social, and cultural life, paying particular attention to the characteristic forms, and evolving possibilities, of democratic intellect. The books will place special, but not exclusive, emphasis on the relationship between intellectuals and American public life. Because the books are intended to shape and contribute to scholarly and public debates about their respective topics, they will be concise, accessible, and provocative.

When All the Gods Trembled: Darwinism, Scopes, and American Intellectuals
   by Paul K. Conkin, Vanderbilt University
Heterophobia: Sexual Harassment and the Future of Feminism
   by Daphne Patai, University of Massachusetts at Amherst
Postmodernism Rightly Understood: The Return to Realism in American Thought
   by Peter Augustine Lawler, Berry College
A Requiem for the American Village
   by Paul K. Conkin
A Pragmatist's Progress? Richard Rorty and American Intellectual History
   by John Pettegrew, Lehigh University
The Next Religious Establishment
   by Eldon J. Eisenach, University of Tulsa
A World Made Safe for Differences: Cold War Intellectuals and the Politics of Identity
   by Christopher Shannon, the George Eastman House

Forthcoming Titles:
Modern Inconvenience: The Social Origins of Antifamily Thought
   by Elisabeth Lasch-Quinn, Syracuse University
Academic Politics: The Colonial Colleges and the Shaping of American Intellectual Culture
   by J. David Hoeveler, University of Wisconsin, Milwaukee
History and Public Memory in America
   by Wilfred M. McClay, University of Tennessee at Chattanooga
Ralph Waldo Emerson and the Problem of Democracy
   by Peter S. Field, Tennessee Technological University
The Murder of Joy: Paul Goodman and the American Battle over Maturity
   by Robert Oliver, University of Wisconsin, Madison
The Public and Protagonist: Tocqueville and American Intellectuals, 1835–2000
   by Matthew Mancini, Southwest Missouri State University

The Next Religious Establishment

National Identity and Political Theology in Post-Protestant America

Eldon J. Eisenach

ROWMAN & LITTLEFIELD PUBLISHERS, INC.
Lanham • Boulder • New York • Oxford

ROWMAN & LITTLEFIELD PUBLISHERS, INC.

Published in the United States of America
by Rowman & Littlefield Publishers, Inc.
4720 Boston Way, Lanham, Maryland 20706
http://www.rowmanlittlefield.com

12 Hid's Copse Road
Cumnor Hill, Oxford OX2 9JJ, England

British Library Cataloguing in Publication Information Available

Library of Congress Cataloging-in-Publication Data

Eisenach, Eldon J.
    The next religious establishment : national identity and political theology in
post-Protestant America / Eldon J. Eisenach.
        p.   cm.
    Includes bibliographical references and index.
    ISBN 0-8476-9618-9 (cloth : alk. paper) — ISBN 0-8476-9619-7 (pbk. : alk. paper)
        1. Religion and politics—United States.   2. Church and state—United States.
    3. Nationalism—Religious aspects.   4. United States—Religion.   I. Title.

    BL2525 .E415   2000
    322'.1'0973—dc21   99-056786

Printed in the United States of America

∞™ The paper used in this publication meets the minimum requirements of American
National Standard for Information Sciences—Permanence of
Paper for Printed Library Materials, ANSI/NISO Z39.48-1992.

*To my students in American Political Thought
for their patience, resistance, and encouragement.*

Contents

Preface

I have written this book because I fear for the future of my country and for the direction of its higher intellectual life. These fears are related because high intellectual culture provides the framework and much of the vocabulary within which we interpret ourselves and our experiences. Our philosophical, religious, moral, and political discourse are "moral orientations," and it is from within these horizons that we shape our individual and our collective self-understandings. In Charles Taylor's words, "We are selves only in that certain issues matter for us. What I am as a self, my identity, is essentially defined by the way things have significance for me."[1] We do not "choose" these orientations; they are our very condition because "it belongs to human agency to exist in a space of questions about strongly valued goods, prior to all choice or adventitious culture changes."[2]

What we can choose is to explore and become articulate in the "moral sources" that constitute our shared moral orientations. We can choose to discover what possibilities they intimate and what shortcomings they hold in clarifying and enriching our common experiences and purposes. This is a creative and a critical task. And while this task falls to each of us in our personal and daily lives, most of us carry it out secondhand in our social and public lives, relying on intellectuals to frame the discussion and political and cultural leaders to embody moral orientations in institutions and practices. Here is where my fears for the American intellect enter. I fear that contemporary moral and political discourse at its most articulate has become so divorced from our experiences as to become incomprehensible and even pathological. Universalistic, formal, cosmopolitan, abstract, and rights-obsessed, this discourse not only seems to deny that we are a particular people—a nation—it also constrains or brackets what can legitimately be publicly stated, so that fewer and fewer Americans feel competent to speak at all. The principled high ground of this formal liberal theory not only limits our possibilities of occupying a common ground, it also condemns all consensually created and substantive common ground (like patriotism) as unjust on its face

ix

because it lacks the legitimating requirement of universality. Its epistemic requirements have come to translate standards of legitimate public speech into a kind of Hobbesian imperial tyranny,[3] adjudicating the terms and the discourse allowable by lesser beings mired in the provinces of particular commitments and prejudices, be they ethnic, religious, sexual, or regional.

This is where my fears for our country enter. Make no mistake, this epistemic empire requires an "overclass" of emperors (and their court philosophers), those who claim to live on this high plane of principle and neutrality. Along with Michael Lind, Stanley Fish, and others,[4] I see both a philosophical and a political connection between "democratic universalism" and a principled multiculturalism that leaves no space for a common American nationality. Multiculturalism as a principle and not as a set of concrete facts and historical struggles requires that we view America as an aggregate of separate tribes or autonomous cultures. This portrait must then include governance by imperial rule if the tribes are not to be at each other's throats. Adjudicators, speaking a language not native to any particular tribe, must ensure that each tribe thinks it is being treated equally. More worrisome to me, however, is that this same class of rulers must also decide what constitutes a tribe and who belongs to each, and designate official spokespersons to speak for each grouping. Imperial rule is centralized and uniform rule. When the law speaks, all must bow down. Under these conditions, one can only hope that the law says very little, because, in this logic, where the law is silent we are "free." But as government becomes more and more intrusive, the law has occupied more and more space called "public," and in that space, only its language and principles can reign. The ideal public square should not only be stripped of formal religion, it should ban all expressed experiences and meanings that cannot be reduced to a universal denominator.

There are two ways to subvert this system of philosophical and political rule. The philosophical subversion is to deconstruct the legitimating language of the overclass, to reveal it as the patois of another, albeit very powerful, tribe with its own narrative identity, substantive commitments, and political agenda. A political subversion would support this philosophical one. This would occur when the allegedly separated tribes refuse to act and think within tribal boundaries but step "out of doors" to shape a language in common with other tribes.[5] By coming to occupy a common cultural and moral ground outside the high ground of imperial rule, tribal differences could be mediated under a canopy of shared substantive and moral understandings that have a real relationship to separate tribal self-understandings and experiences. This common ground can be neither commanded nor enforced by law because it is produced and sustained by innumerable institutions ranging from family life to research institutes and by innumerable practices across all levels of popular and elite cultures. It is informal and voluntarist rather than formal and coerced. Its underlying language is that of narrative rather than principles and rules, and it is this shared narrative—we share a common national past because we imagine a common national future—that serves to define and legitimate the governing principles and rules. The voluntary nation would reclaim the power to authorize the coercive state—one might then call our national government one that is of, by, and for the *people* as a conscious and corporate entity.

The chapters that follow are in response to these fears. They attempt to describe and reflect upon the historical relationships between shared moral orientations—commonly called voluntary or informal religious establishments—and the sequences of national political establishments, or "orders," that mark and periodize our national political experience. I argue that each successive national political order requires ideological justification to authorize it, that this authorization must come from the body of the people as a nation, and that this national identity is a sacred one—a shared moral orientation that takes the form of a "political theology" culturally expressed as an informal religious establishment.

This argument and historical reading makes some unusual demands on the reader. The first is to disassociate "religion" from "church" or churches in trying to make simultaneous sense of the history of our national spirit and our national politics. Church or denominational history only misleads by hiding our shared cultural-religious experience: this history can neither understand nor explain the energy, success, and power of the series of voluntary and national religious establishments that mark our cultural-political history.

The second demand is to open the categories of political theology and political theologian to all ideas that constitute moral orientations and draw on moral sources in our culture to express hierarchies and priorities of goods. Charles Taylor distinguishes between "constitutive" goods as moral sources for personal and collective identity—without them we wouldn't know who we were—and "life" goods (sometimes called "elective" goods) as the array of those resources and powers we need and want to carry out our purposes. Constitutive goods and theories of constitutive goods partake of the sacred or religious because they are transcendent; they inspire our respect and help to empower us. These goods constitute our self-understanding and provide the framework by which we interpret or make sense of ourselves and the world. All who presume to instruct us regarding our national identity, our political obligations, and our moral duties are acting in the role of political theologians. The political theologies that underwrote our voluntary religious establishments in the past were not articulated as the creedal theology of any particular church but can be found in the literatures of religious revival (Jonathan Edwards), political history (George Bancroft), public oratory (Abraham Lincoln), poetry (Walt Whitman), philosophy (John Dewey), and philanthropy (Jane Addams).

The last demand is to conceive of the American university as the primary national church and the humanistic disciplines of the liberal arts as the primary sources and articulations of national identity and shared moral orientations. While this request is more plausible when looking backwards (e.g., moral philosophy in the 1830s at Harvard; liberal evangelicalism and historicism at Yale in the 1870s; sociology and the social gospel at Chicago in the 1890s; liberal anticommunism in all elite universities in the 1950s), I argue that the American university (now including the law schools) remains the primary site where American national identity is contested and defined.

This last demand on the reader is difficult to make because it masks deep doubts by the author that the contemporary university and its liberal arts and law faculties have the required intellectual depth, moral courage, and humility to sustain the vocation of their predecessors. This is especially the case because the twin seductions of multiculturalism and democratic universalism are so pervasive and strong. Succumbing to these seductions rewards academics at both ends with a denial of responsibility. A principled multiculturalism bestows on them the mantle of the innocence of the powerless and oppressed, while democratic universalism gives them a free ticket to psychic membership in the imperial overclass. Combined, these seductions often create an arrogance and a blindness beyond belief. My hope as expressed in the last part of the book is that these seductions can and are being resisted across the range of academic disciplines. Where many conservative public intellectuals see nothing but skepticism, rebellion, and nihilism in the academy, I see in this resistance a reenchantment and a revival of spirit in the liberal arts. Indeed, it is because I also see some faint outlines of a shared moral orientation—a new substantive common faith and source of national identity—that I can hope that the history recounted in this essay has a future.

NOTES

1. Taylor 1989, 34.
2. Taylor 1989, 31.
3. Geoffrey Hill, "The eloquence of sober truth; Clarendon and the opposition to Hobbes's 'monstrous Soveraign,'" *TLS*, 11 June 1999, 11.
4. Lind 1995; Fish 1987, 1997, 1998; and see Rorty 1989.
5. This logic would hold true however many tribes there were; indeed, a classic liberal individualist posits that each person is a tribe.

Introduction

America is having an identity crisis. From issues of multiculturalism and immigration and struggles over the writing and meaning of our national history to philosophical argument between liberals and communitarians, public intellectuals are engaged in fierce contests over America's character and destiny. Because being an American requires some notion of what America is and should become, defenses and assertions of personal ways of life become struggles over the norms and purposes of our lives in common: abstract debates about citizenship, affirmative action, or family policy become concrete struggles about ways of life that should receive national recognition and support. Our identity crisis is both personal and national. To have an identity crisis is to lose one's orientation in moral space, to be at sea regarding orders of significance and what our commitments should be.[1] Religion is deeply implicated in this debate not only because so many Americans find their moral sources and express their individual moral orientations in the great historic religions and their philosophical articulations but because we have symbolized and expressed a common American identity within these same traditions.

The current struggle over national identity is not unprecedented. Our history is marked by the rise and fall of political orders, or "regimes," each of which embodied an authoritative national identity as warrant for the exercise of its national political authority. The rise and fall of each national regime are products of struggles that were at once religious, cultural, and political. To deny the centrality of the rise and fall of national political regimes is to deny our history. To say that the Constitution alone, automatically and indifferently, authorizes every electoral victor is true only insofar as it is trivial.[2] Simple national electoral victory has never bestowed enough authority to govern the nation. If our political history teaches us anything, it teaches us that our constitutional institutions and structures of offices never did and never could govern us without substantial extragovernmental help and that no victory is lasting. In short, our history is marked

1

by the rise and fall of distinct political orders. Each succeeding order had to overthrow or disestablish the standing one before it could establish its own, and to
do this it had either to "conquer" augmenting structures of authority (state and
local governments; powerful institutions in civil society) or create alternative
authorities that could displace the standing ones (new political movements and
parties, churches, newspapers, colleges, reform organizations).

The history of American "party government" is testament to this primary fact
and highlights the centrality of both cultural conflict and extra-governmental institutions. The most obvious instance was the conflict, both political and religious,
between Patriots and Loyalists in the American War for Independence. In 1800,
the Federalist Party, after only twelve years in power, was defeated by the
Jeffersonian Republicans, who remained in power for a quarter of a century. Many
of the defeated declared the Constitution, morality, and law at an end, and even
spoke of secession to preserve the true American nation. When Jacksonian Democracy then triumphed electorally, anti-Jacksonian forces began a long process
of cultural, party, and reform movement mobilization to reclaim America.
Lincoln's electoral victory and the victory of the North in the Civil War irrevocably altered both the national government and American national identity, as the
reach and authority of both governmental and civic or voluntary institutions were
reconstituted and vastly extended.

To parties must be added the whole complex of governing institutions below
the national government, and to those must be added civic and voluntary organizations of all kinds, including what is now termed the media. Without all of these
augmenting institutions and the authoritative messages and values they carry, we
could not begin to make sense of our political history and its relationship to
American culture. Religion is central to this reading of our history because
overarching each victorious national political and cultural order was an informal
or voluntary religious establishment that had come into being by disestablishing
a standing one.

This process can be charted on many levels and in many different ways, from
tracing the religious styles that marked the contending political parties to looking at the religious origins and ideas of civic and voluntary organizations that
were part of—or helped to overturn—a standing political order. We might restate
this in broader terms by saying that every decisive politico-cultural struggle in
America has also been a politico-religious one. Ortega y Gasset remarked that
"the past has reason on its side, its own reason. If that reason is not admitted, it
will return to demand it."[3] This is especially true when we attempt to understand
our religious history. It is commonly accepted that nineteenth-century America
was Protestant and that it is Protestant no longer. This is a cultural and political
conclusion and not merely a demographic one, for it presumes that a clearly identified voluntary or informal Protestant establishment dominated American national
identity and its major national educational, political, cultural, and economic institutions. It is also commonly accepted that at some point in the twentieth century,

this informal religious establishment—and presumably its reigning public theology—was disestablished and that a new post-Protestant or generic Judeo-Christian establishment replaced it. Finally, it is now commonly accepted that, at some point in the recent past, this post-Protestant establishment was in turn disestablished and that we now inhabit a nation whose identity and major national institutions are not only post-Protestant and post-Judeo-Christian but, with a few rapidly diminishing exceptions, wholly secular—call it "post-religious."

While this narrative of establishment/disestablishment/reestablishment/disreestablishment was never intended to be a neat and seamless one, it does assume that neither the constitutional provision against religious establishment in the First Amendment nor the completion of legal disestablishment in the states in the 1830s prevented the creation of de facto national Protestant religious establishments. In seeking to understand this ironic result—was de jure *state disestablishment* a necessary condition for de facto *national establishment*?—many other ironies suddenly appear. Here is one: if disestablishment is the test of religious freedom, was there *more* religious freedom in early-nineteenth-century America—when formal establishment in the states was almost dead and the informal national one had not been consolidated—than in the late nineteenth and early twentieth centuries when the informal and national Protestant establishment was at the peak of its power?

As a concluding preliminary, pair this larger irony with one that is immediately relevant to our perceived condition today. In 1875, James G. Blaine, then Republican Speaker of the House, proposed an amendment to the U.S. Constitution that would make the two religious clauses of the First Amendment (i.e., no establishment and free exercise) binding on state governments. By formal amendment to the Constitution, Blaine sought to accomplish what the Supreme Court did by incorporation in the *Everson* decision—but *seventy-two years earlier*. Blaine's proposal carried in the House by a vote of 180 to 7 but failed in the Senate. Needless to say, Blaine (and almost the entire House of Representatives) was hardly a proponent of religious neutrality and strict separation—let alone representative of a secular-humanist intellectual elite seeking to banish religion from American public life. Blaine, later known for his "Rum, Romanism, and Rebellion" presidential campaign against Grover Cleveland in 1884, was in fact mobilizing Protestant religious passions by attempting to use federal authority to prevent some cities and states from accommodating Catholics in public school policy. His intent, in short, was to maintain the public schools as de facto Protestant institutions in post–Civil War America.[4]

What does this imply for the claims of principled neutrality in the "wall of separation" argument in the *Everson* decision in 1947? Blaine's claims of neutrality and equal rights, like the identical claims of wall-of-separation doctrine today, do not rest on their own foundations of truth but ride on the cultural and religious understandings that prevail. Church-state jurisprudence is in almost total disarray today precisely because those supportive understandings do not exist. Because we are absent a voluntary cultural-religious establishment, we cannot possibly agree on the constitutional meaning of disestablishment.

The religious dimension in struggles over American identity and the meaning of American citizenship continues today in current controversy in political theory between what are called "liberals" and "communitarians" and in the ways in which this controversy plays against the more immediate issue of multi-culturalism. While later chapters address this debate in a variety of contexts, it should be remarked here that each side is attempting to define American identity—that which holds us together (or at least defines us) as a people—by articulating what should be our shared national projects and commitments. I would maintain that, in doing so, each participant is also and unwittingly play-ing the role of national political theologian—even as he might loudly declaim that his argument has nothing to do with such a private and inviolate sphere as religion.

All of us are familiar with neoconservative calls for the restoration of moral and religious values in public and civic institutions. Combined with the political forces mobilized through the media and organizations of the Christian right, these writings are often thoughtlessly dismissed as merely reactionary, a thin cover for the retention of the power and status relationships of an era long past and neces-sarily opposed to the full inclusion of all on an equal basis. But what is one to make of liberal communitarians' writings that echo many of these same themes, albeit without creedal and biblical references and supports? How is one to un-derstand the powerful critique by law professors in the most prestigious and po-litically correct law schools that have attacked prevailing liberal church-state jurisprudence in ways quite compatible with conservative critiques but resting on postmodernist premises and put in the interpretive language of pragmatism and deconstruction?[5]

Some recent writings from the left have begun to bring this religious dimen-sion explicitly to the fore, if often only indirectly and by the use of metaphor or by historical analysis and analogy. The most prominent has been Michael Lind's *Next American Nation* (1995). He asserts that we have been governed by three distinct American "republics." The first two republics, "Anglo-American" (1776–1860) and "Euro-American" (1870s–1970s), each encoded a distinct racial-cultural and religious component of American nationality, and each empowered major American reform projects and achievements (as well as injustices, exclu-sions, and bloody conquests). The current "Multicultural" republic (1970s–present), according to Lind, lacks both a religious and a national component and is therefore disconnected from our past, self-subversive, and without a viable future. His call for a new "Transracial" fourth republic restores a robust national identity and includes a shared religion of "civic familism" to serve as the sacred canopy of a reborn American nationality.[6]

Another recent book from the left is Richard Rorty's *Achieving our Country* (1998). He begins by asserting that no national reforms are possible without pride in one's country, through which one is both shamed and motivated to undertake collective projects in the public good. He recounts the ways that left-liberal reformers and intellectuals from the Progressive period through the 1960s fully embraced American patriotic values and made of the American university something of a national church, integrating, focusing, and deepening American spiritual and moral energies in the name of these national projects and purposes. He calls for the political left in America to incorporate these earlier national and patriotic elements by being more historicist, pragmatic, and vital.[7]

These are only some of the more obvious ways that concerns for American nationality have reintroduced issues of religion and voluntary religious establishment into public discourse. Early versions of this book began when I was invited to participate in two meetings with other academics from a wide variety of disciplines and religious backgrounds to discuss what appeared to be the intractable and incommensurate positions taken on the proper role of religion in American public life.[8] Given my previous writings, I was asked to look at ways in which America can be considered post-Protestant or post-Christian in its self-understanding. As I first shaped my talk and later my paper, a logic developed in my analysis that became, often against my will, more and more unsettling in its implications. Needless to say, all of us at these meetings knew disestablishment language and principles by rote, so my fellow participants quickly grasped one side of my analysis of the dialectical features of establishment/disestablishment/reestablishment in our history. But the other side, an analysis that entailed a serious look at the ideas empowering each voluntary *reestablishment*, was much more difficult to convey and discuss in a way that all could understand and/or come to some agreement about. All of us were inarticulate regarding ideas powering reestablishments because to become articulate *would risk offense*. We were entering the dangerous domain of moral orientations, political theologies, and national/personal identity.

My own attempts to give substance and system to nineteenth- through mid-twentieth-century reestablishment ideas in America occasioned bewilderment by some and principled rejection by others. When I extended this logic to argue that a new voluntary religious establishment is required as a precondition for reaching agreement on church-state/religion-politics issues, I met strong resistance. And when I further suggested that this new informal establishment might already be in process of formation and that its creators are not primarily conservatives and evangelicals outside academia but some "politically correct" liberals inside its walls, I was met with incredulity. Recounting the main features of this logic will indicate some reasons for this dual response and make transparent the organization of this book and some of its sequential connections.

The logic that developed might be stated as a series of propositions:

- The American people were culturally constituted before they were politically constituted: the American nation preexists the American national state and, indeed, any and all constitutions and political authorities, and continues to exist independently from them.

- The United States Constitution standing alone as a series of formal legal rights and powers is insufficient to authorize a common national identity or the undertaking of significant national projects. Indeed, it has usually been used effectively for precisely the opposite ends. It cannot serve as the autonomous ground of authority over the American people nor serve as the underlying basis of fealty to those who exercise national political power.
- The substantive values and purposes constituting American national identity—our shared moral orientations—legitimate the constitutional exercise of national political power through creating and sustaining distinct national political orders, or "regimes."
- American national identity is a voluntarily created and sustained or reconstituted cultural achievement, the product of the institutions and practices of civil society, most notably by educational, cultural, religious, and intellectual leaders and institutions.
- American national identity was shaped in the past by and through a series of voluntary national religious establishments, each of which was constituted by and made acceptable through a corresponding theology. Historically, there has never been a voluntary national religious establishment without a national political theology to give it point, purpose, and direction. Historically, however, specific church creeds and church organizations played only subsidiary roles in the creation and maintenance of this national political theology.
- All American political theologies are national metanarratives within which "timeless" or "principled" constitutional doctrines and public philosophies are voiced. These metanarratives are to public philosophy and constitutional law what paradigms are to science: deep background understandings and commitments that shape our operative beliefs and direct our agendas and purposes.
- Each succeeding voluntary religious establishment and its national political theology both discredits the standing one and shares common features with it, making possible a continuously reconstructed narrative of one American people who, nevertheless, periodically undertake momentous political and governmental actions that irrevocably change the direction, destiny, and national identity of America.
- Each voluntary religious establishment and its national political theology is both an invitation and an exclusion: an invitation to participate in shared national projects and purposes as defined by that establishment and a warning that failure to do so will result in exclusion from full participation in national political and cultural life. In every establishment period some groups proudly and eagerly decline the invitation, some proudly and eagerly accept; some are never invited; some have become so prominent that they must be invited; and some accept because they have few or no viable alternatives. From a value-neutral or universalistic perspective, every invitation and every exclusion is unfair.

- Those included groups whose personal, ethnic, racial, and religious identities are now mediated through and partially incorporate American national identity (i.e., have accepted the invitation) by definition have been required to modify their more local identities (and attendant practices) to fit the national one. By this fact, they or their leaders have relinquished the exclusive power to define and determine these more specific identities. To be a full member of the American national community requires that personal and group identities be negotiated with and through those who do not share those specific identities but who are fellow members of the American nation. No group actively participating in American national political life exclusively controls or defines its own identity and therefore is incapable by definition of imposing its "own" identity on others.
- There are two ways to forestall the loss of personal, ethnic, racial, and religious autonomy. One is to forego full inclusion in the American people—psychologically speaking, to become or remain a resident alien. Another way to forestall this loss of autonomy is to recruit and join with others to overthrow the standing voluntary religious establishment and constitute a new establishment that more fully recognizes and affirms one's identity. This political, religious, and cultural struggle, however, recreates the very conditions of negotiated identity and loss of autonomy that one initially sought to avoid, albeit under more favorable conditions.
- In periods of disestablishment, when American national identity is being bitterly contested, personal, racial, ethnic, and religious identities tend to be very divisive. Conflict is primarily *between* and *among* groups whose boundaries and definition seem fairly fixed, and therefore intergroup conflict suppresses and disguises intragroup conflict. In periods of successful voluntary establishment, when a shared national identity is ascendant, the site of conflict moves inside each group, whose boundaries are now more opaque, permeable, crosscutting, and shifting.

Stating this baldly, without argument, and in the form of declarations, makes me sound much more sure of the arguments that follow than I actually am. Paraphrasing the seventeenth-century philosopher, Thomas Hobbes, I must apologize to the reader for "some things which have more of sharpness, and less of certainty than they ought to have." Hobbes asked for this leave because he wrote as "one whose just grief for the present calamities of his country may very charitably be allowed some liberty."[9] I ask a similar leave.

My hope is that these sharp declarations will encourage an analysis that connects many aspects of our national political history that the reader will probably count as good (American independence, the abolition of slavery, women's suffrage, victory over fascism, desegregation of public institutions, the fall of communism) with political movements and voluntary religious establishments and a vigorous and outspoken patriotism that many readers will probably count as both ˙ embarrassing or bad.[10] Persuasive argument that speaks to their inseparability not only cuts through illusion, hypocrisy, and bad faith regarding our past, it may even help us to confront more directly who we are and might become as a people in the future.

A second benefit is that the kinds of historical linkages suggested in these propositions free us from linguistic and philosophical bondage to abstract constitutional and "rights" talk. To get the discussion of vital issues of racism, multiculturalism, nationality, and political culture out of the courts and free from the imperiously principled language of lawyers and their court philosophers is itself a huge gain. The possibility of subordinating that imperious language to a freer and more culturally and intellectually supple *democratic* discourse has the added advantage of including many more interesting people in the conversation, thereby both refreshing the spirit of inquiry and reconnecting whole areas of current academic scholarship to public discourse.

A third benefit is that analysis of our past and present within the terms set by these propositions might help us to discern the range of possibilities within which American academics and intellectuals might again participate in helping to fulfill "the promise of American life." Herbert Croly, from whom this phrase is taken, had long believed that, among powerful and energetic nations, only America could be committed unreservedly to the cause of democracy: other nations "cannot afford to become too complete a democracy all at once, because it would thereby be uprooting traditions upon which its national cohesion depends." In America, however, "we can trust its interest to the national interest, because American national cohesion is dependent . . . upon fidelity to a democratic principle."[11] For Croly the fate of democracy and social justice, both in America and in the world, rested for good or ill on the fate of American nationality, and, as he wrote late in his life, American nationality required a shared religious faith to counter the disuniting and antidemocratic temptations that always beset us.[12] The particular task for academics and public intellectuals is to articulate the moral sources, moral orientations, and common narratives within which civil and democratic discourse can take place. To deny or to fail in this task will isolate the American intellect from American politics and perhaps reduce our politics to simple contests of interest and power.

There is, perhaps, one final benefit in beginning this way and that is the benefit of self-understanding. In a recent essay, Anne Norton asserted that when we become citizens "our private memories are supplemented by public and political histories." She then recounts the ways in which her own memories have incorporated that larger story.[13] My own biography confirms this. Raised a third-generation, German-Russian Protestant pietist, I have been enabled to incorporate into my personal memory and identity (to name some of my favorites) John Winthrop and Jonathan Edwards and John Quincy Adams and Frederick Douglas and Jane Addams and John Kennedy. Had my grandparents come to America only negatively, to protect their "identity" or autonomy, their individual and confessional rights to live exactly as they pleased, they would have denied my parents and me a larger and fuller life. To their credit and my gratitude, I had lost my German-Russian ethnicity before I was born, and my "native" language immediately thereafter. Rejecting much of my ancestral formal religious creed took a bit longer. For all this "loss" I cannot blame evil WASP hegemons; rather, I can only thank my parents and grandparents for freely and deliberately accepting their invitation.

What was it that made the path of my life—so different from that of my grandparents—possible and, in retrospect, almost inevitable? Surely it was not the Constitution, except insofar as its prohibitions permitted a voluntary religious establishment. Through that common faith my grandparents and parents were enabled to interpret their pietist Christian faith and their ethnic way of life as a series of possibilities opening into a larger and fuller life in America shared with people and traditions they would only later come to know. To envision this common future was to understand their past not as a series of battlements to be defended but as a host of intimations for a more personally and spiritually full life. On these terms, my grandparents' German-Russian-pietist identity was neither lost nor assimilated nor marginalized but, through my parents and through me, I hope more fully revealed and more fully realized. This book is itself a way of meeting the obligations of my birthright and perhaps my good fortune. That is what political and religious freedom is all about. That is what America should be about.

NOTES

1. Taylor 1989, 25–32.
2. Ackerman 1993 and 1996, for a strong statement of this position.
3. Ortega y Gasset 1932, 95.
4. Michaelsen 1971; and, on accommodation, 1969.
5. Tushnet 1985; Fish 1997; Steven Smith 1990 and 1995; Williams 1998; Alexander 1993. Political theorists have supplemented their arguments from a broader theoretical perspective: Macedo 1995 and 1998; Murphy 1997, 1998, and forthcoming; Taylor 1990; Neal 1997.
6. Lind 1995. Another recent book: Kevin Phillips 1999.
7. Rorty 1998. He begins the lectures by asserting, "National pride is to countries what self-respect is to individuals: a necessary condition for self-improvement," 3.
8. The title of the project was "One Nation Under God? A Scholarly Project on the Fate of Religion in American Public Life," sponsored by The Mellon Program in Social and Political Thought, directed by Professors H. Bruce Douglass and Joshua Mitchell of Georgetown University, and held at Georgetown 7 and 8 December 1996, and 19–21 September 1997.
9. Hobbes, *De Cive*, "Preface to the Reader," xxiv.
10. A *New Yorker* critic nicely captures the present ambivalence. She wrote of the recent musical, "1776," "But Edwards and Stone are to be congratulated for making this

story fresh, and for making it possible to feel less cynical and embarrassed for being an American." Franklin 1997, 94.

11. Croly 1989, 266–67.
12. Stettner 1993, 144–53.
13. Norton 1998, 131.

Chapter 1

Identities: Personal, Religious, and National

We are told that America is now in an era of "identity politics." This assertion has many different meanings. An "essentialist" reading would hold that each person is defined by characteristics not of his own choosing and that these characteristics are primary in determining one's identity and orientation to the world. Race, ethnicity, and gender are the primary categories, but others such as sexual orientation, age, and disabilities are also used. According to this understanding, America will not achieve its democratic promise until each group whose members are defined by these and analogous characteristics are accorded equal rights, respect, and dignity.[1] In seeming contrast to this reading, an "individualist" reading would hold that in a free society, each person must be able freely to choose values and practice ways of life that serve as the source of his authentic self. If freely chosen and practiced in ways that do not harm others, these ways of life are not to be ranked and judged or rewarded and punished by the larger society. Groups that form on the basis of shared chosen ways of life are also to be accorded equal rights, dignity, and respect.

While these two readings start from radically different premises and often differ from each other in policy prescriptions, they share two important features. The first is that the state must be neutral by according each group equal respect and treatment regarding these identity differences, whether their origin is in nature or choice. The second is that both understandings seem to begin outside of history and societal experience. The essentialist starts from nature or fate and the individualist starts from a sort of "state of nature" (or a veil of ignorance) in which one should be free to choose how to live one's life. I think that both of these starting points are philosophically and psychologically deficient and politically impossible.

A third understanding, and one with increasing influence today, threatens to undermine both of these positions. This phenomenological and pragmatic understanding holds that personal identity is neither intractably given nor freely cho-

11

sen but historically and socially constructed or scripted and that these constructions or scripts can be tracked historically as the result of contestations, struggles,
victories, and defeats. If there is a *politics* of identity, conflict and struggle necessarily follow: within groups, in negotiating their common identity—that which
makes them a bounded unity capable of common political action—and between
groups, in negotiating the terms of their relationships and struggles within a shared
society and polity.

To repeat: if there is a politics of identity in America today—and it would be
difficult to deny it—then we must grant some truth to the "constructivist" position, even if we must reject the use of it to argue that identity rests only on power
or domination. Another way of saying this is to say that, "the pursuit of identity
always [has] two sides: freedom and discipline," and the disciplinary imperatives
are both internal and external.[2] To complicate this matter further, over time and
even at the same time, the sources or grounds of what might be considered some
basic or determinate identity changes both *in* politics and *for* politics. Political,
religious, and cultural struggles alter our identities—often profoundly so—because political, religious, and cultural institutions differentially reward and pun-
ish how we reveal and represent our identities. In short, we are not entirely in
charge of our personal and local identities, but neither is anyone or anything else
that we might clearly discover and confront.[3] Identity is not a principle but a risky
and continuous constituent of human agency and practice.

Our personal, religious, social, and political identities are mediated and interpreted—by ourselves, with others, and by others. Moreover, historically our politics, our religions, and our culture have been structured and scripted by a whole
range of changing identity sources: race, church, party, language, ethnic origins,
region, gender, sexual orientation, economic status, economic role, to name some
fairly obvious ones. If it is politics and conflict and power that is our main concern, each of these sources, alone and in combination, have variously served as
a primary bond by which groups have been formed and mobilized to resist or to
impose, to make claims or to deny claims, to defend the prevailing political order or to attack the prevailing political order. In this sense, all politics in America
have partly been about identity, directly or indirectly, but no identities in political life are or can be either irrevocably given or autonomously chosen or wholly
constructed by others. But only at particular periods in our history do issues of
personal, social, and national identity come together as deeply contested ones
resulting in a politics where almost all issues and events bear the imprint of deeply
held commitments and rival visions of collective destinies.

CULTURE WARS AND IDENTITY POLITICS

Because identity politics is a fairly recent term, however, one risks anachronism
in attempting to reread our political history through this category, especially if

we drag back into that history the identity sources and markers that happen to have the most purchase today. The primary markers in any given political era suppress, subordinate, and even try to obliterate competing markers (e.g., the distinctions between Catholic, Protestant, and Jewish white males in America today)—indeed, *that is often the very point of the struggle*, in order to give prominence and priority to new groups and identities. But no particular selection or identity can be philosophically validated outside of historical practices and historical commitments to particular moral sources and orientations.

If we broaden the meaning of identity politics to include cultural politics, we not only help to avoid the risk of anachronism, we import a consciousness of shifting and alternative political identities into the discussion at the very start. The term cultural politics is also preferable because it suggests three fruitful directions for expanding discussions of identity. The first direction involves a long-standing body of historical scholarship that has identified the ethno-religious and confessional basis of party loyalty and voting throughout the nineteenth century, as well as explained antiparty movements at the turn of this century that successfully broke the monopoly of party organization both in the electorate and in government itself.[4] This helps us to understand that multiculturalism, or "difference," has been a continuous feature of American political and cultural conflict.

A second direction toward which the term cultural politics points is "Kulturkampf"—culture war—a term from Bismarkian Germany that is now used in America to label a politics of deep convictions between secular and religious institutions or between universalistic-cosmopolitan (state) and more particularistic (confessional) ways of life. In the mid-1960s, a culture war was begun by the New Left, first from within the universities and then from other national institutional settings. For the past two decades, political-cultural conflict has been occasioned by the rise of the religious right, primarily from the cultural and institutional periphery but affecting national government, political parties, churches and allied religious institutions, and now even universities. Conflicts occasioned by initiatives of the Supreme Court against state and local political majorities seeking to retain control over moral and religious values in education and the exercise of police powers have been another precipitating cause for conflict on these same sites, but now extended into law schools.

A third direction this term suggests is the growing importance of "culture studies" in American universities, a field of study that seeks to combine the newer studies of race, ethnicity and gender identities with the more traditional disciplines of literature, history, religion, the human or social sciences, and philosophy. Liberal arts education has always been a primary source and vehicle for articulating American national identity, so we must examine the impact of culture studies on the liberal arts for intimations of how American identity is being reshaped today.

Cultural and identity politics permeate and run parallel to principled arguments about the nature and meaning of democracy and freedom in America because the issues raised are distinct from or radically alter a "normal" or mundane politics of material interests and group advantage. This distinctiveness also tends to prevent resolution by the normal devices of political trade-off, compromise, or court adjudication that all parties accept. The stakes in identity or cultural politics are higher both in terms of consequences and in terms of the kinds of argument required to discuss and resolve them. Insofar as court and constitutional understandings at any given time tend to codify past victories, past establishments, and past political orders, in periods of cultural and identity politics, constitutional law and rights talk are never sufficient. Indeed, in periods of cultural-political struggle, this rights talk tends to lead us up blind alleys of intractable battles of subjectivities and into intellectual and moral incoherence in the law schools, in the courts, and in the general intellectual culture. In these periods, courts and constitutional thinkers need help, and that help can only come by reconfiguring the terrain on which we stand and the articulation of issues that are at stake. So, too, do elected officials and political parties need help: whenever they confront identity or cultural issues that are deeply divisive, their best instincts tell them to run and hide because any decisive action may lead to defeat and even ruin.

To alter the terrain of current discussion, we should recognize at the start that the current battles are not simply for "equal rights to recognition" or "rights to equal respect" or some other abstract and principled variant such as religious freedom, or parental rights—as if the identities of the claimants are fixed by the irreducible facts of nature or free choice. The struggles denoted by identity politics are not and cannot be *only* about recognition or equal respect for groups or individuals defined by whatever markers are used or asserted—that list would, in principle, be almost endless. One cannot simply demand a right from on high and in principle and expect to have it heard.[5]

In democratic politics there is no way in which claims for recognition of one's identity or culture can be put without some *reasons*, and these reasons must be given in terms of a discourse that is understood by the larger society to whom the claim is addressed. This very necessity means that the identity boundaries defining and separating individuals and groups are permeable and shifting. From the start, therefore, we must recognize (1) that personal, racial, ethnic-religious, and national identities constitute a series of differing sets of *interrelationships*; (2) that these identities have different social, institutional, and organizational *locations* at different times that structure these relationships; and (3) that *struggles* for recognition, equal respect, and freedom, both offensively and defensively, necessarily require major shifts in the way these identities are related, expressed, and located.

BOUNDED AND OPEN IDENTITIES

If life were simple and we were all Amish or Hutterites, we would not ask for recognition; we would be happy with our constitutionally guaranteed freedom to practice our religion or way of life free from much interference. The love and mercy of God and the respect and recognition from our fellow believers is all we ask. As long as America does not meddle with them, they will not meddle with America. As Amish or Hutterites they are free according to the secular Constitution—and they would rightly ask, *What are the rest of you complaining about?* Once over the shock of being interrogated by them (who do they think they are?—*Americans?*), we might reply that *they* are the ones who are actually oppressed, that they are Rousseau's "happy slaves" in the grip of false consciousness and religious superstition. But will we then be prepared to articulate and defend true consciousness and true freedom? And would we then be willing to "force them to be free" by denying them the right to practice their own religion and way of life unmolested by us? Whatever the answer, we do know that we— *as Americans*—would never be satisfied with Amish or Hutterite freedom. Why?

These are troubling questions. After all, the Amish and the Hutterites are almost perfect "rights claimants"—they ask nothing but freedom from the state and they have essentially received it—making all the rest of us rights-claimers look like we have larger agendas and moral and political commitments that we should in fairness state and be able to justify. But any such justification quickly leads away from issues of group or personal identity/autonomy and leads us toward the meaning of a good society and its relationship to American national identity.

The Amish and the Hutterites are ethnic-religious communities with very clear boundaries and markers. They do not act to please or be accepted by the rest of us, and if they said that the rest of us were all damned and destined for hell, we would not take offense because we do not consider their religion part of a shared American faith. Neither would we take offense at claims by ultra-orthodox Jews that Jews are the chosen nation and that all other peoples and nations are inferior in the eyes of God. Why is it then that we *do* take offense—and even feel threatened—if a Southern Baptist preacher says that God listens only to Christian prayers? Why, indeed, do we require public recantation and apology by the miscreant or by a chorus of his fellow communicants? Why would we do exactly the same if a prominent Conservative or Reform Jewish rabbi proclaimed that Jews were chosen by God to stand above all other peoples or if a Catholic prelate publicly declared to all America that outside the Catholic Church there is no salvation, and that includes all Southern Baptists?[6]

The answer must be that most Americans, but not the Amish and the Hutterites, hold at least two "religions" simultaneously, an ethnic-church-family-oriented religion that points to a personal and even private identity that no one should meddle in without our permission, and a moral-political-national-oriented religion that points to a public and civic identity that becomes an open invitation for meddling by others and a warrant for our meddling with others.[7] There are a series of possible relationships between these two religions and their respective institutional expressions and embodiments, ranging from continuity and even merging to strict separation, tension, and conflict. These relationships are at once theological, cultural, institutional, and psychological. Relationships that entail continuity and some measure of integration tend to mobilize political power on behalf of national political regimes and projects and often constitute political-religious establishments that persist over long periods of time: they are often aggressive and encourage meddling in the beliefs of others.[8]

Conversely, those relationships that mandate separation are designed to protect regional or local political and personal identities (as well as specific church creeds and doctrines) and try to limit "national political theology" to minimal constitutional-legal values. This latter relationship, however, can also be transformed into attempts to disestablish the prevailing national establishment or at least to provide more effective defenses against its hegemonic claims. Paradoxically, however, these disestablishments have usually been either short-lived or have themselves resulted in new establishments. Put differently, personal or local identities strengthened and forged in rejection and rebellion and protective-rights claims usually end in assimilation and inclusion because the deeper motive for recognition is inclusion in the body of one people, the American people.[9]

What this dynamic suggests is a kind of dialectic between these two identities, especially evident in the rhetoric and actions of "outsiders" who, unlike the Amish and the Hutterites, want to be respected by being included as Americans. Take a hypothetical example: Presbyterian gay men create an organization to condemn the Presbyterian Church for being homophobic, self-righteous, exclusionary, and frozen in the past, closed to new revelation or even to simple acts of love and charity. One obvious response to these demands is to say, "You're Protestants, go form your own church and be satisfied (like the Amish and Hutterites and Hasidim)." Added to this response is the equally obvious thought that the claims made by gay Presbyterians on their own church have nothing to do with politics or civil rights or American citizenship.

These responses are hardly persuasive. In assuming the role of a Jeremiah, this group is acting in a *politically authoritative* role, recalling their fellow churchmen *and the rest of the nation* to a preexisting covenant and seeking to give an authoritative reading to that covenant in God's name. Their claims are rights claims that rest on birthright. This covenant or promise is not "owned" by the legally incorporated, private, and voluntary body called Presbyterian Church, U.S.A., but is the property of the American people. Its theological articulation is not Presbyterian but national—as is its intended audience to whom this jeremiad is actually addressed. Moreover, this larger audience does not even know or care if the members of the protesting group are in fact official members of the Presbyterian Church. The very depth of their condemnation is testimony to the strength of their national hopes and their national faith. "I hate you, I hate you. You are evil and wicked. Please take me in. Please let me join. I desperately want to be a member of your morally debased and rotten society."

If this hypothetical example is unconvincing, perhaps the response of some liberal intellectuals and feminists to the rise of Promise Keepers will illustrate the point more clearly. While its individual members were going about the seemingly personal and private business of joining together to pray, sing, and change the direction of their lives as husbands and fathers, Promise Keepers as an organization was branded as a dangerous right-wing political movement, probably racist and certainly sexist, and subject to long investigative media reports. The personal becomes the political, but only when American identity seems at stake. Conversely, when President Clinton treated the nation as a church by asking *the American people* (not his Baptist congregation) for forgiveness for his sins, these same critics of Promise Keepers bowed their heads or remained silent. Needless to add, these two responses have more to do with national covenantal than constitutional logic.

> Thus stands the cause between God and Us, we are entered into Covenant with him for this work, we have taken out a Commission, the Lord hath given us leave to draw our own Articles we have professed to enterprise these Actions upon these and these ends, we have hereupon besought him of favour and blessing . . . but if we neglect the observation of these Articles which are the ends we have propounded, and dissembling with our God, the Lord will surely break out in wrath against us [and] be revenged of such a perjured people and make us know the price of the breach of such a Covenant. (John Winthrop, 1630)

AMERICAN CATHOLIC IDENTITY

A more complex historical example, and one that speaks directly to the relationship of religion and national identity, is the Catholic experience in America. Arriving in large numbers in the two decades preceding the Civil War, Catholics from Ireland almost immediately embraced a Jeffersonian secular-constitutional understanding of religious freedom and rejected the dominant national culture and national institutions that they perceived were Protestant and overtly anti-Catholic. From universities and professional associations through public schools, reform societies, and national weeklies and monthlies, they saw hostility and threat. Over the next fifty years and under this constitutional canopy of religious freedom,

> The Catholic Church attempted nothing less than creating a completely enveloping state-within-a-state for its own Catholic community. The goal was to make it possible for an American Catholic to carry out almost every activity of life— education, health care, marriage and social life, union membership, retirement and old age care—within a distinctly Catholic environment.[10]

Over time, the paradoxical result was that, while the Church was clearly marked off from the larger institutional religious culture, the "parachurch," or "faith-based" institutions created by the Church, rapidly assimilated Catholics into American civil and political life and therefore into its culture—including its religious culture. Separated from the prevailing religious establishment and its political theology, however, Catholics were forced to defend these institutions and their faith with a secular enlightenment philosophy of political life that their own church theology repudiated. They had to teach that the American government was *at best* godless and, when infused with religious belief, heretical. Here there is an almost perfect analogy between this reading of religious freedom and nine-teenth-century "states' rights": both are defensive claims against the larger national culture and its institutions and both celebrate negative liberty. It was no wonder that there was an elective—and electoral—affinity between Irish Catholicism and the American South through the Democratic Party.

Unlike the South, however, the longer range historical result for Catholicism was not secession and reconquest but voluntary and even triumphal assimilation. Hoping, perhaps, to create a strong and proud Irish-Catholic "nation" inside a Protestant-secular America, Irish-Catholic bishops created instead the institutional structure of *American* Catholicism that became in turn one of the most powerful and effective engines of national assimilation ever seen in America. Given im-migration patterns, the Church could not remain both ethnically Irish-Catholic and *the* Catholic Church in America. What choice did it have if it wanted to cre-ate an American Catholic Church and not a series of separate national German, and Polish, and Italian ethnic Catholic churches?[11] The Irish-American Catholic Church sought to suppress attempts by other ethnic groups to create their own separate Catholicisms and thereby deprive the Irish of their one most important source of pride and identity in America. But the only way this suppression would work is if it were voluntarily accepted by these other groups, and they would only do that if the Church were a common American one and not an Irish one that happened to be in America.[12] By this logic, the "invitation" extended by these Irish Catholic bishops to non-Irish Catholics was *already an American one*, al-ready partly expressing an American political theology, because its appeal em-braced the hope that a unified and transethnic Catholicism would be more pow-erfully and authentically Catholic and thus able to play a decisive role in American national life and destiny.

The initial Catholic response to Protestant America, then, was to defend their identity in purely Jeffersonian terms: in America, they said, religion is private and immune from state interference because politics is secular and public. But this defense and these rights claims were made to enable Catholics to transform America by practicing their religion as Americans in common with other Ameri-cans. To a certain extent, the cultural, political, and legal manifestations of anti-Catholicism were allies to those talented Irish-Catholic bishops busily construct-ing the American Catholic Church, its schools, hospitals, and charities. Like the early Mormon leadership, the bishops not only thrived on but often seemed to encourage derision and attack as a source of group solidarity.

By the 1940s and 1950s, however, Catholic social mobility, Democratic Party victories, de facto institutional assimilation, and the rise of the Cold War com-bined to propel American Catholicism into the very center of American national life. Catholic universities and intellectuals lagged somewhat behind, but the cu-mulative result was clear: Catholicism became an integral part of the Religion of America. Their publicly expressed theology became part of the national political theology, and they became part of the voluntary religious establishment. Indeed, by the 1980s, many Catholic intellectuals were calling for a *restoration* of this earlier voluntary establishment, an establishment that made it possible for Catholics to integrate their religious, social, and national identities. Under that canopy they could be *more fully and more freely* Catholic than before or after because they were more fully American. Catholics no longer had to defend their faith by denying its major teachings: that religion is essential to politics and public life; that religion sustains those civic institutions essential for maintaining legitimate and just government. Under the canopy of a common American faith, the Catholic Church was called to take more *spiritual* responsibility for our common life, including responsibility for Protestants, Jews, and nonbelievers. In the nineteenth and early twentieth centuries, American Catholics as sturdy Jeffersonians were spared this responsibility—just as Jacksonian Democrats eschewed national responsibility for slavery.

There is, of course, a quite different reading of this story: Irish-Catholic immigrants are innocent and powerless victims of religious and ethnic prejudice, seeking refuge in the Democratic Party as the only way to fight back against evil WASP hegemons. After heroic struggle, but keeping their primary identity intact, so this reading might go, they fought their way to religious equality by demanding and getting a more culturally pluralistic and democratic America. But alas, with the power of acceptance came corruption, and they soon joined with their previous oppressors to privilege their hard-won victory. My reading embraces this story only in granting the fact of struggle, but emphatically rejects the assumption that Catholic self-definition and self-representation remained constant. Indeed, the claim that the Irish fought the battle for respect and inclusion *for all other* Catholic ethnic groups is itself a disguised way of justifying its own hegemonic role in assimilating those groups largely on terms initially set by the Irish.[13]

In truth, the passage from Irish-Catholic to American Catholic entailed some significant changes in both ethnic and religious identity by the Irish and by the later-arriving Catholics from Central Europe and Mexico. As Jacksonians and as "victims," Irish-Catholics could first act something like the Amish or Hutterites; i.e., be morally and religiously indifferent to non-Catholics (and even non-Irish Catholics) so long as those "others" did not threaten their own interests. The larger society, in turn, could view the values that the Hutterites and Amish [and Catholics] suffered and died for as mere interests no different from property interests or even hobby interests, because their religion was private or "self-regarding" and of no concern to any but themselves. This kind of Jeffersonian religious freedom is necessarily held at the cost of indifference and even trivialization of the religion of these groups by the larger public.[14]

Irish-Catholic leaders, however, had a vision of a Catholic America. That vision was met with outrage and stoutly, even violently, resisted in the nineteenth century when voiced, for example, in the request for tax funds for de jure Catholic schools on a par with tax funds for de facto Protestant ones.[15] The struggle for recognition

and efficacy required mediation, and that mediation could never be via
Jeffersonian constructions of religious freedom and could never have been done
within the language and logic of the Constitution. Mediation required Catholic
participation in the creation of a national political theology that included Catholicism. This was the signal contribution of Father John Courtney Murray.[16] This,
in turn, encouraged and even required *lay* Catholics to participate in representing Catholicism both to the larger culture and to itself.[17]

It gets worse: not only lay Catholic intellectuals, but Protestant and Jewish and
secular intellectuals could now claim a right to meddle in Catholic self-definition and representation to others by instructing the Catholics through the common American faith of which they are now a part. It would be difficult to imagine a Jewish intellectual getting by with writing a book telling the Amish how to
tailor their faith and their teaching to conform to politically correct and philosophically acceptable standards. It would be equally difficult to imagine a Catholic
intellectual writing a harsh critique of Native American religion or of the faith
and practices of Islam in America. But we accept with equanimity books such
as Martha Nussbaum's, which treats Brigham Young University as an Enlightenment mission project,[18] and the recent shelf load of books written by conservative Catholics, Jews, and Protestants on the many failings of what used to be called
mainstream Protestantism.

One of the many virtues of John Cuddihy's *No Offense: Civil Religion and
Protestant Taste* (1978) is its prophetic quality in this present age of political
correctness. His argument is as simple as it is compelling: the more power and
efficacy a particular church religion has in America national culture, the more it
is seen as part of a shared American faith and, therefore, the less complete its
control over its own doctrine and teachings. The more integration there is between
the prevailing national political theology and the public presentation of any particular church to itself and to the larger society, the more warrant there is for others
to meddle under this larger canopy. This meddling is usually done indirectly, by
setting firm limits on what any particular church can or cannot do or say without giving offense. This explains the thunderbolts of condemnation that struck
the hapless Baptist preacher from Texas when he declared that God did not hear
Jewish prayers.[19] This also explains the equanimity that greeted Martha
Nussbaum's condescending attack on Mormon higher education and the equanimity that greeted President Clinton's request for forgiveness. The measure in
both cases is set by American national identity and its supporting political
theology.

COSTS AND RISKS OF RECOGNITION

Now if Jefferson is right and if America is defined solely by the Constitution read
as both neutral regarding all questions of religion and sovereign over all aspects
of public life within its domain, *any* religious utterance by, or religiously moti-

vated public proposal to, the federal government would necessarily give public offense. In the blunt words of Stanley Fish: "You can't say 'kike' and you can't say 'God.'"[20] But the exact opposite of this prohibition might equally result: if we were ruled only by one Constitution read as wholly indifferent to all expression that didn't directly and palpably injure anyone, we could all go around uttering racial and ethnic and religious insults because these mere private feelings (expressions) are quite irrelevant to a public discourse (opinions), constrained as it should be to include only those topics that all of us from anywhere could discuss reasonably, as in an academic seminar or an appellate court chamber. Whether universities or courts could be institutionally maintained in this uncivil an atmosphere is beside the point.

Every attempt to translate personal and group identity into political efficacy confronts the fact that political efficacy (and group recognition) involves conflict and struggle and therefore demands that identity be negotiated, mediated, and interpreted. But the field on which this negotiation takes place has never been and can never be a neutral or level playing field because it is always an *American* one, the product of our specific history and experience. That field has always been preoccupied with more or less clearly established rules and conventions and tacit understandings.[21]

One might change this image to say that the translation of personal and local identity into national identity usually confronts the fact of a standing national political establishment and a standing national political theology. This theology is a kind of toll booth at the entrance to the path of translation. The price charged is the loss of what I have implicitly termed "Amish rights," a constitutional equivalent to states' rights as the right to control and define one's own identity free from significant outside meddling. Conflict and struggle do not cease with the payment of this toll, but they take new directions. The path now traversed turns into something of a maze, with all sorts of people giving different directions. Very often one loses sight of the group one entered with, or the group itself becomes merged with or confused with other groups (Mexicans become Hispanics; Chinese become Asians; German-Russian pietists become WASPS) and goes off in unexpected directions.

There is worse to come: one soon learns that there is no end point at which the entering group can say they have fully arrived, when inclusion or equal respect or religious freedom has finally been achieved—as if either self-respect or religious freedom were a state rather than a practice.[22] This is as true for the oldest and most well-seasoned travelers as it is for more recent ones. To show this, one only has to ask if Jews in America would feel as religiously free and included if American foreign policy toward Israel in the 1950s–1980s period had mirrored that of the French.[23] Or ask American Catholics if they would feel as free as their counterparts in the 1950s or 1960s if national public opinion and all major national institutions suddenly declared that any public interference with rights of abortion or assisted suicide or even euthanasia is an unwarranted interference of private religious beliefs into politics. Or ask mainstream Protestants what would happen to their sense of belonging to America if a coalition of disparate marginals abolished the public school system and imposed a wholly free-market voucher system that permitted any and all groups to form schools on whatever religious or secular foundation they happened to choose. These, of course, are only hypothetical exercises to demonstrate the contingency that is inseparable from identity and cultural politics and to show how that contingency is neither mitigated nor abolished by recourse to constitutional understandings and determinations.

All this does not deny that in any given historical period, especially under conditions of successful voluntary religious establishment and consensual national identity, all this particularism and contingency is presented and understood as universal constitutional legitimacy and common sense. On the bedrock of every historical consensus, truth appears obvious, and the doctrines, rules, and principles reflecting this truth are enforced as common sense. Each political regime underwritten by this religious establishment will by definition receive the blessings of leading political, legal, and moral philosophers, each proclaiming that American institutions and practices, now or in the reformed future, mirror the very nature of universal morality and truth.

This translation from agonistic and contingent religious practice to coherent and seamless secular theory was as true in the early nineteenth century as it was in the early twentieth century. The textbooks of moral philosophy and natural theology used at evangelical Yale and Princeton in the 1840s were as philosophically convincing then as was John Dewey's and James Tufts's *Ethics* fifty years later—the latter a Protestant-Progressive and nationalist textbook that dominated the American college curriculum from its publication in 1908 through its last continuously published edition in 1942. The public intellectuals (and therefore public theologians) in each of these generations tried to express and explain America *through the best and most convincing forms of knowledge prevailing in their day*. In this way, they encoded in reason and social science and common sense a shared national and religious covenant/revelation and, through philosophy, constructed a national political theology that was part of our highest intellectual culture.

Like each succeeding generation, through Minerva's owlish eye we too can see that these claims of reason and truth were, at best, overstated; we too can see the hand of New Englanders and then northern Protestants writing those philosophies and those national political theologies. From this insight, we might even be tempted to call these authors agents of "hegemonic domination" if we like, but this uncovering, this exposure, does not thereby free *us* as authors by placing us on some objective pedestal above our history and our own experiences. We, after all, are also Americans and even their direct intellectual progeny and products; many of us inhabit the same university buildings they inhabited and serve as members of the same academic departments and disciplines they founded. Like it or not, they were the teachers of our teachers and we must both understand and bear some responsibility for them if we ourselves are to think and act with any degree of self-awareness and moral-intellectual honesty.

Here a caveat is required. My very use of the term "we" might suggest that I am speaking only to insiders, winners, and current hegemons, and this is only true. But American outsiders, losers, and subalterns are also part of the "we," if not through these philosophical and social-scientific discourses, then through their embrace of the Constitution that permits and then legitimates the creation and destruction of voluntary religious establishments and therefore the determination of American national identity. One must not equate successful religious establishment with triumphalism. Insofar as this national political theology is covenantal, each formulation had first to stand in judgment on the understandings of its predecessor and therefore on the prevailing institutions and practices it sanctioned.

Political theologies are available to dissidents as well as to adherents. It is no accident that Yale's liberal evangelical Congregationalism and Harvard's romantic Unitarianism were primary resources discrediting the national political regime supportive of slavery—just as the Social Gospel and Progressive social theory and political economy in the late nineteenth century discredited the rights-based and party-oriented Gilded Age regime (1876–1896) that had prevented national political and economic reform in response to industrialism.[24]

LOSERS

But further objection might be made to this reply: what about the *real* marginals, the Irish-Catholic immigrants in the mid-nineteenth century, and the Eastern Europeans and the newly-freed African Americans at the turn of this century? And what about Native Americans and Hispanic Americans? Do we see any traces of them in these earlier establishments and their theologies? The answer must be no, but with the addendum that they cannot even be classified in these earlier periods as losers insofar as they were not then even players in the game. Their condition was truly one of fate, not loss.

If one is searching for real losers in both of these periods it should be those who once considered themselves fully American but were then summarily and even violently reduced to the status of resident aliens: the white South in the latter half of the nineteenth century and evangelical Protestants who refused to become modernist-liberal Protestants in the early twentieth century. The white South could remain fully part of the nation only if American political and cultural and religious life was *not* nationalized. Every step toward national integration, be it national roadways and commerce, professional, philanthropic, antislavery and charitable organizations, or a national common law, threatened to marginalize the South—a fact that was even obvious to Tocqueville in the 1830s.[25] Imagine, then, the threats to regional, local, and personal identities in this manifesto of the American Republican (Whig) Party in 1844:

> We wish, fully and entirely, to nationalize the institutions of our land and to identify ourselves with our country; to become a single great people, separate and distinct

in national character, political interest, social and civil affinities from any and all
other nations, kindred and people on the earth. . . . We have all the elements of becoming a greater people, a mightier nation, and more endurable government than
has ever held a place in the annals of time. (*American Republican* [Whig], 7 November 1844)

Here was a true declaration of a culture war. One national house has no rooms
for slavery, and the South seceded. With the victory of the North (and liberal
evangelicalism) in the Civil War, this nationalization of governmental and educational and cultural and religious and parachurch organizations effectively excluded and marginalized the South for more than a century.[26]

Now reflect on northern, border state, and midwestern evangelical Protestants
at the turn of the century. Between the 1880s and World War I, their churches,
colleges, seminaries, and clergymen were integral parts of the Republican Progressive coalition. Their clergymen and lay leaders were full and active members in the huge complex of national parachurch and reform organizations and
publications that dominated political and moral discourse. They were welcome
and, indeed, often headed the leading national colleges and the new national
universities.[27] They shared a common social gospel with Jane Addams and John
Dewey, and they saw themselves in the moral and intellectual vanguard in the
national movement for social justice.[28] Their leaders and organizations were
proudly listed alongside all of the most prestigious secular leaders and organizations in *The New Encyclopedia of Social Reform*, compiled by William D. P.
Bliss in 1908 and representing America as the leading force for social justice in
the world.[29]

First the South and then the fundamentalists were crushed by these respective
politico-religious establishments, and we can only imagine what America might
be—who each of *us* might be today—if they had not been crushed. The invitations that voluntary establishments offer are not and can never be fair. Liberal
evangelicalism cum theological modernism was required by the Protestant establishment at the turn of this century in order to include German Jews and much
of the founding generation of academics in the new national universities. Only
this formulation was capacious enough—Hegelian enough—to accommodate and
to direct the American national spirit and American material power. Fundamentalists, like Southerners, who fought only to protect their creeds and their local
identities and cultures or to consolidate and exploit past victories—like aging
rentiers in a land of ambition and enterprise—were summarily hived off as a li-
ability, making possible the later inclusion of liberal Catholics and at least the
national or "presidential" wing of the Democratic Party. My point in all of this
is not to ask that we grieve for either the South or the fundamentalists as victims
(they were hardly *innocent* victims) but to help us reflect on the interdependence
of personal, local, and national identities, their agonistic foundations, and their
shifting institutional locations.

ALTERNATIVE AMERICAS

Imagine American history under very different conditions. One such condition would be that originally envisioned by many founders: separate and more or less powerful legal religious establishments and official theologies in many or most of the states, each conceived as a small republic under the protection of a limited and secular liberal *imperium*. The combined result would be cultural-religious homogeneity and an intense "thick republican" patriotism at the state level, and a "thin liberal" constitutional order at the national level. Neither Madison nor Jefferson could object to religious establishment in Massachusetts (though thinking Virginia's system of equal religious freedom superior) any more than they would grant John Adams the right to object to slavery in Virginia (though thinking Massachusetts's system of free labor superior). Like today's principled multiculturalism, this dogmatic liberalism declares that one should not be judgmental across particular and officially recognized subnational boundaries.

A parallel imagined condition would be autarkic institutional religious pluralism spread across the entire country, with each church in control of its own identity and existing exclusively for its own members. Each denomination would be encouraged (or even compelled) to act as if it were an ethnic church whose overriding purpose was defense of the particular religious creed—and perhaps the language—brought from the country of immigration. There would be no American Catholic Church, for example, but only its self-enclosed ethnic parts; no Protestant evangelical popular fronts such as antislavery and prison reform and temperance movements; no ecumenical institutions and parachurches, including national private colleges and universities; no political speech integrating religious, moral, and political commitments; no general religious press or publications; no national history and literature reflecting shared spiritual struggles and commitments. There would be no religiously founded charitable, educational, philanthropic mission or outreach activity by the churches in the larger society. All church-related institutions (often called parachurches) would serve only their own members. All religious expression and exercise would be contained within the separate churches and would therefore tend to consist of religious creeds, rituals, and doctrines combined with narratives of ethnic solidarity that would be endlessly reproduced and handed down to each new generation.

Because ethnic and religious identity would be codependent under these conditions, the decline of ethnic identity would parallel the decline of the church and, therefore, the decline of religion itself.[30] For this reason, issues of intermarriage, language, and education—indeed, the entire problem of modernity and cosmopolitanism—would be intractably and deeply religious problems as well. All attempts at national integration (and a larger sphere for personal freedom) would be threats both to religious and to ethnic identity. This is something of the democratic-pluralistic world urged by Horace Kallen and Randolph Bourne (and misreadings of Dewey) to prevent the dreaded condition of assimilation into middle-class Protestant America.

However fanciful these scenarios, two facts are undeniable. First, both conditions would require a powerful but limited national government imposing strict value neutrality on all national governing institutions and, in the second case, on *all* governing institutions. Strictly within the terms of the U.S. Constitution, *complete religious freedom* (and complete neutrality between belief and unbelief) would be absolutely guaranteed by virtue of the fact that the national government *would have nothing whatsoever to do with religion.* In the first scenario, the national government would look something like the British Empire in America prior to the 1760s and represent the vision of Jefferson, in which almost all domestic governance would be state and local. In the second scenario, the national government would have to be centralized to the extreme, overseeing or absorbing any and all levels of government that would have a tendency to translate local beliefs into public policy through democratic politics. Pluralism would be guaranteed by and through the minute supervision of society by cosmopolitan (and necessarily secular) "overclass" elites perceived as value neutral and above the always potential battles. Like benign imperialists keeping the tribes from warring against each other, they would be the sovereign Universal in a world of concrete Particulars. Whether either of the kinds of governments required of these imagined conditions would have been politically and culturally feasible is an open question. Whether either of them would be recognizably American by Americans living today is not.

To reflect on our real national experience is to enter a world that combines and mediates the sacred and the secular because it combines and mediates personal, local, and national identities. We must therefore address more directly how national identity relates to national government and how legitimate voluntary religious establishment is related to legitimate (and coercive) national political orders. With the privilege of hindsight and extensive bodies of historical scholarship, we can do this most easily by tracing the primary connections between the rise and fall of national governing regimes and the rise and fall of voluntary religious establishments.

NOTES

1. Iris Young 1990, 40, lists "women, Blacks, Chicanos, Puerto Ricans and other Spanish-speaking Americans, American Indians, Jews, lesbians, gay men, Arabs, Asian, old people, working-class people, and the physically and mentally disabled." And see Young 1995.

2. Howe 1997b, 209.

3. And see Taylor 1989, 25–32.

4. On the second party system and the Civil War era, Benson 1961; Carwardine 1993; Kleppner 1970; Gienapp 1987; Greenstone 1993; Jaenicke 1986. On the post–Civil War

era and Progressivism, Jensen 1971; Kleppner 1987; Swierenga 1990; McGerr 1986. Generally, Gerring 1997 and 1998; Kelley 1979.

5. In Judith Butler's words, "Whether a [universalistic/principled] claim is preposterous, provocative, or efficacious depends on the collective strength with which it is asserted, the institutional conditions of its assertion and reception, and the unpredictable political forces at work." From Nussbaum 1996, 46.

6. Terms and argument from Cuddihy 1978.

7. Michaelsen (1970), 1–3, provides a useful three-part distinction in ways of holding religion: personal, church, and national; and see Cherry 1989. See also Mead's classic essay, "The 'Nation with the Soul of a Church,'" 1975. A three-part distinction captures the contemporary phenomenon of members of the same institutional church holding rather different religious orientations, often sharing more commonality with members of other churches than with many of their own. See Ribuffo 1993; and Wuthnow 1988. But whether one speaks of a two- or a three-way division—or more properly, of a spectrum— there is a common recognition that some aspects are private and should not be interrogated by others and some aspects are public and should be held accountable to a shared standard. Where these lines are and how they differ for different religious traditions are politically and culturally negotiated and change over time. Each successful voluntary religious establishment represents a temporary resolution. A good local example is the use of a two-religion argument in the "school war" in Cincinnati, Ohio, 1869–1870, recounted in Michaelsen 1969.

8. Today, most of this meddling by the reigning establishment is justified on the grounds that the meddlers are neutral, above politics, and without a substantive agenda of their own—they are only protecting *others* who are too weak or inarticulate or complacent to put up a defense of their own against larger cultural and political forces. They are tribes that need imperial protection.

9. Moore 1986.

10. Morris 1997, 164.

11. Dolan 1985, 180–94, on attempts to preserve ethnic-national Catholicisms in America. The great agent of intra-Catholic or "Americanist" assimilation was the parochial school. See Dolan 1985, 241–93.

12. Morris 1997; Dolan 1985, 297–303; and see Cuddihy 1978.

13. Dolan 1985, 143–44, notes that in 1900, 62 percent of bishops in the United States were Irish, and over half of those were born in Ireland. As late as 1972, 32 percent of the American clergy and almost half of the hierarchy identified themselves as Irish.

14. This is Stephen Carter's argument critiquing contemporary church-state jurisprudence and views of religion in American universities, 1993 and 1987.

15. Billington 1964. On public schools as tied to mainstream Protestantism: Michaelsen 1971; Glenn 1988, chapters 6 and 7; Handy 1990; Howe 1997b, 214; and see discussion in Marty 1997, 50–61.

16. Hunt and Grasso 1992; Hittinger 1999, 32–35.

17. Morris 1997, 334–35, on laicization of Catholic theology. But see Burtchaell (1998) for a reading of this as a "secularization," even though sponsored and carried out by clergymen.

18. Nussbaum 1997, 278–91. It is perhaps a sign of Mormon arrival that Nussbaum as a prophet of a new common faith would condescend to take on their failings.

19. Dionne 1991, 211. This same phenomenon takes place on a microlevel among intellectuals. See, for example, the way in which Stephen Feldman's *Don't Wish Me a Merry*

Christmas" was treated by Father Neuhaus in *First Things* (January 1998). See also Levinson (1990) on the Americanist loyalty ritual that Catholic judicial appointments to the Supreme Court undergo in Senate hearings.

20. Fish 1998, 81.

21. This is the organizing thesis and conclusion of Miller 1988, 234.

22. This distinction is taken from Steven Smith (1995), regarding religious freedom.

23. Compare Cohen (1992) and Kraut (1989) on differing readings of the 1960s. Both assume, however, that a state of equality and equal respect can be (or has been) reached.

24. On the Social Gospel, Eisenach 1994; Curtis 1991. On Unitarian and Congregational theology, Howe 1970; Stevenson 1986; and see Marsden (1980) on the later divisions within Protestantism in the 1920s.

25. "The civilization of the North appears to be the common standard to which the whole nation will one day be assimilated" (Tocqueville 1981, vol. 1, ch. 19, 265).

26. In the first 72 years under the Constitution, Southerners (and slaveholders) held the presidency for 49 years; held 23 of 36 Speaker of the House positions; 24 of 36 president pro tem of the Senate positions; and 20 of thirty-five positions on the Supreme Court. After the Civil War, a century passed before another Southerner was elected president; a half century passed before there was a Southerner as Speaker of the House or president pro tem of the Senate. And in those same fifty years, only five of the next twenty-six justices appointed to the Supreme Court were from the South. McPherson 1991, 13. The Baptists and Methodists in the South split from their national groups in 1845, effectively cutting them off from participation in shaping the emerging civil religion that was to define the American nation for the rest of the century. Insofar as racial desegregation was an absolute necessity in order to fight the Cold War in Third World countries with any success (Dudziak 1988 and 1997), the South remained marginalized until the 1960s.

27. Longfield 1992a, 46–74; Crunden 1984. See chapter 4 for the extent of clerical leadership of both private and public colleges and universities.

28. Eisenach 1994; Crunden 1984.

29. Eisenach 1999b. Bliss (1856–1926) was a leading Progressive reform leader and intellectual. Eisenach 1994, 32, 126, 140, 233.

30. German Catholics who wanted a separate ethnic church argued that "language saves faith," and therefore "national" parishes were a religious requirement. Dolan 1985, 162.

Chapter 2

Regimes: Religious Establishments and Political Orders

The story of the rise and fall of voluntary religious establishment in America is full of irony. For starters, take Virginia. Statesmen like Jefferson and Madison thought that purging the statutes of Virginia of Anglicanism would result in a self-canceling religious pluralism presided over by an enlightened and cosmopolitan gentry. What resulted was pluralism of a sort, but one that multiplied centers of shared religious enthusiasm and revival. The Baptist revivalist Isaac Backus was a better prophet than the Republican statesman Thomas Jefferson. For Backus, as for Roger Williams before him, the separation of church and state was an evangelical imperative to clear the way for the creation of a holy American nation. There is an added irony here: Massachusetts, which had local, largely Unitarian, legal establishments until 1833, erected the more effective defense against religious enthusiasm in politics than did Virginia. But, like Connecticut and New Hampshire before it, the established churches in Massachusetts were finally destroyed, with the result that the new religious energies and passions unleashed in the Second Great Awakening were more readily released into New England society and culture.

Whether intended (Backus) or not (Jefferson), legal and constitutional disestablishment in the states was the precondition for the formation of a voluntary and national ecumenical and liberal-evangelical Protestant cultural establishment in the nation. The teachings of this establishment were conveyed through sermons, fiction, poetry, academic moral philosophy, and, later, evolutionary theories of history. Its norms penetrated into and shaped churches, families, public schools, charitable and reform associations, and, of course, politics.[1] Its first popular political expression was through anti-Jacksonian party and reform movements, which together coalesced into the Whigs, or National Republicans, creating what political historians term the second party system, which persisted until the eve of Southern secession. This increasingly powerful new politico-religious establishment was consolidated in the Republican Party and, with Lincoln's presidency and the victory of the north in the Civil War, was for a time expressed as a new and powerful civil religion.[2] Although weakened and depressed during the party stalemate period of 1876–1896, through Progressive intellectuals and reformers, a reconstituted and more inclusive establishment increasingly dominated our national public discourse and institutional life well into the twentieth century, this time articulated primarily in the new graduate universities and academic disciplines in the social sciences and literature.

This history suggests two very different understandings about the kinds of ideas that empower movements for religious disestablishment in America. The conventional reading holds that church disestablishment in the states was a secularization of politics, so the ideas driving this disestablishment are, perforce, secular. Here Jefferson and Virginia are normative even if they were not at all prophetic of what happened soon thereafter. On the counterassumption that legal or church disestablishment in the states was only a rest stop on the path to a new voluntary religious reestablishment in the nation, a very different reading of ruling ideas is required. These ideas must themselves be both political and religious, if not to attack the old state/colonial legal establishments, then to usher in a new national and voluntary one, to undermine a pluralistic set of coercive state religious establishments, and to clear the ground for establishing a new voluntary and uniform one.[3]

These differing sets of ideas also exhibit different structures. The former ideas are formal-legal, static, and grounded in fixed and abstract universal dualisms: secular and sacred, state and church, public and private, reason and faith, science and belief, law and conscience. The latter set is dialectical and more experiential: animating values and spirits are embodied in and work through differing institutional forms, migrating over time and space and changing their power and significance. This understanding of ideas is familiar to anyone who has read Hegel, Dewey, or the Bible. Put in terms unfamiliar to most Americans, the former ideas encode a type of scholastic or formal philosophy and the latter, a type of experiential-pragmatic and historicist philosophy.[4] I think that the former ideas are a barrier to understanding our past, our present, and, therefore, our future. If this formalistic mode of self-understanding were sufficient, then America, for all practical purposes, attained full religious freedom somewhere in the 1830s.

Difficult as it is to sustain a formal-legal reading of the early national period,[5] this understanding of our history cannot begin to explain the relationship of religion and politics in the nineteenth and early twentieth centuries. If the legal-constitutional disestablishments of 1776 and 1788 and the 1830s were underwritten by secular enlightenment values and represent democratization, what ideas powered the succession of informal or voluntary national reestablishments of religion in the nineteenth and twentieth centuries? To say that American values or the American creed reassert themselves with every successful *disestablishment* does little to explain whose values were responsible for each succeeding and successful *reestablishment*.

The equation of democracy with secular disestablishment ideas is also problematic. We often celebrate the national political eras that run simultaneously with voluntary national religious establishments as representing the high points in American democratic history, even as we seem to deny the importance of the ideas, institutions, and practices that brought these eras into being.[6] Must we hold that the anti-Jacksonian political constituencies that later came together to constitute the Republican Party and were the victors in the Civil War held religiously retrograde, anti-intellectual, and politically antidemocratic values—a real irony of fate,[7] given their leadership, constituencies, institutional alliances, reform programs, and policy positions? This irony would only be multiplied in the case of the Progressives after the Civil War, who were also driven by national-evangelical imperatives and projects.[8] How and why did good Americans in all of their organizational and creedal diversity put up with this informal cultural-religious domination and sustain for decades on end the political majorities that carried that domination into politics? Where were our political leaders seeking to win elections on the platform of religious freedom and denominational and cultural pluralism? Where were our constitutional lawyers, judges, and other men of legal principle? In truth, to call on constitutional principles was often to be branded an enemy of reform and democratization. Calling these successive political-religious reestablishments hegemonic only changes the charge on our ancestors—especially our nonevangelical Protestant ones—from cowardice to that of false consciousness or gullibility.[9]

But there is another possibility. Take the case of the Republican Party and the Civil War. Here, the reimposition of a morally disciplined and spiritually confident politico-religious establishment was the necessary surcharge on the cost of undertaking the project of emancipation and, in a deep sense, refounding the American nation. But if that was the case then—that enlightenment philosophy and its bare-bones Constitution were powerless without the canopy of an authorizing theology—might it also have been the case earlier, placing both Jonathan Edwards and Roger Williams at the founders' table (with Hegel as a late arrival), where we both reaffirmed past covenants and created our identity as a distinct people?[10] Might this also be the case later, during periods of war or great domestic and foreign challenges—*even now*? That is, *any* large national political and moral projects might be inconceivable without a shared faith and common creed, one that the Constitution alone could never supply.

National Republicans (Whig): We wish, fully and entirely, to nationalize the institutions of our land and to identify ourselves with our country; to become a single great people, separate and distinct in national character, political interest, social and civil affinities from any and all other nations, kindred and people on the earth. . . . We have all the elements of becoming a greater people, a mightier nation, and more endurable government than has ever held a place in the annals of time. (*American Republican* [Whig], 7 November 1844)

Democrats: 1. That the Federal Government is one of limited powers, derived solely from the Constitution, and . . . ought to be strictly construed. 2. That the Constitution does not confer upon the General Government the power to commence or carry on a general system of internal improvements. 3. That the Constitution does not confer authority. . . . 4. That justice and sound policy forbid. . . . 5. That it is the duty of every branch . . . to enforce and practice the most rigid economy. . . . 6. That Congress has no power to charter a United States Bank. . . . 7. That Congress has no power . . . to interfere with or control the domestic institutions of the several states. . . . 8. That the separation of the money of the government from banking institutions is indispensable for the . . . rights of the people. 9. That the liberal principles embodied by Jefferson in the Declaration of Independence, and sanctioned in the Constitution . . . makes ours the land of liberty. (*Democratic Party Platform*, 1840, repeated *verbatim*, with slight change in order, 1844, 1848, 1852, and 1856)[11]

Abraham Lincoln as National Republican: That this nation, under God, shall have a new birth of freedom—and that government of the people, by the people, and for the people, shall not perish from the earth. (Gettysburg Address, 1863)

Senator James Beck as Democrat: There is that contemptible word *Nation*—a word no good Democrat uses, when he can find any other, and when forced to use it, utters in disgust. This is no nation. We are free and independent States. (*New York Tribune*, 13 August 1875)[12]

Woodrow Wilson as Democrat: There is no such thing as corporate liberty. Liberty belongs to the individual, or it does not exist . . . [and] liberty is the object of constitutional government. . . . Constitutional government can exist only where there is actual community of interest and of purpose, and cannot, if it be also self-government, express the life of any body of people that does not constitute a veritable community. Are the United States a community? In some things, yes; in most things, no. (*Constitutional Government in the United States*, 1908)

Woodrow Wilson as National Republican: Our participation in the war established our position among the nations . . . the whole world saw at last . . . a Nation they had deemed material and now found to be compact of the spiritual forces that must free men of every nation of every unworthy bondage. . . . The stage is set, the destiny is disclosed. It has come about by no plan of our conceiving, but by the hand of God who led us into this way. We cannot turn back. We can only go forward . . . to follow the vision. It was of this that we dreamed at our birth. America shall in truth show the way. (Speech to the Senate, 10 July 1919)

Given the alternatives available, which path, the constitutional or the national one, leads to greater personal and collective freedom? Which kind of envisioned society provides more room to shape one's own identity and destiny? Which alternative provides the best hope for racial justice? Which political order opened itself to the voice and claims of women and of minorities and to victims of tyranny, oppression, and injustice abroad?

By reading the cycles of establishment and disestablishment as one national story combining religious and political authority, we can see more clearly the alteration of dominant discourses even as we must concede that only one of them—that of establishment—is constitutive of a national identity thick enough to yield collective purpose and actions engaging the deepest values of its citizens. This is the case because, in the words of Richard Rorty, "national pride is to countries what self-respect is to individuals: a necessary condition for self improvement. . . . Just as too little self-respect makes it difficult for a person to display moral courage, so insufficient national pride makes energetic and effective debate about national policy unlikely."[13]

This reading also shifts our attention away from church and denominational readings of our party and religious history,[14] and it forces us to look more candidly at the ways in which successful religious establishments and political theologies mobilized support by articulating shared political, social, and moral projects that drew from but did not impose particular church or creedal religion. More to the point, this approach helps us unravel some paradoxes in our more recent politico-religious past that underlie our current condition. If, as is commonly written, the second (third if you count the Jacksonian period, 1828–1840s, as the second) major disestablishment was substantially completed in the 1920s,[15] what do we make of the crusade in Europe against fascism and communism and of the moral-religious fervor of the civil rights and antiwar movements in the 1960s? If, instead, we date the start of serious disestablishment in the 1970s,[16] it surely was not a *Protestant* (or a Republican) establishment being disestablished. But if not, how do we describe and discuss the shared moral orientations and moral sources that were being overthrown? More fundamentally, what were the religious and moral sources of that moral consensus?

Historians of American politics and historians of American religion seem to agree on two major points. The first is that both political and religious history must be understood as *periodized* in the sense that one can isolate eras defined by the dominance of particular groups, regions, values, concerns, and purposes. The second is that transition between these periods is clearly delineated by events or actions marking the repudiation or end of one era and the start of a new and different one. In short, reading both political and religious history this way makes that history periodized and apocalyptic. This process can best be described as dialectical. In political history, periodization is marked by what are called "realigning" or "critical" elections, the American equivalent of revolutions, but within a relatively uniform set of constitutional forms. Thus, the election of Jackson in 1828 not only marked the end of a national gentry politics, it ushered in mass-based electoral politics and unleashed an inherent localism and populism in national political discourse—including a much more positive defense of slavery, states' rights, and strict constitutional constructions. Conversely, the formation of the Republican Party consolidated disparate anti-Jacksonian forces, destroyed the prevailing parties, and, under Lincoln, nationalized many of its constitutional understandings.[17] Following a stalemate period, 1876–1896, in which neither the

Republican nor the reconstituted Democratic Party could win a stable majority, the critical election of 1896 resulted in an era of decisive Republican victories that lasted until Franklin Roosevelt's landslide election of 1936. This latter election consolidated the New Deal coalition and established a Democratic political order that ruled until the 1970s.

This history of national regime periods intersects with another story, that of the rise and fall of political parties as the dominant institution establishing and disestablishing political regimes. In the decades following Andrew Jackson's victory, elections and governments dominated by extensive party organizations and party leaders became the norm. From McKinley's 1896 victory onward, the role of parties and elections began a steep decline even as the power of national industrial, professional, educational, religious, and reform interest groups rose in efficacy and power in national political life. Because party government tends to be devolutionary, local, and interest coalitional, this shift also centralized and nationalized politics. This same shift away from parties entailed a shift from legislative- to executive-centered politics and the growth of administrators and experts in both government and civil society. The expansion and reach of the national media, especially weekly magazines and monthly journals, paralleled the growth of its rapidly expanding cosmopolitan middle-class readership. The election of 1896 politically consolidated those groups and interests who supported the nationalization of government in ways that more accurately reflected the earlier nationalization of culture, commerce, religion, and the economy that had been taking place since the late 1870s.[19]

Mass-based electoral and patronage parties in America almost inevitably push power downward and outward. This political environment is inherently hostile to the formation of national religious establishments. Lacking overriding national projects or goals, elections under their regulation and control become local, and all national and most state party organizations consist of coalitions of local party organizations and interests. That is why patronage and "honest graft" are essential to effective party government.[20] And that is why parties of national reform are antiparty in their values, beginning with the first anti-Jacksonian political movements and continuing through the National Republican Party. After 1896 and the antiparty, antielection, and antipatronage regulation that followed, no mere party victory guaranteed effective power. Parties were forced to share power with many other national institutions, and the legislative power that follows from elections was forced to compete with the administrative and executive power that is partly anchored in the authority it receives from national institutions in civil society: industrial, professional, labor, cultural, educational, and religious.

One can restate this logic in another way. Party government as the leading principle is the best weapon against national religious (and political) establishments. Their rise as thick, locally based organizations signals the repudiation of a standing establishment but does not provide a sufficient basis to create a new one. In that sense, party government is a standing negative majority of locally based and somewhat disparate marginals perfectly captured in the Democratic Party platforms from 1840 through 1856.

The resurgence of party and party politics in 1932 was a minor reversal of these trends, but in the New Deal political order that finally resulted, the Democratic Party was only one institution among many that constituted its power and reach. What came to be known as the liberal establishment of the 1940s through the 1960s had home bases in national institutions (media, finance, unions, corporations, universities) and not party organizations. The Democratic Party, in all of its pluralism and despite all of its historic distrust and even hatred of national elites and national institutions, was forced to share power with the national Progressive side of the Republican Party and its national institutions. This side naturally gravitated toward and was institutionally tied to the presidency and federal administrative bodies. Franklin Roosevelt, like all twentieth-century presidents before and since, could not govern without that support.[21]

Before looking at the contemporary period, it is worthwhile to point to connections between this party-political story and the parallel religious history. Jackson's victory in 1828 founded the Democratic Party as a coalition of disparate and angry marginals—regional, religious, economic—against what they perceived was an aristocratic cultural, economic, and political core. This party was locally based but held together nationally by three bonds: a common enemy (domestic elites and England), a set of elaborate rules to protect the vital interests and ways of life of each group or region in the coalition, and, every four years, a presidential candidate minimally acceptable to all members. Members of this party shared few substantive or "inner" convictions except, perhaps, the paradoxical one of a "constitutional faith" that, in their understanding of the document as a compact among the states, mandated no shared substantive or inner convictions.[22]

In marked contrast, the anti-Jacksonian movements and parties—for shorthand, we'll call them all "National Republican"—were principled parties in the sense that their membership tended to share common convictions about national purposes. These parties were similar to and often arose from national moral reform movements—and they often shared the fluid character of these reform movements in their tendency to splinter, divide, and regroup in response to changing events and issues. Whatever their forms, however, they shared an historicist, organic, or convenantal understanding of the Constitution. While Lincoln best expressed this ideal at its highest moment of power, it was John Quincy Adams, the first National Republican, who provided the clearest formulation. For Adams, the Declaration of Independence formally authorized the American people as a corporate body and empowered them to act as a unity. The Declaration was "a social compact, by which the whole people convenanted with each citizen of the United Colonies, and each citizen with the whole people. . . . Each was pledged to all, and all were pledged to each by a concert of souls, without limitation of time, in the presence of Almighty God, and proclaimed to all mankind."[23] The national constitution of 1787 was only the last and highest in a series of such covenantal agreements in the states and localities and in the complex of free institutions in civil society such as churches, schools, and the family.

The decisive cultural factor that marked the differences between the Jacksonian electoral party and the National Republican parties was religious: the latter movements and parties were formed, led, and supported almost exclusively by liberal evangelical Protestants (including Unitarians)—rich and poor, urban and rural, old family and newly arrived. Conversely, in addition to the slave interest, the Democratic Party was composed of traditional evangelicals (later to become termed fundamentalists), Episcopalians, Catholics, nonbelievers, and fringe religious groups such as the Mormons.[24] This pattern of allegiances held fairly constant for more than a century, as had the spirit and policies of their respective party platforms.[25]

Historians of American political ideas have noted other divides that import a moral-religious dimension into the political ideas distinguishing the Democratic Party from this series of party opponents. The Democratic Party has typically held a static view of America because it defined the basis of unity in formal-legal, contractual, and constitutional terms.[26] Its vision of America was to extend this framework of freedom across the continent, endlessly re-creating political environments that maximize local and individual freedoms, defined as independence, from the rule or control by others—especially others who do not share its particular values and ways of life. Thus, homogeneous localities can govern themselves closely but must stoutly resist power coming from outsiders, viewed as elites or aristocrats not sharing common local values.

In this sense, the Democrats were from the start strong supporters of group rights, if by group one means local and state political jurisdictions. Theirs was a defensive politics, a politics protecting present identities and prevailing ways of life. Reformers are to be feared and resisted as much as distant government, for they represent the imperialism of a moral aristocracy: indeed, in the eyes of good Democrats, *these two aristocracies are often indistinguishable*. Finally, to nineteenth-century Democrats, public and private spheres are clearly known, fixed, and should not be breached: church and state, property and state, economy and state, and family and state are to remain forever separated. These and related ideas are the intellectual and emotional glue that bound Northern Irish Catholics to Southern slave owners to simple farmers to cosmopolitan Eastern gentry. Their one common property was the Constitution, because each group read that document as a charter of their particular group's freedom—freedom defined negatively as independence or autonomy.

The Whigs, the Republican Party, and the host of other anti-Jacksonian/anti-Democratic parties and reform movements that came and went during the second- and third-party eras (e.g., the Anti-Masonic, Liberty, and Prohibition parties, and the suffrage, abolitionist, and temperance movements) not only shared a common background of church affiliations and ecumenical reform institutions,[27] they shared a common national political theology and political style as well. They saw

America as consisting of an historic people founded with the first settlers in New England and religiously bound thereafter to discover and to undertake certain purposes in the world. These substantive purposes both underwrote and took priority over America's formal political and other institutional structures. The spirit behind those purposes not only changed institutional locations, it was the force that established, overthrew, and reinvigorated formal-legal institutions. The Constitution seen in this same light—as one more institutional marker of the progressive American revelation—must be read both historically and organically as a living Constitution to legitimate and protect ever higher stages of personal and national development.

In the words of one astute analyst of the cultural divide between these two kinds of parties, the liberalism of the Democratic Party was humanist and the liberalism of its series of opponents was reform.[28] In the image of another, the former liberalism was anchored in space, the latter, in time or history.[29] The Democrats' internal polity was procedurally constituted—and they interpreted the Constitution that same way. The National Republicans were constituted by shared national projects and purposes—and they interpreted the Constitution that way.[30]

Freedom for the Democrats, whether individual, local, or national, meant liberty as the freedom from interference by others, thereby protecting extant ways of life, including first the institution of slavery and then legal segregation. The protocols of their party forbade questioning the values or the ways of life of any of its members. The party stood for no substantive national purposes or projects that one set of members or one section of the country might embody to a higher or fuller degree than any other set of members or section of the country.[31]

National Republican ideas of both freedom and equality were understood in quite a different spirit. Their conception of freedom stressed having the resources, character, and will for improvement or self-development—improvement and development that entailed a larger responsibility for social and national improvement or development. Neither one's identity nor way of life was fixed or even wholly owned by oneself. In that sense, identity itself is a kind of character-building project or achievement that only makes sense if it is a part of a larger project. One's biography or character achieves its meaning through its connection to a larger history and prophecy—a direct analogue to the long-standing religious tradition of writing one's spiritual biography within the biblical framework of sacred history. Political, social, moral, and religious reform, therefore, is never something external—a mere interest that one happens to have or to have chosen—but a key constituent of one's character and identity.[32]

Given these differences in composition and ideas, it is easy to see how National Republican parties could harbor antiparty ideas and why they were so unstable and so vulnerable to destruction by ever purer political movements condemning the selfishness and expedience attending even minimal compromises needed to attain party-electoral victory. The condemnation of party by John Dewey (a loyal Progressive Republican through the 1920s) in his ethics textbook is almost indistinguishable from the earlier jeremiads of Social Gospel ministers and the still earlier Whig condemnation of Jacksonian Party practices. In all three cases, party was seen as a "subtle and silent . . . tyranny" tempting one away from the demands of responsible citizenship by exchanging private advantage for a vote. "A good partisan cannot be a good citizen."[33] Great or national parties representing shared visions of the public good may be necessary and should be able to attract the best citizens actively to participate, but this institution should not be held hostage to the narrow claims of private and parochial interests.[34]

Until relatively recently, the writing of American religious history served as something of a barrier to understanding and establishing these connections between religion and American political orders and eras. Dominated by faculty in sectarian, denominational, or mainline Protestant divinity schools, American religious history was mainly defined by church and church by denominations, numbers of members, differing creeds, ancillary institutions, and their relative social status and "market share."[35] This denominational story could then be read largely as a demographic story of the shifting numbers, power, and status among the different church bodies in America. Read this way, it often distorted our political history as well. For example, because the first Progressive intellectuals and publicists were so overwhelmingly old-family Congregationalists and Presbyterians, their movement was seen as an attempt to retain their status against newly emerging religious and ethnic groupings—a slightly distorting but not unfair reading of Richard Hofstadter and countless others raised in the New Deal era.

On one level, this explanation is absurd on its face: both of these churches had represented a small fraction of Protestantism since well before the Civil War. What this story also misses is that the only alternative was a more or less reactionary Democratic Party, and it cannot begin to explain how these Progressive elites were able to create a political culture that not only attracted a host of educated and talented immigrants, especially German Jews, but created the very institutional structures that powered reform in America for the next half century, including much of the New Deal. The national universities, academic disciplines, professional organizations, and journals, and an interconnected set of journalistic and reform institutions brought together labor, progressive business interests, ethnic leaders, women's organizations, intellectuals, academics, journalists, and church leaders.[36] If Progressivism was a subtle exercise in mainline Protestant domination, it certainly did not work, because it further marginalized the role of mainline Protestant church organization by transferring power and initiative to nonchurch or parachurch institutions and leaders. Here both national universities and the public school system at the turn of the century are the prime examples.

To write American religious history as if it were church history entails a further difficulty. It implies that the transition from ecumenical Protestant churches to ecumenical Protestant universities was a process of secularization because the talent and energy were increasingly not inside the churches. This reading is misleading because it cannot explain why it was that churchmen and active lay religious leaders were the very ones who conceived and carried out this transfer and relocation—a phenomenon common in both British and American Protestant religious history since the seventeenth century.

If one suspends belief for a time in the thought-stopping thesis of secularization embedded in church history, a new set of self-understandings and historical explanations suggests itself. The first is that our religious history can now be read as part of our larger cultural-political history. One set of common period markers would be those denoting formal-legal or electoral shifts in the nature and meaning of religious liberty: the adoption of the First Amendment to the Constitution; the fall of state religious establishments in the 1820s and 1830s; the appointment of Jews and Catholics to the Supreme Court; the election of John Kennedy. Even these markers, however, tied as they are to denominational history, miss the deeper cultural and religious events and changes. Surely the primary formative event was the American Revolution, now increasingly understood as a titanic religious as well as political struggle.[37] And surely the most transformative event in our political-religious history was the Civil War and, therefore, the religious and moral mobilization that preceded it. The "burnt-over" district of New York produced a whole raft of these movements and organizations in the period 1820–1840, from distinctly religious expressions in Mormonism, Sabbatarianism, and Sunday schools to what are now viewed as quite secular calls for female suffrage, health foods, and eugenic and sexual experiments.[38] When, to these periods, are added the religiously based reform energies that began consolidating in the voluntary sector in the 1880s and 1890s—well before Progressivism emerged as a national electoral force—one has the outlines of a parallel periodization that suggests the formation of a religious establishment either as a powerful counter culture that eventually comes to prevail (e.g., the First and Second Great Awakenings) or as a foreshadowing in civil society of what became institutionalized through elections and other means into a national governing regime.

Another way to bring political and religious history together is to look at the structure of the narrative and rhetorical conventions that bind together political and religious discourse when one national politico-religious establishment is being discredited and a new one is in formation. In overthrowing earlier religious establishments and national political orders, the dissident leaders portray *their* new regime as the attainment of a higher form of religious freedom and political democracy. They can do this because they successfully expose and repudiate the limits (i.e., injustices, inequalities) of the earlier regime. The successful insurgents (and their apologetic historians) declare to themselves and to the nation, "We have *finally* got it right and achieved our promised freedom."[39] These narrative conventions barely hide their theological (and Hegelian) roots and, with it, the deep structures of faith essential to American national identity, namely, that religious freedom and democracy are *revealed at a higher level* with each overcoming. What the apologetic history does successfully hide, however, is the spiritual, intellectual, and institutional debt that each succeeding victor owes the

earlier, now defeated, victors and how the language of the vanquished is both appropriated and extended. This debt is built into the very dialectical structure of
periodization, serving to bind the generations and the political-religious eras into
a common story. The narrative meaning of the American people and the moral
sources of our national identity must always be a call for more democracy and
social justice and human rights in the world—in the language of political theology, affirming the intimation of a transcendent kingdom of God or, in the language of political philosophy, of the good.

This binding together is also recognized in a second narrative convention.
Continued inclusion in the new establishment of leading participants from the
rejected one requires contrition by those earlier elites. *Mea culpas* must be made
by them (or by their apologetic historians) for past failings, past injustices, and
past exclusions. Forgiveness must be asked of the body of American people *that
now includes those who were wronged.* Previous participants who do not do this
are summarily (the fundamentalists) and even violently (the South) ejected from
full membership in the nation. This contrition requirement is not to be disparaged. Every national political order tends to failure and often responds to new
challenges in self-serving, arrogant, and oppressive ways.[40] Acts of contrition,
forgiveness, and rededication are also testament that the jeremiad—itself a dialectic—remains the dominant rhetorical form of our political discourse.[41] This
rhetoric is not "mere," for it reveals, in ways that formal-legal and constitutional
discourse cannot, what moral meanings are being negotiated.[42]

A distorting impression made by these and similar narrative conventions, however, has been that *earlier* establishments in America were more authentically
Protestant, or more authentically Christian, or even more religious, but that
yesterday's (or tomorrow's) are not. Even this convention, however, serves necessary political and religious purposes by preserving a common story. One purpose is to contrast the narrowness, exclusiveness, and elitism of the earlier establishment to the inclusiveness of the prevailing one—indeed, to the implicit
denial that the emergent one is an establishment at all rather than an open invitation to all Americans of good will to join in a series of worthy projects.[43]

What this secularization thesis overlooks is that each denominational or faith
tradition in the new and more inclusive establishment has, *in the very process of
accepting the invitation*, modified its own self-understandings and the way it
presents its beliefs to its own members and to the larger community. So long as
church organizations form, reform, and thrive, moreover, a linear secularization
thesis would require that we portray the churches in America as inevitably becoming less and less religious, less Protestant, less Catholic, less Jewish—as if
those making these Olympian judgments are in possession of the definitive measures of religious identity. Those who want to decline the standing or future invitation to join tend to call the establishment theology "too thin"—*even as they
might fear its politico-religious energy* both in and through other churches and
in the culture at large.[44] Indeed, those making these charges might not fear the
alleged irreligion and godlessness of this national political theology as much as

they do its competing and perhaps more compelling religious spirit—a fact obvious in retrospect regarding Jewish, Catholic, and now Mormon histories of rejection and acceptance in informal American religious establishments. Rejection, after all, is often an effective way for church leaders to police the boundaries and maintain the power of their organizations.

The persuasive power of Larry Moore's *Religious Outsiders and the Making of Americans* rests on charting just this kind of process. One might add, however, that principled rejection (often in prophetic anger) often exacts *spiritual* costs on those churches and their theologies. To insist that one's creedal or denominational theology—and perhaps one's corresponding ethnos—defines and occupies the entire content and space of the religious spirit is to pay high costs in a religiously pluralistic and democratic society. The highest cost is removal of that religious (and ethnic) community, its institutions and ideas, from participation in the larger spiritual and intellectual life of the nation and, through that, of one's own time. Indeed, at its best, American political theology has often been the path by which particular church theologies confront the world, grapple with its new knowledge and powers, and thereby instill a greater depth and reflexivity back into their own theologies. Rather than being conceptually thin and ethically shallow, American political theology is often *too demanding* for many churches, so they retreat into themselves. Fortunately, however, most rejections in the long run have proven to be more strategic than principled, a means of gaining voice and joining the conversation.[45]

A final way to bring these political and religious histories into the framework of a single story might best be illustrated by the American experience leading up to and following our participation in World War I. This period is rightly understood, I think, as representing both a kind of apotheosis of the Protestant-Progressive establishment and as its last hurrah. This was the last time that ecumenical Protestantism spoke with one overwhelmingly powerful voice *as the American religion*. This period is both triumphal and tragic because it so starkly illustrates the temptations that inevitably come to corrupt and subvert all successful politico-religious establishments in America.[46]

By 1900, most Progressives shared the view expressed by one of America's foremost political theologians, Lyman Abbott, the editor of *Outlook*: "We are a world power; we are likely to be a leader among the world-powers. We could not help ourselves if we would; we would not help ourselves if we could."[47] As close followers of European events and long-time participants in international mission, reform, charitable, and disaster relief causes, Progressive political, educational, and religious leaders were the first to urge "preparedness." While preparedness included governmental plans for military mobilization, its initial thrust was moral and voluntarist—a call for all Americans to prepare themselves for a momentous test of resolve and will. Without question it was Progressive intellectuals, publicists, and political leaders who led the way.[48] Their very willingness to prepare for some as yet unknown collective sacrifice was itself proof that national republican virtue was more important than individual material comfort—

proof that, in the words of Theodore Roosevelt some years earlier, we are not a nation of "well to do hucksters . . . sunk in a scrambling commercialism."[49] Once the struggle in Europe was framed in terms of the fate of democracy in the world, Progressives did not doubt that America would be called to take a leading role in its defense.

Here is where the seeds of both triumph and tragedy are sown. When defense of democracy at home and abroad is also a defense of a certain kind of sacred American national identity, the call for preparedness takes on the ideal of national regeneration through atonement—the selfless sacrifice by the "innocent" and "righteous" for the evils of others. Politics itself becomes salvific, especially when a weak formal government is attempting to benefit from and control an exceptionally well organized and powerfully mobilized set of righteous and self-confident national institutions and a supporting national media. To oppose the call is un-American in both a political and a religious sense. As preparedness turned to mobilization, and mobilization to war, it was almost as if four decades of cultural and political preparation by the Progressives had at last found an object worthy of its impulses.

Lyman Abbott's *The Twentieth Century Crusade* (1918) stands as a sort of "proof text" for the flood of books and articles written by Progressive publicists and intellectuals, revealing both the grandeur and the hubris of effective establishment for the achievement of great national ends.[50] American civic virtue, according to Abbott, is best embodied in her mothers and their young sons, two groups officially excluded in 1918 from the constitutional status of voter. The mothers are asked to sacrifice their sons to the larger cause of justice and democracy; the sons are called to exercise physical courage and risk their lives to atone for the sins and failings of others—including, presumably, their own voter-fathers.[51] Despite their sentimentality, Abbott's nine letters to mothers are a robust call to arms. The first letter recalls Lincoln and the Civil War, telling the mother that her son "has joined the noble army of patriots." By the fifth letter, he is contrasting the "glory in tribulation" to the sordid ends of personal happiness.[52] The sixth and seventh letters remind the reader that democracy is not a form of government but a way of life, a faith in human brotherhood that informs the character of all American institutions, religious, industrial, educational, and political. Our democratic republic is portrayed as the modern Israel, a holy nation opposing "Rome" in all its forms. Lincoln and Wilson, Abbott tells us, stand for Hegel and Christianity; Germany and the Kaiser represent materialism, paganism, and power. The concluding letters are triumphal. Democracy and social justice are marching to victory. They "who have offered their lives, not merely for their country, but for an unknown people, of a different land, a different language and often of a different religious faith" will be crowned with immortality "not as a hope for the future [but] as a present possession, . . . the consciousness that I am more than the body which I inhabit."[53]

This politico-theological understanding of American identity and civic virtue gave early preparedness campaigns and later war mobilization a decidedly voluntarist cast, creating a powerful engine of moral, religious, and political coercion without commensurate state machinery to locate responsibility and set limits on the exercise of this power.[54] While this was most evident in the thousands of Americans who served in expeditionary units prior to the declaration of war, it was also manifest in the way in which small federal governmental units functioned through very large voluntary organizations and efforts.[55] The crowning achievement of this style of mobilization was military conscription itself. Almost the entire apparatus of the draft functioned outside of the official federal government—and, therefore, outside its constitutional procedures and limits. Of the 192,000 workers administering the draft, just 429 were salaried federal employees. Only a nation already integrated and mobilized in spirit for many decades could have accomplished what still appears almost miraculous today. Two weeks to the day after Congress passed the Conscription Act, nine and one-half million men presented themselves to local draft boards. With only the most rudimentary federal administrative apparatus, the American nation did what the most powerful and centralized European states could barely imagine.[56]

What are we to make of this experience? A negative reading is simply to point to the domestic victims of preparedness marked by the "Red Scare": left populists, the Industrial Workers of the World (IWW), antiwar socialists, and the peace churches were joined by isolationists and traditionalists, including many fundamentalist churches, in rejecting the preparedness crusade, and they all paid dearly for it. Read this way, the war was both a means and a pretext for capitalists and conservatives to intimidate and forestall the triumph of radical reform and perhaps even democratic socialism.[57] A positive reading is to see in this political and economic mobilization the kinds of administrative capacities, moral resources, and (discounting the excesses) political leadership that all great undertakings require. Given our system of divided government and the dominance of particular interests, this sort of popular and "corporatist" model is an extreme case of what all major national undertakings require, whether the ends be industrial and racial justice at home or combating fascism and communism abroad.

Combined, these conflicting readings suggest a more dialectical and ironic one. In situations when informal religious establishments become so entwined with formal government that they become almost indistinguishable, governmental power expands exponentially. What was previously a consensus which each group could differentially join or ignore tends to becomes a uniform and coercive standard. Formal hierarchy and elite rule soon become the norm. Instead of the voluntary nation authorizing the coercive state, the coercive state now appears as the sovereign, itself presuming a sacred character and demanding worship.[58] Political theology becomes a civil religion, and establishment churches risk becoming adjuncts of the state. A merely ironic response, however, is not sufficient. All effective democratic national government in America both requires and risks these conditions. The choice is not between innocence and evil but between responsible and irresponsible exercises of power under these conditions.

Whatever America did or did not learn from this experience, we do know that this triumphal story ends in the dissolution and defeat of Progressivism as an animating political force. The gap between triumph and defeat can be measured by comparing the election of 1912 to that of 1924. In 1912 all three leading presidential candidates had some impressive Progressive credentials; in 1924 the Republicans nominated Calvin Coolidge, and the Democrats, John W. Davis, a Wall Street lawyer from West Virginia who ended his career defending states' rights before the Supreme Court in *Brown v. Topeka*. The only "progressive" candidate was Robert LaFollette, but it was difficult to tell which of his followers were progressive and which nostalgic reactionaries. The results for Protestantism as a coherent cultural and moral source were equally clear. Liberals and modernists paid a heavy price when they mercilessly attacked more traditional evangelicals for not joining the preparedness campaign—at least not soon enough. Fundamentalism discovered and organized itself. Culturally and intellectually the results were more complex. Walter Lippmann both opted for rule by liberal elites and made common cause with the leading fundamentalist theologian, Princeton's John Machen—thereby stripping theology of its political dimension and consolidating the ideal of secular-cosmopolitan elite rule. Lippmann's disenchantment in *Preface to Morals* (1929) is mirrored in similar disenchants and retreats in the books of other intellectuals such as John Crowe Ransom, Harry Elmer Barnes, and Joseph Wood Krutch.[59] Even John Dewey, who maintained both his national democratic commitments and his deep religious spirit, desperately searched for a formula for a faith that would empower but not divide the nation.

This brief period proved both the power and the weakness of a national political theology. What it did not prove is that we can get along without one. This period also demonstrates the deleterious effects on the American intellect when a common canopy no longer speaks to and inspirits America. Whether the response be authoritarian, nostalgic, utopian, or reactionary, public intellectuals writing in the late 1920s and early 1930s should be viewed as "beautiful souls" with little or nothing coherent to say to America at that time or at any other. They could not find a voice with which to speak to the nation because the nation had, for a time, disaggregated. Their proper job, and one that John Dewey seemed to take seriously and responsibly, was to reshape a narrative structure and vocabulary that would again channel the varied moral spirits and intellectual impulses of America into a common stream, but now wider and deeper than before.

NOTES

1. Howe 1979 and 1997b; and see Kohl 1989.

2. The best discussion of Republican Party formation is Gienapp (1987). Discussion of Republican Party rhetoric as a civil religion is found in Tuveson (1968) and Bellah (1968). Care must be taken to distinguish the concept of civil religion from the larger idea of political theology. The former suggests (but neither Tuveson nor Bellah do) more

a purely legitimating function for both churches and religion generally; the latter is a more comprehensive orientation that embraces both state and church within a comprehensive biblical-historical framework. This is discussed in the next chapter.

3. This distinction, appropriate for discussing different relationships of the nation and federal government to religion, slights the very real and persistent presence of formal religion in various state constitutions in the nineteenth century (Gaustad 1987, appendix B), and see Lowi (1995), chapter 1, on the use of state police powers to regulate morality.

4. Some recent studies of American political thought that recognize and use this distinction are Eisenach 1990 and 1994; Greenstone 1993, 48–65; Howe 1979; Kohl 1989; Major Wilson 1974.

5. Two examples illustrate this difficulty. The Jeffersonian and populist historian, Vernon Parrington, declared it only "a curious irony of fate" that Jonathan Edwards, "a reactionary Calvinist . . . became the intellectual leader of the revolutionaries" (1927, 164). The Catholic theologian, John Courtney Murray, dismisses the normative status of Roger Williams as "a seventeenth-century Calvinist who somehow had got hold of certain remarkably un-Calvinist ideas on the nature of the political order in its distinction from the church" (in Miller 1988, 219). Here, secular Jeffersonian and Catholic join hands—and not for the first time—in insisting that no "Protestant" theology, or indeed, any "church" ideas, can be taken as constitutive of American nationality by incorporating them into readings of the Declaration of Independence, the Constitution, or its Bill of Rights. On Parrington's reading, religious freedom in America is the product of a secular philosophy that provides the necessary articles of peace in a religiously pluralistic society. For some religious readings of these same documents and events, see Ferguson 1996, 44–79; Miller 1988; Bercovitch 1976, 597–630; Bloch 1990, 44–61; Eisenach 1979, 71–98; John Wilson 1990, 77–91; and Gordon Wood 1997, 173–205.

6. Here the origins of the Republican Party and its relationship to earlier fringe parties and religious movements and to a rather virulent anti-Catholicism is the most obvious example. Gienapp 1987. Greenstone responds to Gordon Wood's statement that John Adams's ideas were anachronistic (while Jefferson's foretold the future) by asking why Adams's untimely traditionalism "kept repeating itself" (1993, 75). Wood, like Hartz, cannot account, for example, for the increasing influence of John Quincy Adams in national political discourse after his defeat by Jackson, nor, indeed, for the rise of the Republican Party from Federalist, Whig, and even Know Nothing sources.

7. Here the issue is the widely differing perceptions of the Jacksonians and the Whigs and other anti-Jacksonian parties and movements. Because the anti-Jacksonian parties were composed primarily of evangelicals, the related issue is whether this social force and the movements it supported were progressive or reactionary. An excellent discussion of the origin and persistence of National Republican [Whig] ideology is Gerring (1997 and 1998); and see Howe 1970 and 1997b.

8. Eisenach (1994), chapter 1, on intellectual creators of their critique of America and their similar backgrounds.

9. What is pride in success and assimilation in one generation is occasion for painful reappraisal in the next. This is especially the case among Jews, whose German leadership exercised persistent pressure to integrate newer immigrants into national institutional life, following their own extraordinary success in doing so between the Civil War and World War I. See Cohen (1992), charging these leaders with timidity by accepting Protestant leadership, and Ginsberg (1993), who sees the 1920s as a sort of proof that

the successes as parts of national governing coalitions in the prior half-century were an illusion. The irony of this is that both authors could not have even conceived of writing such books and occupy the positions in the institutional and cultural milieus they do without the hegemonic strategies of the German Jews over the new arrivals. Both of these books are evidence of the paradoxical processes Laurence Moore describes in *Religious Outsiders and the Making of Americans* (1986); also Cuddihy in *No Offense: Civil Religion and Protestant Taste* (1978).

10. This would explain, too, the consensual language of John Jay and George Washington, who seem almost deliberately misleading according to our readings of colonial religious diversity today. Jay, in *Federalist Paper* no. 2, claimed that "Providence has been pleased to give this one connected country to one united people . . . professing the same religion"; Washington, in his "Farewell Address," reminded his countrymen that, "with slight shades of difference, you have the same religion" (in Miller 1988, 322 and 244).

11. Donald B. Johnson and Kirk H. Porter 1975, 1–2.

12. Quoted in Keller 1977, 252–53.

13. Rorty 1998, 3.

14. See introductory essay, Stout and Hart (1997). One problem with many of the ethno-religious interpretations of party allegiances and realignments cited in chapter 1, n.2, is that using church denominations as markers tends to make churches stand for and contain religion itself.

15. See Handy 1960, 3–16, and 1971, 184–225; and Marsden (1994) on equating disestablishment per se with the end of mainline Protestant church hegemony in the 1920s.

16. See Ahlstrom 1972; Roof and McKinney 1987; and Mooney (1990) on religious pluralism supplanting a common faith of Judeo-Christian ecumenicism in the 1970s.

17. The definitive study here is Gienapp (1987); see also Kelley 1979.

18. McCormick 1986; Silbey 1991; McGerr 1986; Burnham 1970.

19. That is the major argument in Eisenach 1994; and see Skowronek 1982; McCormick 1986; and Gerring 1998.

20. Woodrow Wilson defended this in *Constitutional Government* in 1908. See Eisenach 1994, 127–29.

21. Shefter (1978) and Plotke (1996) are best here; and see Eisenach 1995.

22. Unlike the anti-Jacksonian parties, for example, the Democratic Party required a two-thirds majority to nominate a presidential candidate, a rule that demanded extensive negotiation and trade-offs to reach agreement because it gave strong blocs effective veto powers. Jaenicke 1986; Greenstone 1993; Kohl 1989.

23. Quoted in Eisenach 1994, n50.; and see Elazar 1998, 1–98.

24. Benson 1961; Swierenga 1990; and Carwardine 1993. The Episcopal Church was a bastion of the Democratic Party in the North in the second- and third-party-system eras. Given the dominance of evangelicalism and, later, the Social Gospel, in other Protestant bodies, the evangelical wing of the Episcopal Church in America was much less strong than its counterpart in the Church of England. Indeed, the Episcopal Church became something of a refuge from the intense evangelicalism and revivalism in the other American churches. See Howe 1997b, 217–18 and n.48.

25. See Gerring (1997 and 1998), especially on the issue of national authority and national institutions. He correctly points out (1999), however, that party platforms and competition between parties are usually expressed in economic policies, with the cultural and religious components usually hidden or expressed obliquely. This is not only mandated

by election strategy but also by the fact that the cultural component is usually fought out first *within* each party and, once settled, subordinated to economic issues. See Glenn 1988, chapters 3 and 7, on the Democratic Party opponents of Horace Mann and formation of common schools.

26. The wording and order of its national party platforms were essentially unchanged from 1840 through 1856, and all planks stressed constitutional limitations.

27. These ecumenical organizations and institutions were crucial for establishing shared political identities because they were often lay-led and not immediately implicated in denominational market-competitive interests. Combined with key colleges and universities, they represented the penetration of National Republican values in culture and civil society.

28. Greenstone 1993. The political historian Harry Watson put this same difference this way: "The Democrats saw themselves as the party of liberty, while Whigs claimed to be the party of improvement" (in Howe 1997b, 213).

29. Major Wilson 1974.

30. Jaenicke 1986; Kohl 1989; Greenstone 1993; Eisenach 1990 and 1994.

31. This also meant that Southerners, as experienced and educated local elites, tended to dominate national leadership in the Democratic Party and, before the Civil War, American national leadership. In the first 72 years under the Constitution, Southerners (and slaveholders) held the presidency for 49 years; held 23 of 36 Speaker of the House positions; 24 of 36 president pro tem of the Senate positions; and 20 of 35 positions on the Supreme Court. McPherson (1991), 13. Tocqueville's distinction between equality and liberty perfectly captures this negative ideal. Equality, or freedom as noninterference in another's self-chosen ends, is available to everyone. To taste its pleasures one only had to live. What he meant was that one could wake up every morning with no duties to others except those one had freely agreed to. Tocqueville 1981, vol. II, bk. 2, ch. 1, 390–98.

32. This understanding is philosophically articulated in Charles Taylor's distinction between "constitutive goods" that lie behind "the morals of obligatory action" and "life goods" that do not. Taylor 1989, 92–93. And see John Morris 1966; Abrams 1973, 71–139; Peterson 1986. John Stuart Mill's concept of individuality was grounded in this same biographical-historical ideal. On the *Autobiography* of Mill as written in the same framework as spiritual biography, Eisenach 1987; and Carlisle 1991.

33. Eisenach 1994, 113. Dewey's textbook reads: "These agencies are the 'machines' of political parties, with their hierarchical gradation of bosses from national to ward rulers, bosses who are in close touch with great business interests at one extreme and those who pander to the vices of the community (gambling, drink, and prostitution) at the other; [combined with] all sorts of devices for holding together and exciting masses of men to more or less blind acquiescence" (in Eisenach 1994, 114).

34. Eisenach 1994, 117–22. And see Tocqueville's contrast of great and small parties (1981, 89–91). In contrast to these writings, Woodrow Wilson defended traditional party government and the patronage that necessarily held it together. See Eisenach 1994, 127–29 and 135. On this difference, see also Greenstone 1993; Jaenicke 1986; and Gerring 1997 and 1998.

35. Stout and Hart 1997, 3–11.

36. Eisenach 1994; Crunden 1984; and Fitzpatrick 1990.

37. Gordon Wood 1997; Eisenach 1979; Bercovitch 1976; Clark 1994; Paul Johnson 1995; Phillips 1999.

38. Cross 1950; Moore 1994.

39. This is convincingly argued by Steven Smith (1995). A good example of the illusion of arrival is the first sentence of a definitive study of religion in the public schools written in 1912, *The Secularization of American Education as Shown by State Legislation, State Constitutional Provisions and State Supreme Court Decisions*: "For somewhat over a century there has been going on in the United States a gradual but widespread elimination of religious and church influence from public education" (Brown 1967). And see Glenn 1988, chapters 6–8.

40. See Skowronek 1993, for a masterful analysis of this process in the context of the presidency; and Morone 1998, on the limits of popular mobilization on a national scale.

41. Bercovitch 1978.

42. This is perhaps another way of making Charles Taylor's point that one discovers the personal moral commitments of contemporary analytic and "value free" philosophers by attending to the rhetorical denunciations of the religious and philosophical errors (and the damage they do) of their opponents (1989, 338).

43. Perhaps the reason that Rogers Smith's *Civic Ideals* (1997) has received so many public awards, apart from its many scholarly virtues, is because it almost exactly replicates these rhetorical strategies. For a critical discussion and rejoinder of *Civic Ideals* on these terms, see Eisenach 1999a and Rogers Smith 1999.

44. This duality is nicely charted in Glenn (1988) in recounting the success of the religious understanding of the proponents of common schools against both Catholic and conservative Protestant opponents.

45. This argument is not meant to make light of this kind of Barthian stance—indeed, just the opposite. It does, however, point to the inevitable ambiguities of a prophetic stance that is positioned in but not of the world when the institutional standpoint is one church in a plurality of churches and whose audience is both inside and outside that body of the faithful. Here the writings of Stanley Hauerwas are the most instructive.

46. Morone 1998, starting from different premises, reaches this same conclusion.

47. Abbott 1901, 266. Abbott was the editor of *Outlook,* a leading Progressive weekly, and pastor of the leading Congregational Church in America. Anti-imperialists were largely confined to the South and to Unitarian Boston, by then both marginal cultures, and to the remaining pockets of populism throughout the country.

48. See McClymer (1980), chapters 5 and 6, on social workers; Kennedy (1980), 33–44, on the universities; Wynn (1986), 36–38 and 43–44, on Progressive journalists, reformers, and women's rights activists; Schaffer (1991), 90–95, on women reformers, and 127–48, on the universities; and Ernst (1974), 35–69, on liberal evangelical churches and ecumenical associations.

49. In Giankos and Karson 1966, vol. 1, 52–53.

50. Abbott 1918; and see discussion of this and similar books in Eisenach (1994), 243–50. Dwight Eisenhower's history of World War II was titled *Crusade in Europe* (1948).

51. The counterpart of this image is that adult males embody liberal individualism and truncated ideas of citizen as voter. This argument is developed in Kann 1990.

52. Abbott 1918, 52–54.

53. Abbott 1918, 106 and 103.

54. Here the parallel to the early Civil War is almost exact, except the extra-governmental power then was almost exclusively located and coordinated through the Republican Party organization.

55. From George Creel's Committee on Public Information, with its volunteer army of 150,000 intellectuals, writers, and speakers, to Herbert Hoover's Food Administration, with a paid staff of 1,400 directing 750,000 volunteer housewives allocating and rationing the nation's food supply, it appeared that official action was only the final procedural act, not the substantive animating source, of the war effort. Even the initial funding for allied loans was raised voluntarily. In June 1917, four million Americans joined in offering the government $3 billion in "Liberty Loans"—an amount that increased to more than $25 billion within two years.

56. This was also true regarding the War Industries Board (WIB) that directed the entire wartime industrial economy. Created by Woodrow Wilson without any statutory authorization, it functioned with state and local councils appointed by governors. Eventually consisting of almost 200,000 members, these councils and the WIB provided legal sanction and enforced agreements reached within each industrial and regional group on wages, hours, production quotas, and prices. See Eisenach 1994, 245–46.

57. Murray 1964; Peterson and Fite 1957; Weinstein 1984. On this measure, the most progressive state in America was Oklahoma.

58. As Morone (1998) so thoroughly recounts, given Americans' distrust of powerful bureaucratic institutions, this resolution contains the seeds of its own destruction.

59. See Conkin (1998) for an excellent discussion of these writings in the context of the Scopes trial.

Chapter 3

Theologies/Ideologies:
National, Political, and Religious

Every effective religious establishment, voluntary or legally coerced, relatively tolerant or relatively intolerant, must have some theology defining, directing, and binding it together. Every effective political order, whether relatively open and democratic or relatively hierarchic, closed and authoritarian, must have some ideology performing these same integrative and directing functions. In a democracy, both theology and ideology must also serve to generate and maintain popular support against the competition of indifference and of political or religious alternatives. However a standing regime comes to be discredited and destroyed, given the succession of religious establishments and political orders in America, both countertheologies and counterideologies must eventually be created to authorize new leaders, constituencies, programs, spirits, and values.

There is one further requirement: both theology and ideology must prevail not only among the more immediate and enthusiastic leaders and constituencies, they must also hold sufficient sway over the more passive and even opposed leaders and their constituencies to convince them to accept the legitimacy and obey the authority of both the establishment and political order, if only passively and only at the national level. The forms of this acceptance and obedience are, of course, quite different regarding a voluntary and informal religious/cultural establishment and a coerced and formal legal government, but acceptance and obedience are necessary if society is to sustain social peace, cooperation, and mutual trust.

A common term used today to describe both the establishment/regime and the opposition that accepts its authority and legitimacy is "hegemony." For leaders and rulers, hegemony is a *solution*, not a problem, for without it, their capacity to lead or to rule would be extremely difficult if not impossible—especially in democratic, decentralized, and pluralistic America. In America, however, we do not like the authoritarian sound of hegemony (nor its derivation from the Gramscian branch of Marxist thought), so we express the same idea with the softer terms of "consensus" politics and "common" or "shared" religious beliefs. John

51

Jay, in *Federalist Paper* no. 2, claimed that "Providence has been pleased to give this one connected country to one united people . . . professing the same religion"; George Washington, in his "Farewell Address," reminded his countrymen that, "with slight shades of difference, you have the same religion." Jefferson, in his 1801 inaugural address proclaimed, "We are all Republicans, we are all Federalists."[1] These men are accounted founders not because they won elections and prevailed at ratifying conventions but because they helped to *establish a people*. Whether this is termed hegemony or consensus-building, these victors nevertheless won not only an external or institutional victory, they won the ethnic battle as well by capturing the hearts and minds of enough of the opposition to marginalize as extremists or malcontents those standing outside the canopy of consensus. If pushed—and leaders were sorely pushed during the Revolutionary War and the Civil War—victors will go so far as to demand loyalty oaths and label some outsiders "un-American."[2]

If periods of religious establishments seem to run parallel to or, at a minimum, significantly overlap periods of distinct national political orders, then the theology of the former should run parallel with or significantly overlap the ideology of the latter. More importantly, since both the religious establishment and the political order are *national* ones—with lots of local and regional room for indifference, divergence, and even active disobedience—there should even be a convergence. This is the case because both national religious establishments and national political orders have as a common and often overriding goal the infusion of authoritative purpose into the American people and the creation or re-creation of America as one people against the centrifugal and even anarchic tendencies built into both religious freedom and decentralized and limited constitutional governments.

Two historical examples may be useful. John Quincy Adams echoed Tocqueville's charge that unchecked democratic individualism is incompatible with sustaining a common nationality because, with individualism as a defining value, America "has no forefathers, it looks to no posterity, it is swallowed up in the present, and thinks of nothing but itself." A century later, the Progressive reformer Mary Follett put this same opposition more bluntly: "To substitute for the fictitious democracy of equal rights and consent of the governed, the living democracy of a united, responsible people."[3] Follett, of course, did not seek to destroy either equal rights or consent of the governed and, Andrew Jackson to the contrary, neither did John Quincy Adams. Both Adams and Follett were addressing a perennial American problem that is neither distinctly church-religious nor distinctly governmental-political, but cultural-national—who we are and what we are about *as a people*. Their instrument was persuasion and their medium, intellectual culture and public opinion. Like all who seek national leadership and the undertaking of common projects, both Adams and Follett knew that an authoritative public opinion that integrates personal, social, and political roles also and necessarily ranks and measures ways of life. While this is often blandly called "civic education" or "political culture," it is a shared moral orientation that necessarily distinguishes between lower and higher forms of citizenship and between more and less admirable ways of life. All significant acts of national democratic political life and all attempts to create and sustain common purposes entail these choices.

While theology and ideology overlap, however, there are significant differences both in their institutional settings and in how they work. Because political ideology is primarily a discourse of electoral politics and regime creation, maintenance, or overthrow, it often has a somewhat disjointed and discontinuous content. Effective majority coalitions must be sustained under very difficult and changing conditions that a general partisan consensus cannot always overcome. And the very existence of an organized opposition, even one that accepts the moral framework of the governing party, means that failures, indecision, or incoherence will quickly be exploited. When events—wars, economic depressions, labor unrest, and race riot or other instances of domestic violence or insurrection—overwhelm the political order, political discourse must respond, both to frame the event and to indicate appropriate policies. Moreover, some signal events so discredit a standing political order and its ideology that their electoral opponents are simply handed victory without a coherent set of alternative governing ideas to replace those of the overthrown regime. The clearest instance is Franklin Roosevelt's victory in 1932.[4] Finally, parties contesting general elections often deliberately subordinate the moral and cultural issues of their core supporters in order to attract support on other grounds. Because moral-cultural issues tend to be fought out in intraparty battles, economic issues that encode but do not explicitly state these background values are stressed.[5]

The case of informal religious establishments is quite different. The heart and soul of their discourse is that of moral orientations, usually expressed in the discourse of improvement and reform. Often their major opposition is portrayed as indifferent, uninformed, and withdrawn. Because of the variety and the continuity of nationally based intellectual, academic, religious, charitable, and cultural institutions, the theology holding any single religious establishment together is not only less immediately programmatic, it might be held in quite different ways by its various leaders and constituencies. The authority exercised by voluntary national religious establishments is neither legal nor direct, so it often functions from within the ordinary practices and institutions serving other direct purposes, for example in the norms and practices of the professions, in the humanities and social science curriculum in universities, in the priorities and training imparted in schools of education, and in the rhetorical themes of presidential inauguration and commencement speeches.

Wherever this theology is articulated and manifested, however, it is never the same as the specific doctrinal religious creed of a particular institutional church or even the common doctrinal religious creeds of a group of strong churches. *Indeed, if this theology were ever perceived that way or can be made to be perceived that way by large numbers of people or even by a significant sector of American leaders, its authority is immediately undermined.* This same negative can be put in positive terms: the theology of every successful establishment in America must consciously disavow allegiance to any sectarian doctrine even as it avows allegiance to that which binds "all" Americans together.[6] No matter how exclusionary or narrow such establishments might appear in retrospect, every successful theology is a standing invitation to all who are thought (or think themselves) capable of joining. This has been true of all successful establishments and their corresponding theologies. The clearest evidence of this is the formation of the public school systems in the mid-nineteenth century and their continuous adaptation and success in the twentieth century.[7]

The parallel to political ideology here is almost exact. The ideology that a victorious party must share to govern nationally must seem to embrace many of the values and purposes of their opponents as well.[8] *Indeed, if this ideology were ever perceived as only the values and projects of the electoral victors or could be made to be perceived that way by large numbers of people or even by a significant sector of American leadership, its title to rule would only be because they were merely stronger (they had more votes) and its authority would soon be undermined.*[9] Thus, the moral authority to govern the nation can never be grounded in simply winning an electoral game.[10] Electoral games alone can produce "negative" majorities but not necessarily governing ones. Positive national majorities are required, not only because the U.S. constitutional game is not the only game in town, but because that Constitution contains such severe formal prohibitions on the use of federal power that no national government could possibly govern only within its rule framework, its own institutional structure, and its explicit grants of power. That is why, from the start, national elites quickly formed into party caucuses and created the party press, why mass-based electoral party machines were constructed, and why the whole panoply of quasi-governmental national establishments, from universities through the national press, quickly emerged when parties lost their monopoly. Truth to tell, even parties—those seemingly more directly "political, public and secular" institutions—were never effective in constructing powerful national political orders except as they also served as holding companies for the religious, economic, cultural, and sectional values that aspired to national leadership.[11] Without that animus, they could only govern negatively by repudiating and disestablishing the prevailing order.

NATIONAL POLITICAL THEOLOGY

These factors, along with the history of periodization in both religious and political establishments, suggest that some term must be used that encompasses both theology and ideology and takes into account the fact that so much of our political, moral, and intellectual energies are addressed to the problem of sustaining and enriching American nationality as the source of religious, cultural, and political authority. The ancient term and one that was reissued into American circulation in the 1960s by Robert Bellah, was "civil religion." But this term cannot really do to convey the argument made here because its long historical usage (but not Bellah's) suggests a false unidirectional causal path: the use of a common religion to "legitimate" governing authority. To be sure, American religious establishments have served as cheerleaders for the powerful but they have also stood in prophetic witness against them. Neither function, however, captures its other elements and activities that are national and authoritative but not directly governmental. Indeed, in the late nineteenth century, as parties lost their monopoly control of elections and as party loyalty dissipated and began to lose its ethno-religious determinates, even this connection and mediation that encouraged civil religion (at least for the Republican Party) has disappeared.

Some other terms to connect theology and ideology are also in circulation but also must be rejected. One is "common" or "shared" faith. These, too, are inadequate because they too readily suggest a common denominator *left over* from allegedly more real and demanding church faiths and because they disguise the *politically authoritative* element that must be present. Another commonly used term is "public religion." This term suggests authority (public) but also suggests formularies and rituals as its chief component, reducing it to those ceremonial occasions when we want to say, "This event is really significant" and mark it by draping the stage with patriotic bunting and parading clerical representatives of the major faiths across the platform. None of these or similar terms captures the ways in which the theology of voluntary religious establishment does much more than legitimate governors and often has little to do directly with churches and other sectarian institutions. Last, and perhaps most important, none of these terms suggests a distinctly philosophical or intellectual component. For all of these reasons and for others that should become apparent later, I have chosen the term "national political theology" to denote the body of ideas that combines both the theology of voluntary religious establishment and the underlying ideology of national political orders in America.

In every establishment period, national political theology not only legitimates national regimes by mobilizing church, government, culture, media, schools, voluntary organizations, and even families on behalf of national projects and purposes, it also declares what kinds of parties, churches, schools, voluntary organizations, entertainment, and their corresponding forms of expression and beliefs are appropriate for full inclusion in national political deliberation. Because it serves this two-sided legitimation function, ever since the rise of *informal* religious establishments, the primary institutional location of our political theology has rarely been the denominational churches. Many of its leading theologians have transcended their church identity while many others have not been members of the clergy or even affiliated with a particular church at all.

If the *nation* is the church invisible as both the object and subject of national political theology, its major institutions must be persuaded to understand themselves within a common framework and to treat all who do so with the respect they deserve as fellow members: this is true in both politics and religion. Moreover, given the role that national political theology plays in political regime destruction and formation, it is clear that this theology can never be as thin and derivative as suggested by such terms as "overlapping consensus" and "common denominator" or, indeed, any concept that suggests a disparate package of discounted "remainders," as if the items of real value and power are the sole possession of separate churches or faith traditions, or of ethnic, linguistic, or racial groupings, or of subjective choice by sovereign individuals.

Under the combined auspices of powerful politico-religious establishments (or disestablishment movements seeking to replace the prevailing one), American national political theology has often been a stern and intellectually demanding faith quite willing to excommunicate, define heresies, and impose ritual obedience, and quite able to recruit the energies, talents, and sacrifices of America's most intellectually sophisticated and morally serious members. Another name for this history is nation building; still another is national democratic political life under conditions of religious pluralism and intellectual and religious freedom. It is discourse *within* national political theology that permits the many and various groups in America to speak to each other as equals, to explain and justify themselves to others, and to interpret and understand themselves and others *as Americans*. It is *by* national political theology that the people in America become and remain bound to each other *as Americans* with mutual obligations. It is *through* national political theology that the people in America authorize and empower—and chastise and weaken—their various and changing political, cultural, religious and social institutions.

National political theology is the substantive expression of American identity in its highest and most articulate intellectual form; it is the concrete expression of what we mean when we say that we are "one nation . . . indivisible." But here one confronts the contemporary rub. Just because this nation and its national political theology were always presumed "under God" (a phrase added to the Pledge of Allegiance in 1952), can we presume that this is still the case? If we cannot, if we are joined together only by sheer self-willing or by self-constituted obligations, can we even imagine a national political theology today and, if not, can we *have* a coherent national identity? Self-willing and self-constituting are the products and appropriate behaviors *within* free government and constitutions, but free government and constitutions are not self-constituting. Can we remain one nation, indivisible *without* an authoritative national political theology and without an informal religious establishment that attests to these origins? Walt Whitman was only one in a long line of American intellectuals who called for and helped to shape "a sublime and serious Religious Democracy sternly taking command, dissolving the old, sloughing off surfaces, and from its own interior and vital principles, reconstructing, democratizing society."[12] Has this line— should this line—become extinct?

The history of authoritative national political theologies in America can be understood in many different ways, but surely one overriding feature is its consistency in form and purpose. National political theology in America incorporates an inner imperative to engage with and adapt to the changing economic, political, demographic, religious, and intellectual facts and events in American life. It, therefore, can never be reduced to formal institutions, principles, and rules, because it is purpose- and action-oriented and is part of a continuous history of purposes and actions that long preceded it and will long succeed it. These features are also suggested by the way in which national political theologies have survived and flourished in the face of massive demographic changes in denominational and creedal distributions of members and resources. We not only remained a nation without a distinctly and necessarily Anglo-Saxon Protestant establishment that prevailed through the Civil War, we became more of a nation and a more just one. Even when we seemed to have disestablished the succeeding and more embracive European-Protestant establishment that came into being in the 1880s and remained powerful into the 1920s, we not only remained "one nation, after all," we soon embraced an even more inclusive Judeo-Christian-Western Civilization establishment that informed and directed the leading institutions of our national life and foreign policy from the 1940s through the 1960s.[13] What are the common intellectual, moral, and political threads in this string of successive and successful transformations? And what about now?

It often appears today that our leading public intellectuals, including ecumenical religious leaders, higher journalists, the judiciary, and academics in the humanities and social sciences, have embraced an understanding of America as a "nation of nations" under the boundless canopy of an abstract set of universal liberal principles but not with distinctly national values. This set of principles is recommended precisely because it is *not* grounded in our national experience and politics—indeed, because it can and should be read largely as a *repudiation* of that experience—and therefore comes to us with aspirations and ideals but without a history. Its highest institutional expression is the federal appellate court. Can this hypothetical and philosophically intuitive canopy, this universal empire of rules without horizon in time or space, permit us to imagine ourselves back into nationhood? If it has no real history, can it have a real future? The question that both our history and our current identity crisis raises, then, is whether we can conceive of ourselves as one nation with authority sufficient to define and to rule ourselves without the authorization of a national political theology that necessarily posits that we exist as a people under the authority of God.

Putting the issue this way might appear odd and even embarrassing—it certainly was to me when I found that I could no longer avoid it. After all (one might rejoin and deflect), might not the history of religion in America point to precisely this secular fulfillment?[14] Each disestablishment was partly carried by these universalistic and formal dualisms: church-state, private-public, inner belief-outward actions. Even the fact that, up to the recent past, most of the strongest votaries of these philosophically abstract ideas *were themselves religiously motivated* does not automatically make these secular principles theological ones; it only shows that one should desire these ideas for their claims to universal truth and public communicability and not for the concrete advantages they may bring in advancing one's own subjective religious ideas in the public realm. Moreover (this rejoinder/deflection continues), the fact that each disestablishment was often and loudly proclaimed a final and complete *attainment* of religious freedom only shows how little they knew then and how much we know now. I will even grant you (this rejoinder concludes), that disestablishment in the past always required the empowerment of God's authority to overthrow the prevailing establishment and to make the new religious establishment more inclusive and the new political order more just. But (to put it bluntly) the power and authority of God is not only no longer needed, it is now a barrier to inclusion and to the political fruits of a wider justice, an inclusion and a justice *we* are quite capable—judges and justices willing—of freely choosing and freely imposing on ourselves by ourselves. If this hope requires renouncing both the history and the future of American national identity, that is a cost we—whoever this *we* is that presumes to speak for the nation—are quite willing to pay.

This is a strong rejoinder—especially if this "we" were bound together strongly enough to be capable of willing at all—but I do not think it can be answered without first reviewing the structure and content of our past national political theologies and the lives, motives, and intentions of its leading theologians. Through this exercise we may attain a different perspective on the current struggle over American identity between a dominant and supposedly secular rights-based liberalism and their host of critics—postmodernists, pragmatists, communitarians, civic republicans, conservative Catholics and Jews, and Protestant evangelicals.

I will try to show at the end of the essay that contemporary liberalism has increasingly been compelled (often against its will) to rediscover America by defending itself in more historical and national terms. That reoccupied common ground gives to attackers of contemporary liberalism and to its defenders, arguments and forms of rhetoric that pattern and often mirror both the form and the content of earlier national political theologies in America. These contemporary arguments might seem to differ from those in the past because they are conducted without ever having to use the G-word—most of today's combatants loudly disclaiming any religious foundations to their arguments. But this is hardly unique. In many past conflicts over American identity, our national political theologies were constructed in the noncreedal and nonbiblical languages of natural theology and moral philosophy, of sociology and political economy and literary studies, and of a pragmatism that was at once an historicist philosophy, democratic sociology, and moral psychology.[15]

What did our past political theologies teach and what can their history teach us? The first lesson is that national political theology in America is nation centered, not state or church centered. It insists that only under conditions of religious and intellectual freedom can the voice of God—the source of our "possession" of America as well as of our democratic political authority—be heard by the whole people.[16] Here is the president of the University of Chicago, William Rainey Harper, speaking at the University of California at Berkeley at the turn of the twentieth century.

Democracy has been given a mission to the world, and it is of no uncertain character. . . . [T]he university is the prophet of this democracy, as well, its priest and its philosopher . . . the university is the Messiah of this democracy, its to-be-expected deliverer.

As the visible Church of the American Religion, the American university, Harper continued, must be self-governing and free from interference by either state or church to fulfill this national role.[17] An authoritative political theology, therefore, is *in* but not *of* the government, its laws, and offices, and *in* but not *of* the separate churches and their particular creeds. It is, however, both in and of the American people, articulating the norms for a voluntary and shared "moral government of God"[18] sufficient to define us as one distinct people and to authorize common political and social projects. American political theology is also international, or world historical, in that it supplies the intellectual framework for writing our national history through a narrative framework by which and through which we can understand and share a common experience in the world.[19]

Four major tenets of national political theology in America are: (1) that God's revelation and spirit are continuous and progressive until the end of time, a progress marked by God's word increasingly inspiriting all social institutions and practices; (2) that God speaks to peoples or nations and that the American nation or people is the primary unit through which God now speaks to the world and in history; (3) that a measure of religious belief, both individual and social, is active participation in the achievement of goodness and justice in the larger society; and (4) that there is a real relationship, but never an identity, between righteousness and democratic citizenship.[20]

National political theology presupposes a national covenant and therefore raises a standing question of performance. Because revelation is continuous, faith requires that each generation use its own best knowledge to discover God's word for them and to reinterpret past revelation accordingly. God rules both through reason, corresponding to the legal term *jus*, and through revelatory actions of power, corresponding to the legal term *lex*. Because this reason/revelation is cumulative and progressive, knowledge gives to faith—especially to biblical revelation—increasing clarity and confidence. This is the core of what can be called its "Protestantism" or, more properly, its periodized, progressive, and somewhat apocalyptic style. This same core, however, is evident in the shaping of American Catholicism, first in its battles against the calls for separate national ethnic churches by German and Polish immigrants,[21] then in its social doctrines, and finally in its contemporary understanding of religious freedom. This same political-theological core has also supported a host of relatively free-standing bodies of knowledge, ranging from Lockean rationalism, Scottish moral philosophy, social evolutionary and historicist social theory, and finally, the new social sciences established in the American university at the turn of the century. Although the Bible was always the implicit authoritative text of this political-theological core, it was often read through the texts of these free-standing bodies of knowledge—to such an extent that it was difficult to distinguish core support from interpretive superstructure.[22] Means of diffusing this knowledge into the body of America are equally various and range across religious and secular boundaries and from high to low cultural institutions, in fact, across and through all of the instruments by which a common culture is shaped.[23]

One hundred years ago, Jane Addams, who attended no church, and Richard Ely, who wrote primarily as a political economist and economic reformer, equaled any clergymen of their day both as religious figures and as religious spokesmen. A religious life, as defined by this national political theology, is not opposed to that defined by the separate churches and creeds, but requires extension into the home, the community, the school, the laboratory, the business enterprise, the political party, and the state. Unlike the nineteenth-century constitutional order, the more Progressive side of establishment theology, both before and after the Civil War, not only included women, blacks, and immigrants, it often accorded them central roles in the achievement of American destiny.[24]

According to this understanding, the state itself is not seen as a constitutionally created set of separate public and governing institutions but, at particular times, as the highest expression of a nationally shared democratic faith. Thus, Samuel Batten, a prominent Baptist Social Gospel minister, declared that "in the last analysis the State is the organized faith of a people," and Mary Follett, a high priestess of Progressive political science, concluded that "[t]he state must be no external authority which restrains and regulates me, but it must be myself acting as the state in every smallest detail of life."[25] Each of these sites can serve either as a bearer of or a barrier to the coming of the kingdom of justice. The evangelical imperative in the Progressive era to Christianize the society is equally an imperative to democratize and Americanize the society by infusing all of its institutions and practices with shared national values of social justice.[26]

POLITICAL THEOLOGY AS SOCIAL GOSPEL

Two features especially mark this persistent feature of our national political theologies. The first is that all of them are a social gospel, a set of overarching national projects, and the second is that they are all strongly concerned—even onto obsession—with the state and condition of American public opinion. While the term "social gospel," or "social Christianity," was coined to describe the reform response to industrialism by some northern Protestant clergymen and reformers in the 1880–1910 period, one could use these same terms to describe every and all successful religious establishments and national political theologies in America.[27] Indeed, the centrality of Hebraic and Old Testament typology in American Puritanism made American religion Hegelian and mission-oriented from the start in the sense that God's progressive revelation was seen as immanent in the political, moral, and material world.[28] The persistence of this Hebraism was not only continuous, it was periodically revived and reinterpreted through the national jeremiads that resulted from each political, moral, and material crisis.[29]

These jeremiads are ways of translating crises into opportunity by reading them as tests for affirming the national covenant. This social gospel is also, and more dangerously, evident in American worldly success, both individual and collective, as this success is read as inspirited, as God's special favor bestowed on his almost chosen people. But from both directions, this social gospel, or "reform imperative," this need to generate national projects for national regeneration, become internalized as part of individual projects for individual regeneration. Just as religious revivals—often the seed bed of new national religious establishments—conflate these national-individual redemptive elements, so, too, do political revivals and reform movements. To the extent that these two collective-personal revivals often flow into each other, they constitute a social gospel that is continuous with a national political theology.

Postulating that *all* national political theologies and informal religious establishments in America are implicitly social gospels, however, points to two different trajectories. The first might be termed a dialectical trajectory: as each politico-religious establishment becomes successful, its inspiriting religious gospel becomes increasingly ritualistic and empty while its social (especially economic) power becomes increasingly decisive and self-serving. Two such periods that stand out are Gilded Age America and the 1920s. Worldly success inevitably tempts prophetic witness into priestly advantage, as spirit becomes law, vision becomes common sense, and ordinary interests become encoded as science.[30] Failure, renewal and rebirth, therefore, describe periodic conditions, and together they frame the dynamic element in the history of American political theologies.[31]

A second trajectory, more commonly accepted but, I think, less defensible, might be termed "secular-linear." It posits that each succeeding establishment gets more social-worldly and less gospel-spiritual, more secular-ethical and less religious-transcendent, than the preceding one. While Hegelians and Christians might accommodate this linearity within the dialectical argument that Spirit becomes progressively immanent in the world, its institutions, and practices, we must address this trajectory theory on its own terms. The argument for a secular-linear trajectory might go something like the following. Granting the power of these establishments and the reach of their national political theologies in the nineteenth and early twentieth centuries, this string of successes, especially in the articulations and sponsorships by Progressive intellectuals, was the cause of the decline of religion generally, and mainstream Protestantism in particular, from the 1920s onward.[32] This argument can be buttressed sociologically by chanting the now familiar mantras, "religious pluralism" and "the secularization of the American university." Setting aside how the truth of this charge might be adjudicated, the important question to ask is *whether this adaptation/translation constitutes a weakness or a strength for national political theology.*

This question is similar to the one that asks whether the extension of religion into popular culture—Sunday schools, summer camps, advertising styles, dietary fads, music, self-help and pop-psychology manuals (the list is almost endless)— helps to destroy or helps to preserve and extend religion in American life. Inso- far as these very secular manifestations did not prevent the rise of a powerful establishment theology in the 1940s through 1970s—one that successfully brought together not only Jews, Catholics, and Protestants, but those professing no for- mal religion at all—this is at least a latent spiritual strength.[33] The charge of pro- gressive and linear weakness and decline might really be postponed for about half a century—the 1970s—when this later liberal and Cold War establishment was successfully challenged. Given the general instability and fragility of national political and cultural authority in America, to call either of these establishments (1880s–1920s and 1940s–1970s) self-subversive and weak invokes the obvious response: weak compared to what? What alternative sources of national politi- cal governance were both creditable and available?

One might be even more blunt in rejecting this charge of a progressive loss of spiritual energy and force. Here, one would point to two sets of predictions re- garding the future of ethnic and religious assimilation into American society made, respectively, in the disestablishment periods of the 1920s and the late 1960s. Horace Kallen, the foremost theorist of cultural pluralism of his time, maintained with complete assurance that the assimilation of the new immigrants into a common America was neither possible nor desirable. It was no more pos- sible than imagining Hungarians routinely marrying Poles or Czechs in America, not to mention marrying someone from an older immigrant group such as Ger- man Protestants or Irish-Catholics. For Kallen, ethnic identities were quite fixed and defined separate cultures so the only way to overcome them and achieve national integration would be by massive and coercive efforts at assimilation. By the 1950s, Kallen's arguments were hardly worth attention and appear now as demographically absurd as Jefferson's predictions of an Anglo-Saxon America.[34] Not only had Kallen's European national-ethnic groups quickly lost their ethnicity in America, they did so largely *in and through their own religions, their own churches, and their own leadership.* What was precisely impossible in Europe seems inevitable in America, attesting to the capacious, adaptive, and protean character of our national political theology and a voluntary religious establish- ment.

A second radically wrong set of predictions was made in the late 1960s and early 1970s, symbolized in two popular books, *The Rise of the Unmeltable Ethnics*, by Michael Novak, and *Beyond the Melting Pot*, by Nathan Glazer and Daniel Moynihan.[35] In retrospect, these books and the host of ancillary writings are a sort of echo of Kallen. Like Kallen's they can be read as really wrong pre- dictions born of the social and racial conflicts in the 1960s attending the great migrations of blacks from the South into the white ethnic neighborhoods and neighborhood schools of northern cities. Unlike Kallen, however, their analyses can also be read as part of an outsider strategy for reinclusion in the national ruling coalition: American jeremiads that call for more respect for white ethnics and for Catholicism by political intellectuals whose commitment to civil rights and racial justice tempted them to paint blue-collar and lower-middle-class ethnic Catholics as Southern racists.

Only in the second sense can the arguments of these two books be salvaged, but this second sense is a repudiation of a common assumption in both books, namely, that ethnic Catholicism is an autonomously fixed or core identity that must be accommodated by more tolerance and more pluralism.[36] By the time of the Nixon and Reagan presidencies, ethnic Catholic social and family values were again as firmly a part of America as they had been in the 1950s. Indeed, they had never really left. Not only did America succeed in reassimilating these groups, this assimilation was so deep as to appear ironic: ethnic-Catholics have now been deracinated into one, undifferentiated, Euro-male oppressor group. This irony was possible because difference and pluralism are now increasingly defined in the new and supposedly fixed categories of race and gender.[37]

There is a serious question suggested by a linear secularization understanding, but I think it applies to the very origins and nature of national political theology arising and sustained under conditions of religious freedom. To what extent is a reform-oriented, ethically centered and national political theology a religion or a religious faith at all? Might there be an inherent danger of subverting particular faith traditions simply because this national theology can serve to inspirit and authorize national moral, social, and political reform movements and projects and can serve to transform self-contained racial, ethnic, and religious difference into a shared American nationality? That it had neither subverted nor destroyed church-centered religion in the past might only be due to the historical contingencies of immigration patterns, undemocratic hegemonic domination, and (bad?) luck. In short, might it be inevitable that our political theology as social gospel is, at some point, going to end up fulfilling itself as a wholly secular moral, social, and political program without any distinctly religious foundations? This would leave us floating in a public philosophy that is neither Protestant nor Christian nor Judeo-Christian but only some bloodless and abstract creed that we could simply choose to take or leave.

My simple answer is no, that this reading is something of an ahistorical illusion regarding the stability of religious doctrine within Judaism and Christianity, within the various American churches themselves, and within and through the many organizational and institutional forms through which Jewish and Christian religious beliefs are articulated, understood, and practiced in the larger culture. No church and no religion *in and of America* has remained "indoors"; all must be or become evangelical either directly or indirectly through educational, charitable and economic organizations they create and sustain to serve the larger society.[38] Moreover, this projected fate into a disenchanted universalism cannot begin to explain the history and practices of American churches in popular culture—let alone why tens of millions of committed Christians and Jews from many differing churches and doctrinal positions could see this national political theology as publicly *acknowledging* their more specific church and ethnic identities and thus *strengthening* their identities as Christians or Jews because they are also Americans.

Creedal and doctrinal specificity—even market differentiation—are necessary results of religious freedom and institutional religious pluralism in America; but so, too, is ecumenicism and voluntary religious establishment, for without this canopy, religion and religious freedom itself would retreat into pure subjectivity and thus be removed altogether from civic and public spheres. Religious freedom would then be an empty postulate and not an experienced practice. Churches as buildings for containing worship and creeds are only a small part of institutionalized religious expression in America. Subtract all of the other institutional and cultural creations of churches and religious movements from America and our civil society would be almost as naked as the public square is now alleged to be. Our concern with whether the institutions of civil society are doing their job is further attested by the obsession with the condition of American public opinion regarding toleration, hope for the future, and, most importantly, trust in each other and in American institutions and their leadership.

POLITICAL THEOLOGY AND PUBLIC OPINION

Just as a social gospel is inseparable from a national political theology, so is its obsession with the state of moral or public opinion in America. If the difference marking church doctrines and creeds were imported directly into civil society and if all parachurch or faith-based institutions merely carried and expressed these differences, we would have very little civil society at all and perhaps no common American culture. But that, of course, cannot happen because, with exceptions noted earlier, each different religion presents and represents itself to the larger society through a mediating national theology—and all or most of these institutional representations to the society at large appear under a shared American canopy. This is where persuasion and public opinion as sources of self-interpretation are most crucial.

For a voluntary religious establishment to succeed, it must do so through public opinion. One path of success is the institutional conquest of the major forums of opinion, from public schools, higher education, the national media, national business and government down to the family, the churches, and local media, business, and governments.[39] That public opinion and political theology are intimately related is seen in the fact that recognition and articulation of the centrality of public opinion arose immediately with the decline and death of state legal establishments in the early nineteenth century. Three early prominent "republican theocrats"[40] of voluntary establishment, Nathaniel Taylor, Timothy Dwight, and

Lyman Beecher, wrote during the first three decades of the nineteenth century. For them, the first step in the creation of a national political theology for an independent America was to undermine those creedal elements in the main Protestant churches that seemed to require or encourage the direct civil imposition of biblically based religious commands. Hard Calvinism had to go: churches, church publications and church-founded colleges that did not reject it were consigned to a marginal sectarian and therefore divisive status in American national life. Because men "as free moral agents . . . sin knowingly and voluntarily" and can only escape from that condition "under the renewing influence of the Spirit of God," civil laws and punishment can never directly cause righteousness, either individually or collectively.[41] Persuasion is the only means by which this can take place, and the most effective means of persuasion is not law but instruction and example. Together, churches, schools, charities, literature, popular entertainment—all informed by an articulate and persuasive natural and biblical theology—will create a climate of influences in which Americans will grow together in faith and virtue.

> It is public opinion . . . which gives to conscience all its power. Were a corrupt public opinion to dispense with the moral and religious instruction of children, with the institution of the Sabbath, with the revelation which God had made of himself, of his law, and of human destiny, with all the appointed vehicles of conveying moral truth to the mind conscience would become extinct in the soul of man. And what, then, would be the power of human edicts?[42]

Sixty years later, this same theological revision and stress on public opinion was restated in the first sociology textbooks and endlessly repeated in those texts through the 1920s and beyond. John Bascom's 1898 sociology text spoke of the way in which "the free, the spiritual, the personal are to triumph over the fixed, the mechanical . . . and religion is to become a pervasive atmosphere of the largest life . . . free, plastic, progressive . . . ever embodying itself in new forms as the ages unfold." The modernist churchman Theodore Munger gave direct theological support: "The New Theology does indeed regard with question the line often drawn between the sacred and the secular . . . a line that, by its distinction, ignores the very process by which the kingdoms of this world are becoming the kingdom of the Lord Jesus Christ."[43]

In one of the early and most influential sociology texts of this period, Charles Cooley wrote that public opinion "is no mere aggregate of separate individual judgements. . . . It may be as different from the sum of what the individual could have thought out in separation as a ship built by a hundred men is from a hundred boats each built by one man." One can combine "a very slight regard for most of what passes as public opinion with much confidence in the soundness of an aroused, mature, organic social judgement."[44] Whether this resource was called public sentiment or public conscience (Arthur Twining Hadley), rational assent or social judgments (Franklin Giddings), reflective consciousness and purpose, or public will, or organic social judgment (Cooley), all agreed with Hadley when he said that public opinion conceived this way, as an architectonic and authoritative structure of beliefs and ideas, constitutes individuals into one sovereign people,

> represented by a common public sentiment which includes all good men, minorities as well as majorities, who support the government not as a selfish means for the promotion of their own interest, but as a common heritage which they accept as loyal members of a body politic, in a spirit which makes them ready to bear its burdens as well as to enjoy its benefits.[45]

Well after most of these ideas were encoded in college textbooks and in the identities and purposes of academic social science disciplines, Herbert Croly and John Dewey drew out more clearly some of its political and intellectual implications. In Croly, the law represents a form of "bondage to a mechanical conception of social causation . . . which assumed an essentially automatic harmony between individual and social interests." Genuine democracy, in contrast, is a faith that "carries with it the liberation of democracy from this class of social pseudo-knowledge." This shared faith expressed as a coherent and authoritative public opinion "is indispensable to social progress" because it encourages skepticism toward legal-individualistic solutions to social problems and because its democratic expression is grounded in the most sophisticated forms of current knowledge, i.e., pragmatism and modern social psychology.

> It has been reserved for recent social psychologists to give a concrete account of the way social minds are formed, and consequently to bring the idea of social minds into relation with the fundamental idea of society as a process. . . . Genuine individuality is also essentially an idea which does not become of great value to men and women except in a society which has already begun to abstract and cherish a social ideal. . . . The American nation is no longer to be instructed as to its duty by the Law and the lawyers. It is to receive its instruction as the result of a loyal attempt to realize in collective action and by virtue of the active exercise of popular political authority its ideal of social justice.[46]

It remained for John Dewey to state the appropriate social psychological, moral, and political conclusion:

> Only a voluntary preference for and interest in a social good is capable, otherwise than by coincidence or accident, of producing acts which have a common good as their result. . . . In truth a common end which is not made such by common, free voluntary cooperation in process of achievement is common in name only. . . . It has to be continually buttressed by appeal to external, not voluntary considerations; bribes of pleasure, threats of harm, use of force. It has to be undone and done over.[47]

PUBLIC OPINION AND PUBLIC KNOWLEDGE

From before independence to the Civil War, Protestant churchmen shaped public opinion by forging the links between a biblically based national political theology and natural theology and moral philosophy, drawing on English writers such as Paley and Locke and the host of Scottish commonsense philosophers. This linkage was incorporated and supplemented in romantic theories of national history (e.g., Bancroft) and in imaginative literature.[48] Through the mid–nineteenth century, moral philosophy was the common curriculum of Unitarian Harvard and evangelical Yale and Princeton and in most of the more narrowly based denominational colleges. Without its biblical-exegetical and Protestant-Christian apologetic purposes it could and did function as a nonchurch and noncreedal means of inculcating common personal, moral, and political values in the American people in ways that received direct support from their particular religious beliefs. In the decades immediately preceding the Civil War, and despite growing denominational schisms, romanticism as a psychology, a moral theory, and a way of writing national history became another secular vehicle by which one linked reason to revelation. While Channing and Emerson are seen as the originators, it was primarily the New Theology of Yale and Andover Seminary that reaped the politico-theological intellectual harvest after the Civil War.

Informing these newer writings explicating the theology of voluntary establishment in nineteenth-century America was an explicit social evolutionary view of human destiny that extended biblical understandings of progressive revelation into philosophy, secular history, and the social sciences. Darwinism was not only understood but embraced both as biology and as an idealist theory of history because this form of history *was already commonplace in Protestant thought*. The merging of evangelical theology, philosophy, and philosophy of history was first articulated in Germany by Hegel (1770–1831) and Schleiermacher (1768–1834) and became normative in American theology first at Unitarian Harvard and then, through Andover Seminary, Princeton, and Yale, within liberal evangelical Protestantism generally.[49] While it is common knowledge that a vast majority of the founders of the social sciences in America were trained in German historical scholarship in the 1870s and 1880s, it is not so well known that their philosophical and theological mentors had preceded them in this study. Most of the early post–Civil War faculty of religion and divinity at Harvard, Andover, Yale, and Princeton, and the editors of the leading theological and philosophical journals, had studied in Germany in the 1830s through 1860s. Thus, in post–Civil War America it was difficult to distinguish theologian from philosopher from social scientist from public moralist and reform intellectual. This, in itself, is proof that a broad-based and voluntary establishment theology is in force.[50]

By the turn of the century, the study of English letters was incorporated into the American university curriculum, and here, too, national political theology thrived under its intellectual auspices. The study of literature as inquiry into the moral sources of our personal and national identity became a sacred calling. One of the defining textbooks in this field was written by Vida Dutton Scudder, professor of literature at Wellesley College (1892–1928) and a prominent labor reformer. Her textbook, *Social Ideals in English Letters* (continuously published from 1898 to 1923), interpreted American national literature and its English antecedents through a national political theology and thus into a means of a continuing revelation regarding the public good. Here is a sampling:

> To realize a spiritual democracy for the victims and outcasts of the Old World is a task before which we may indeed quail. . . . But, turning back to the lives of our fathers, surely we see in the warfare against slavery of the negro a prophecy of our larger conflict against evil [exploitation of immigrant labor] less evident, but more deeply imbedded in the social body. . . . Belief in democracy is the last demand of idealism. We are not likely to forget this: we whose national Credo must be spoken in the presence of the seething throngs of the outcasts of Europe. To look our national situation squarely in the face and say that the cure for democracy is more democracy requires a reverential trust toward humanity at large such as only the mystic who avoids men has in the past been able to hold with any degree of steadiness. . . . It is difficult, it is impossible, to define or describe a tendency [of the age] of which we are all disciples; but so much it is safe to say,—that with the intellectual impulse toward the reconstruction of social theory, and the practical impulse toward the activity of social service, is blending more and more a spiritual impulse deeper than either of these, imperatively desiring and seeking the realization of the Kingdom of God on earth.[51]

Sixty years later not much had changed regarding the location, tenets, and purpose of national political theology. In an editorial in *Theology Today*, "National Ethos and the Church," the writer outlines three tenets linking church and state and religion and politics in America.

> At the very time the denomination failed to function as the church, the nation came more and more so to function. Thus, American Protestantism endowed the nation with churchly attributes, with three theological notes in particular. . . . (1) Gradually in America the nation emerged as the primary agent of God's meaningful activity in history. Hence Americans bestowed on it a catholicity of destiny similar to that which theology attributes to the universal church. . . . Old Testament concepts and idealistic philosophy [of history] supported this view. (2) It was also true, especially during the nineteenth century, that the nation became the primary society in terms of which individual Americans discovered personal and group identity. It was the one unity which absorbed all pluralities and in connection with which full personal life was realized. . . . Public schools forged this unity. While Protestant in religious outlook, they were nationalistic in fostering a sense of corporate identity. . . . (3) As the nation became the primary community for fulfilling historic purposes and realizing personal identity, did it not also assume a churchly function in becoming a community of the righteous?

This editorial was written in 1963, at the height of power of the liberal Judeo-Christian-Western Civilization establishment and by a highly respected Protestant theologian and editor of its leading theological journal. But he wrote not to only praise this achievement (tenets nos. 1 and 2) but to question (no. 3) and then partially bury it. "Instead of Christianizing the nation, the [Protestant] churches have been nationalized."[52] Was Smylie urging a final disestablishment or was he preparing for a new one—or both?

NOTES

1. Miller 1988, 322 and 244; Mead in Elwyn Smith 1971a, 254.

2. The long history of loyalty oaths in America not only combine politics and religion, they ceremonially reaffirm membership in the nation. See Levinson (1988) and Elazar (1998) on oaths, covenants, and constitutionalism.

3. In Eisenach 1990, 186 and 210. Tocqueville's oft-repeated quotation reads: "The woof of time is every instant broken and the track of generations effaced. Those who went before are soon forgotten; of those who will come after, no one has any idea: the interest of man is confined to those in close propinquity to himself" (Tocqueville 1981, vol. II, bk. 2, ch. 2, 396).

4. This sudden victory might account for both the intellectual incoherence of the early New Deal governments and their dependence on the older tradition of National Republicanism as part of its governing structure, especially in foreign policy and international finance. Plotke 1996; Eisenach 1999b.

5. Gerring 1999.

6. Lyman Beecher argued, for example, that when church membership was a requirement for political office under colonial New England legal establishments, it "produced the lax mode of admission to the churches . . . followed by the long and dreadful declension from evangelical doctrine and piety" (in Elwyn Smith 1971b, 175). This same idea gets extended by Progressive intellectuals, often clergymen, into critiques of churches per se as preventing the Christianization of America. Bascom 1898; Strong 1915; and see Eisenach 1994, 57–62.

7. Even strong critics of the liberal Protestant hegemony over the public schools testify to its success in mobilizing the energies and support of nonliberal Protestants and those from many other religious backgrounds. Glenn 1988.

8. This inclusion of the defeated opposition can also be a threat: Jefferson's inaugural address following his victory in 1800 included the phrase, "We are all Republicans, we are all Federalists." In the gentry and antiparty politics of the day, this was the veiled threat that those who do not cooperate with his administration will be isolated as disloyal Americans and driven from national political life.

9. This is why presidents elected in an era dominated by the opposition party (e.g., Cleveland, Wilson, Clinton) must not only repudiate many of the values of their strongest party supporters, they must often act "without principles" in order to be effective at all. Skowronek 1993.

10. On the Progressive contempt for Gilded Age partisan politics because they were modeled on and driven by the external rules of electoral games, see Eisenach 1994,

111–22. Progressive Party reform weakened party organizations and the power of patronage and, therefore, weakened elections per se as a title to rule. This is also discussed in Shefter 1978.

11. In this sense, party government per se and as an autonomous ideal is a better instrument for mobilizing negative majorities and disestablishment and explains why antiparty values are so effective in mobilizing positive, national political majorities.

12. Whitman 1955, 531.

13. This periodization loosely tracks Lind 1995.

14. "History has sobering surprises for us all. Surveying now, after two centuries . . . one can say that a long-delayed outcome is now arriving. Although in its narrower definitions religious liberty was achieved fairly early in the nation's existence, in its broader definitions, and in the cultural issues it brings in its train, its full complexity rising into view, 200 years after the Virginia statute was enacted. Moreover, this larger significance comes into place as the long de facto Protestant establishment has clearly ended, and as no other candidate for that effectively dominant cultural-religious position can successfully take its place—not any other religious persuasion, nor any combination of religious groups, *but also not, despite the noisily articulated fears of the conservative religious community, 'secular humanism' either.* Establishment by law ended in the nineteenth century. Establishment by cultural domination ended in the twentieth" (Miller 1988, 350). This Hegelian reading without any substantive fulfillment (we are all free to do what?) ends up confirming a national political theology and denying that a nonreligious theology can take its place.

15. Eisenach 1994; Howe 1970; Hutchison 1992; Marsden 1994, Part 2; Reuben 1996; Turner 1992. By distinguishing religion from theology and equating the former with the life of the intellectual and man's highest spirit and the latter with narrow sectarianism, the religious spirit could be expressed in and through the liberal arts curriculum.

16. See Smylie 1963; Elwyn Smith 1971a; and Mead 1975.

17. In Marsden 1994, 249–50.

18. In Elwyn Smith (1971b), 161, quoting a book title by Nathaniel Taylor, a mid-nineteenth-century liberal evangelical theologian at Yale.

19. See Bercovitch (1976), for example, on this theological structure in George Bancroft's history of America. On the internationalism of American nationalism in the Progressive era, see Eisenach 1999b.

20. Examples of these four tenets are found in Strong (1915), Bascom (1898), and Batten (1898 and 1911). These books draw heavily on other writers and summarize the liberal and modernist movements in Protestant theology generally. The definitive work here is Hutchison 1992. A summary similar to mine is found in Smylie (1963), 313–14, and used by Mead (1975), 73. These tenets were not the sole preserve of liberal evangelicalism. In the words of Archbishop John Ireland at the turn of the century, "We cannot but believe that a singular mission is assigned to America, glorious for itself and beneficent to the whole race. . . . With our hopes are bound up the hopes of the millions of the earth. The Church triumphing in America, Catholic truth will travel on the wings of American influence, and encircle the universe" (in Dohen 1967, 109). The definitive hermeneutical analysis of political theology is O'Donovan (1996).

21. Charles Morris (1997), on German Catholics; Dolan (1985), 181–85 and 299–301, on Polish Catholics, and 297–99, on German Catholics.

22. This is another way of saying that God's post-biblical revelation is found in these texts, which are then used to reinterpret the Bible in the same way that later prophets in

the Hebrew Bible force reinterpretations of earlier ones and the events and prophecies of the New Testament occasion reinterpretation of the Hebrew Bible.

23. E.g., Douglas 1988; Howe 1997a and 1997b; Handy 1971; Moore 1994; Eisenach 1994, chapters 1 and 3; Edwards 1997.

24. Walters 1977; Howe 1997b, 217; Eisenach 1994, 81–87, 181–86, 195–204, 207–8; Fitzpatrick 1990.

25. In Eisenach 1994, 130–31. Earlier, Batten echoed John Dewey and most other Progressive intellectuals of this time in holding that democracy "is less a form of government than a confession of faith; it is the confession of human brotherhood. . . ." Batten 1898, 253; and see Eisenach 1994, 62, for others making this same argument.

26. There are not many deep differences between pre– and post–Civil War establishment theology. Compare, for example, Howe (1990), 121–45, to Handy (1990), 281–301; and see Gerring (1997) on the consistency of National Republican ideology between 1829 and 1924.

27. See McClay 1994, 152–59.

28. See Hutchison (1992), especially chapters 3–5, and Hutchison (1987), on foreign missions and American identity. On home and foreign missions as part of the dominant Protestant culture in the nineteenth century, see Michaelsen (1970), 24–28, as it effected the formation of the common schools. The continuities in foreign policy between Josiah Strong's mission-oriented call at the turn of the century and American internationalism in the post–World War II era are quite striking. Reed 1972; and see Meyer 1973 and McClay 1994.

29. "In times of prosperity Christians tend to become Greek in their theology; in times of adversity they again become Hebrew" (Hutchison 1992, 305, quoting Luccock). Substitute "Americans" and "national political theology" and it beautifully expresses periodicity and the use of jeremiad. On Hebraic themes in Progressive thought, Eisenach 1994, 62–63 and 252. The American appropriation of the holocaust is the most recent example of the continuity of this feature of American political theology and American identity.

30. This is the organizing argument of "anti-foundationalist" legal theorists because courts are particularly tempted to construct "objectivist" and therefore putatively "neutral" principles to legitimate the status quo, e.g., Sunstein (1993). For a discussion of the wider implications of this position and its relationship to pragmatism and democracy, see Williams (1998).

31. Morone (1998), traces these same trajectories in the context of mobilizing support for major public policies.

32. Handy (1960), reads American religious history as mainline Protestant church history in describing the religious "depression" of the 1920s. And see Bass 1989.

33. See King (1989a) on exactly this issue. See also King 1989b; Voskuil 1989; Marty 1996, vol. 3. See McClay 1994; Reed 1972; and Meyer (1973) for antecedents. A parallel argument could be made regarding the changing ideology taught in the public schools.

34. Lind 1994. Dolan's brief history of nationality conflicts within American Catholicism nicely summarizes the point: "[Orestes] Brownson wanted the Irish to become American; [Archbishop John] Ireland cajoled the Germans; and [Archbishop George] Mundelein worked on the Polish (Dolan 1985, 301)."

35. Novak 1972; Glazer and Moynihan 1970.

36. Oddly, this argument lives on. See Levinson (1990) on Catholic nominees to the Supreme Court, written as if Catholic justices *must necessarily* be torn between Catholicism and constitutionalism, when an embracive national political theology invites both

personal integration and social reconciliation. Whatever some conservative Catholic churchmen might argue, the justices do not seem torn by inner conflict.

37. The logic of a principled multiculturalism makes this ironic resolution paradoxical: Are Euro-males part of the imagined new America or are they to become a newly created class of resident aliens like the South after the Civil War or Protestant fundamentalists after World War I? Might they retake a naturalization test?

38. See Monsma (1996), and note the current debate about the role of faith-based institutions in America. Half of all tax-deductible charitable giving in America goes to religious institutions.

39. Wuthnow 1994.

40. The term is from Elwyn Smith 1971b.

41. Taylor and Dwight quoted in Elwyn Smith (1971b), 165. The origin of this attention to public opinion as a sort of invisible and atmospheric public conscience that penetrates and shapes private conscience is the traditional Christian distinction between the power of external law and the influence of inner faith and grace. Dwight put it this way: The power of civil government "is felt only within certain limits, and on particular occasions; whereas the Scriptures extend their influence to every place, time, and action, seek out the offender in solitude . . . sound the alarm at midnight . . . enter into the recesses of the bosom, watch the rising sin, and threaten the guilty purpose, while it is yet a shapeless embryo" (in Elwyn Smith 1971b, 173).

42. Taylor in Elwyn Smith (1971b), 177. "When the great majority are unselfish they will create a righteous public opinion which, with democracy rapidly extending throughout the world, is becoming more and more nearly omnipotent. . . . New social sciences, like so many powerful search lights, are illuminating its path, and public opinion becoming as intelligent as it is disinterested, reforms will be as fleet and as sure of foot as Mercury" (Strong 1915, 119).

43. Bascom 1898, 119 and 178; Munger 1883, quoted in Hutchison (1992), 76. Bascom's college sociology textbook is an excellent example of an early Progressive statement of political theology: it is antichurch because faith should infuse all national institutions (82–83); morality should replace creeds (117–19); moral reason should increasingly supplant creeds and biblical literalism as revelation (160–83); churches and creeds are often barriers to new revelation (164–65); and we should understand America within an Hegelian framework of history (258–64).

44. Cooley 1909, 121–25 passim, in Eisenach 1994, 75.

45. In Eisenach 1994, 76.

46. Croly, 1914, 175–77, 183, 197–99, and 210.

47. Dewey and Tufts 1908, 297 and 304. And see Kuklick (1985), 230–49, and Kuklick (1989), on the religious origins and dimension of this conception of democracy; and Westbrook 1991, 144–48 and 154–56, on the philosophical basis of this argument.

48. See note 15 above, especially Turner 1982.

49. Hutchison (1992), is the definitive work in this area, but also see Eisenach 1994; Howe 1970; Kuklick 1985; and Stevenson 1986, for the role of this theology in broader reaches of American intellectual life. For these same features in English theology and philosophy in the nineteenth century, see Murphy (1955) and the splendid collection in Helmstadter and Lightman (1990).

50. For biographical sketches of nineteen such Progressive academics and reform intellectuals, see Eisenach (1994), 31–47. Yale was the center of liberal evangelical

theology in the mid–nineteenth century and produced the founding presidents of the three major new national universities: Andrew Dickson White of Cornell, Daniel Coit Gilman of Johns Hopkins, and William Rainey Harper of Chicago. John Bascom, who straddles the transition from churchman to academic philosopher and social scientist, illustrates this integrative reach: G. P. Putnam's Sons published fourteen of his books, whose titles include aesthetics, rhetoric, comparative psychology, English literature, philosophy of religion, natural theology, political economy, ethics, sociology, evolution and religion, historical interpretation of philosophy, and, inspiriting them all, *The Words of Christ as Principles of Personal and Social Growth*. A graduate of Andover Seminary (a center of German historical scholarship), Bascom was president of the University of Wisconsin, 1874–1887, and professor at Williams College, 1891–1903.

51. Scudder 1898, 210–11, 246, 287, and 314.
52. Smylie 1963, 313–18 passim.

Chapter 4

Institutions: Theocracies and Clerisies

Given the argument to this point, it would seem that both voluntary religious establishment and its political theology are without specific institutional location. Neither state- or church-centered, this establishment might appear to be floating in the zeitgeist without a church or theologians to call its own. This conclusion, however, is not warranted. The very continuities in the styles, structure, and teachings of this national political theology suggest an institutional base that underwrites this continuity. This is the first topic to be addressed. Secondly, while attempts to institutionalize voluntary establishments in and through national organizations of denominations and churches have persistently failed, another set of national institutions, namely, the American university and, to a lesser extent, common (public) schools, has persistently succeeded. This is the second topic addressed: how the success of the American university as a powerful and unified set of national institutions independent of both church and state might be understood as the authentic national church of voluntary religious establishments. This is done by exploring the relationship between the continuities in style, structure, and teachings of American political theology and the continuities in the missions, moral teachings, and political practices of the American university. One final introductory note: Without recent revisionary scholarship on the history of the American university and the academic disciplines, this exploration would hardly have been possible nor could the connections suggested here have been drawn. The recent appearance of this history, in turn, suggests a future for the American university that is continuous with this rediscovery of the religious spirit and functions of the American university.

THEOLOGICAL CONTINUITIES

American national identity is grounded in a national political theology. If one looks at the persistent impulses and styles that have marked this identity, there

75

is a remarkable consistency in this political theology. This consistency can be stated as a series of interconnected imperatives. One of the most obvious is an evangelical or mission imperative: to be an American is to participate in common projects to better the world.[1] Whatever the forms and locations in which these acts are undertaken, American political theology will incorporate them into the prevailing national social gospel and thereby raise the meaning of those acts into public honor and significance. This honoring and signification incorporate private, voluntary, or sectarian activities into shared public purposes and, in turn, impose constraints and directions on those activities if they are to be so honored.

A second imperative is freedom, or "voluntarism." One of the American origins of this imperative is the Calvinist insistence that individual and collective redemption by "works" alone is impossible. Without grace and faith, externally set standards or externally imposed rules are always insufficient and ineffective: "It has to be undone and done over." This antilegalism not only subordinates individual church polities and creeds, it relegates government and law as well to this individual/national inner imperative of character and motive.[2] The subordination of political institutions to constitutions and constitutions to popular sovereignty is a central feature of American self-understanding.[3] The subordination of religious institutions resulting from this same imperative is not so clearly understood. This subordination is itself theological, and not simply a default position necessitated because no particular church and church theology are nationally strong enough to be legally established.[4] Decades before the American Revolution, the revivals begun by Jonathan Edwards and carried through by churchmen and lay leaders from many separate churches affirmed this imperative both theologically and practically—as did every later politico-religious revival movement. Public opinion is the religious counterpart to popular sovereignty, and both require a national political theology to connect the self to the society and to the polity. Together they embody something of an anti-intellectual component in the sense that sincerity, intentions, morality, and character take precedence over doctrinal coherence or ratification by experts.[5]

A third imperative is inclusiveness. All political theology is by definition "kingdom" theology. As an earthly kingdom America must be a democratic one; the "promise of American life" is a democratic promise.[6] So strong is this "millennialist" understanding that each of our voluntary religious establishments has, in turn, routinely been accused of hypocritical complacency by equating, respectively, Protestantism, Christianity, or Judeo-Christianity as such with "the American way of life" as embodied democracy, rather than measuring our institutions and practices by the promise. These accusations, however, are usually and most powerfully voiced from *within* these respective establishments because, for them, the American way of life as fulfilled in democracy and social justice is never an achievement but always a covenanted goal that can only be intimated or more fully disclosed, but never fully achieved, in history. National institutions deserving the highest respect and power must be shown to be both inclusive and dedicated to service in the form of furthering the ends of democratic community both in their internal practices and in their external teachings and effects.

The continuity of these imperatives of evangelicalism, voluntarism, and inclusiveness can be seen also in the impressive series of overlaps in the express and substantive teachings of the successive establishments. I will mention only a few of them. The first overlap is a consistent "Hebraism" and therefore the acknowledgment of a national covenant and corporate obligations. It is commonly said that only in the post-Christian America that emerged in the 1950s has our voluntary religious establishment (and, presumably, its theology as well) been both Christian and Jewish; that is, full membership, already accorded to Protestants and Catholics, was now extended to Jews. While there is a superficial and demographic plausibility to this, the deeper fact is that from the very colonial start, American political theology has been Judeo-Christian—even philo-semitic—because the very idea of a political or national theology would make no sense unless the autonomous relevance of Judaism and the Old Testament were retained in Christianity.[7]

This biblical hermeneutic is confirmed in American theology and practice. Jews were accorded civil status in New England much sooner and much more enthusiastically than were Catholics (or, for that matter, Quakers). In the pre–Civil War period, German-Jewish immigrants immediately joined National Republican parties and movements, and therefore the ruling national parties, which were dominated by evangelical Protestants and were systemically anti-Catholic.[8] Reform Judaism and Conservative Judaism, if not exclusively "made in America," immediately became the ethno-religious representations of American Judaism; their theologies and their "ecclesialogies" were continuous from the start with the national political theology.[9] In the Gilded Age, German Jews participated as major shapers of the formative critique that brought national Progressivism into prominence and were accorded high status and positions in leading national Progressive institutions.[10] Every generation of writings articulating the theologies of voluntary religious establishment has reaffirmed this biblical-theological Hebraism and in every generation of American experience until the present, Jews have more easily and more readily affirmed their ethnic-religious identity within the framework of the reigning *national* politico-religious establishment than have Catholics.[11] Nowhere has this been more true than in American national universities, where, starting in the 1880s, nonorthodox Jews have been more at home than either conservative evangelicals, or Southerners, or Catholics.[12]

A second overlap is the special place accorded women and Blacks within our national political theologies. This inclusion is implicit in the Hebraism of Black Christianity and its biblical hermeneutic: kingdom theology is a powerful passageway in both directions. The special role that women played in evangelical Protestantism thinking largely flowed through its stress on the family as a major center of religious life and through the many and various parachurch reform and charitable activities in which women played decisive roles, ranging from the

Sunday school and temperance movements through abolition and urban settlement houses. The "feminization" of American Protestantism and literary culture
has been dated in the early decades of the 1800s, following state disestablishments
of religion, the same period in which antislavery movements and, soon thereafter, anti-Jacksonian movements and parties began forming. Later, female novel-
ists from both England and America used these popular forms to spread their
inclusive and socially oriented public theologies.[13]

The inclusion of women and Blacks is made more obvious when one contrasts
Democratic Party anti-establishment coalitions with the Republican Party, its
allied reform movements and supporting auxiliaries, under the canopy of a voluntary religious establishment. Women and Blacks were excluded in principle and
by design first from Jacksonian and then from Democratic Party organizations,
activities, and supporting bodies. The reason was, paradoxically, the hyperlegalism
and constitutionalism of the party, its overriding commitment to individual and
states rights, its fear of national elites and centralized government, and its civic
republican commitment to (white male) equality as personal independence.[14] Conversely, the very nationalism of the reform parties and their stress on voluntarism
blurred the lines between home and church and parachurch and party and polity,
thereby automatically making room first for women and Blacks, and then, but
less uniformly, immigrants as well.[15]

There remain two other indices for the persistence and continuity of voluntary religious establishments and political theologies in America. They are less
obvious because they can only be stated as negatives. The first rests on the fact
that there is a consistency in the kinds of oppositional alliances that establishments call forth that suggests a consistency in what these oppositional alliances
oppose. Each period of successful voluntary religious establishment calls for resistance to it during which a political alliance is struck between those who are
hostile to supernatural religion per se (on putatively more universalistic or cosmopolitan grounds) and those who seem almost wholly defined by religious localism, either geographical or ethnic, and devoutly practice and display these local
religious identities. Each side of this alliance, but for quite different reasons, thinks
that the mixing of religion and politics through voluntary religious establishment
is wrong. Both of these parties also agree, but again for different reasons, that
American nationalism is inherently dangerous and that nationalism is the core
principle of religious establishment and its political theology. The cosmopolitans
are opposed because it makes America too narrow, provincial, and patriotic, especially compared to Europe, which is understood not as a series of different nations but as a single high culture. They prefer a very thin nationality expressed
largely through an enlightened language of abstract principle.

Religiously sectarian locals resist because voluntary establishments tied to
national political regimes pressure their own churches to become *too* worldly or
secular or national-cosmopolitan. Every nationalization of the society and culture is perceived as a loss in their own autonomy, status, and power. They, too,

prefer a thin and secular nationalism and very weak national institutions. Universalist-cosmopolitans often discover a natural affinity with these locals because both parties want to keep religion "where it belongs," inside the churches or bounded by ethnically or religiously homogeneous localities, where the integrity of religious, regional, and ethnic tradition is preserved. The more this attenuated relationship of religion to public life is maintained, the more hope there is that religion and religious passions will gradually fade from national public life and culture. This alliance often rests on a strict or literal construction of the Constitution, derived either from a particular historical reading of its origins or from the affinity of its principles with certain strands in liberal-democratic political philosophy.

The long-standing alliance of enlightened Jeffersonian and Jacksonian secularists with Southern evangelicalism, Mormonism, and, later, Irish-Catholicism, is a prime example, but this pattern was characteristic of Democratic Party coalition formation throughout the nineteenth century, lasting well into the New Deal period.[16] A little known but important example of this phenomenon is the alliance struck by Walter Lippmann (an agnostic Jewish Episcopalian) and the most prominent and articulate fundamentalist of his day, J. Gresham Machen. Their respective attacks on religious liberalism shared a view of Christianity that was fundamentalist both in the sense of being reducible to a few uncontestable tenets or creeds as objective tests of Christian belief and in the assertion that God and history remain permanently separated until the end of time. Both Lippman and Machen feared that religion understood this way was being corrupted by the penetration of secular culture through historical biblical criticism and the Social Gospel, making the culture hypocritically self-righteous and religion increasingly thin and intellectualized, no longer capable of appealing to and shaping the behavior of the average person.[17]

If one thinks that this alliance struck more than sixty years ago was purely opportunistic and almost accidental, consider the almost identical oppositional alliance begun more than two decades ago and still strong between nonpracticing Jewish neoconservatives and evangelical Christians, but now including (perhaps as its intellectually strongest element) conservative Catholics.[18] The elements uniting these persistent alliance structures are not fortuitous; indeed, a similar pattern appeared in the alliance in England in the 1860s between Comtean secularists and the High Church party in their opposition to the Broad Church party, which defended Christianity and urged the reform of Oxford and Cambridge (and thus the Church of England) by incorporating modern forms of knowledge in their project.

INSTITUTIONAL FAILURE

A second piece of negative evidence for the continuity of political theology in America is directly institutional and requires more extensive discussion. This evidence is the persistent failure of formal ecumenical church alliances or federations to incorporate the national political theology and thereby constitute itself as the fixed institutional embodiment of the religious establishment.[19] If my characterization of our national political theology is correct, these church-institutional attempts face a series of formidable barriers to success. The hostility of national political theology to the particularism of churches and creeds as divisive and a barrier to a national faith does not lessen when some of these churches and clergymen create a federation.[20] American national political theology is inherently anticlerical. This religiously grounded anticlericalism is a necessary part of the religious nationalism of political theology under conditions of church pluralism. This same anticlericalism implicitly and strongly supports the three imperatives of national political theology discussed previously (evangelical, voluntary, inclusive) under these same pluralistic conditions and constitutes an additional barrier to the success of church federations.

This reading does not receive support from most commonly accepted histories of religion in America. These histories describe the series of voluntary religious establishments in America as if they were essentially a series of de facto or de jure ecumenical organizations—almost a series of "clubs" of particular churches—that have a progressively more inclusive constituent membership.[21] Since many ecumenical organizations had been formed in the past and were "federal," i.e., consisted of church bodies and their representatives, so this reasoning goes, voluntary religious establishments in America can hardly be thought anticlerical if the federation consists of churches and their leadership consists of the clerical representatives of those churches.

My response to this rejoinder is to grant this argument with the same proviso that many of these same church-oriented histories also make: *every attempt to federate or institutionalize voluntary establishments has met with almost immediate failure*. Attempted institutionalizations have not only not become the church and clerisy of the national establishment, they have more typically been the cause of division and the pretexts for endless arguments about the permissible grounds and extent of inclusion. One might state this same conclusion another way: national ecumenical church organizations claiming to represent a voluntary religious establishment tend to form when a successful informal religious establishment is beginning to come apart. Combined with and contributing to this institutional failure have been the results of religious freedom itself: revivals; new religious bodies; schism and division in older ones; and, from the outside, the sporadic streams of new immigrants. No church or combination of churches can maintain institutional and cultural control under these conditions.

Voluntary religious establishment only works well when it is understood and seen as the property of the *nation* and not this or that particular mix or combination of churches.[22] Attempts to consolidate a voluntary establishment through constitutional federation on the model of state governments to federal government have often helped to undermine the voluntary establishment and the effectiveness and reach of its national political theology.[23] Any federated church of churches would demand *some* creedal grounding, but any formal expression of such grounding having normative weight and substance would either divide the constituents from within or be perceived from without as so thin and insubstantial as to be the object of derision *as an authoritative moral source and moral orientation for the nation.* Moreover, since no formal federation could embrace all institutional embodiments of American Protestantism—not to speak of American Catholicism and American Judaism—without facing this dilemma, the very institutional presence of a unified and powerful federation would also appear aggrandizing and oppressive.

Even assuming an initial measure of efficacy and power in a newly formed federation as the only national and transdenominational game in town, there would soon result a call for counterfederations to speak for religious groupings with different voices and accents. The constitutional norm of religious equality would then immediately trump federation claims to national authority. This result is worse than before the dominant federation was formed: these counterfederations, under the constitutional principle of religious freedom and equality of churches, would, on principle, be granted *equal formal public status no matter what their beliefs,* resulting necessarily in weakening the power of churches and religion generally in public life.[24] The only way out of this trap would be to construct ever larger and more embracive federations with ever more diverse constituent bodies. But this path reaches the same destination: the only faith remaining in common would be a "constitutional faith" that, in itself, affirms nothing except that all faith is private and that freedom of individual conscience is the highest value.

Our history confirms this logic. The Federal Council of Churches, formed in 1908, was intended as the institutionalization of the Social Gospel. Its founders consisted almost exclusively of northern Protestant churches and churchmen. Formed well after Progressive reform had consolidated and organized in other quarters, it immediately became embroiled in political and religious controversy because it seemed to commit its constituent churches to taking overt political positions. The first instance of this was taking the side of workers in the acrimonious Bethlehem steel strike in 1910. This not only created divisions within each of these churches, it stimulated the later schism between liberal-evangelical modernists and conservative-evangelical fundamentalists. In no sense could the federation be seen as the formative church of the voluntary establishment: it formed too late and quickly lost its efficacy.[25]

By the time its successor organization, the National Council of Churches, was formed in 1950, its constituent churches were higher in cultural status than in numbers, evangelical energy, and will to power. The National Council represented itself to America as the enlightened voice of the Protestant religion and its social conscience, a sort of high-minded Progressive remnant, but it no longer presumed to interpret the voice of God's word to the American people. Speaking more or less in a transreligious ethical voice, it was not so much actively opposed as ignored by other faith traditions, meeting with them mostly at high ceremonial occasions. Given the persistence and power of a *real* national political theology under which it *in fact* existed, the National Council must be seen as only a part of a much larger voluntary religious establishment, and not an entirely comfortable part.[26] Like all other churches, this ecumenical church federation could accept the invitation to join this larger establishment, but only if it subscribed to a much more powerful and demanding national political theology than its own, one that mobilized America in a series of national crusades to fight against totalitarianism and a remnant European colonialism abroad and for economic and racial justice and against left- and right-wing extremists at home.

But the most ambitious federation initiative of all was that attempted between the formative eras of the Federal and National Council of Churches. This initiative was called "Interchurch." In the years immediately following the conclusion of World War I, when Progressive intellectual, religious, and political leaders became disabused of their hope that the spirit and unity of preparedness and mobilization would continue to animate the national government, they shifted their hopes to other sectors of American society. This was especially true of wartime leaders who came from Protestant ecumenical organizations that had enjoyed unprecedented prestige and support during the war.[27] In the words of one prominent religious publication, "War drives for world freedom [were] passing into Christian drives for world redemption. . . . Christian churches mobilize when armies demobilize."[28] And mobilize they did.

The most ambitious of these plans was to create and fund a gargantuan umbrella organization called the Interchurch World Movement. This organization, American liberal Protestant in initial funding and leadership, would embrace not only *all* the churches in America representing all faiths in America, but would call on the support of nonchurch-affiliated leaders in government, labor, and industry as well to help underwrite a sort of national voluntarist "Church of America," a super-state/super-church to organize and spearhead the drive for democracy and justice at home and abroad. In 1920, Interchurch, with a paid staff of 2,600 in New York City and expenditures exceeding a million dollars a month, began its drive to raise more than a third of a billion dollars over a five-year period. With the support of prominent Progressive wartime leaders from all sectors of American society and help from major national advertising agencies, the funding campaign to fulfill the kingdom covenant at home and abroad was finally launched. While the campaign within most of the thirty founding church denominations for their own use was quite successful, support for this post-Protestant ecumenical organization itself was a colossal failure. Not even 10 percent of the goal was met. The denominational underwriters of the venture (Methodist, Baptist, Presbyterian, Congregational, Disciples of Christ) quickly bailed out, and Interchurch simply faded away. This failure paralleled a precipitous decline in the major Protestant ecumenical and student organizations as well.[29]

INSTITUTIONAL AND THEOLOGICAL SUCCESS

In hindsight, it is clear that the rise and fall of these three federation experiments were quite independent of the rise and fall of powerful voluntary religious establishments and the national political orders they defined and supported. Their strongest connection to this larger history is an ironic one. Their formation was really a sign of the impending demise of the establishment they were trying to consolidate, in the same way that state-mandated [Protestant] Bible reading in the public schools only became the norm by the middle of this century—just when national elite support for the practice was dissolving.[30] Another way of saying this is that American denominational or church history cannot tell us what we need to know about the institutions and clerisies of voluntary religious establishment and national political theology in America. The proper place to look for both the institutional and the clerical wellsprings of the national political theology that underwrites voluntary religious establishment is the American university.

First, contrast the institutional continuity, national power, and protean reproductive energies of Harvard, Yale, and Princeton Universities with that of their respective denominational founders, sponsors, or successors, namely, the Unitarian, Congregational, and Presbyterian churches.[31] Next, contrast the contributions to American intellectual and cultural life of clergymen in and of those church bodies, to the clerical and lay faculty in and of these universities. Now contrast the ability of these universities to colonize—to extend and enforce their standards, values, and curriculum into newly formed institutions of higher education—with the ability of their sponsoring churches to do the same in newly formed churches outside their direct control or through ecumenical federations. Finally, compare their respective powers and wills to humiliate, ostracize, exclude, and discipline recalcitrant or resisting units within their respective domains. Finally, from the final state disestablishment of Unitarian Massachusetts in 1833 onward, compare the growing national public status, public recognition, and public power of the handful of leading American national universities, their presidents and faculty, to the power of the most prestigious and powerful Protestant churches and their leading churchmen.

The obvious response to this invidious comparison of Protestant church failure to national university success is to pronounce the comparison unfair. The universities, this counterargument goes, succeeded as national institutions because they were *not* churches. We all "know" that only the smallest remnant of formal religion remained in universities by the turn of the century; indeed, the road to secularization and science was taken with no turning back much earlier, in the foundation of the new modern research universities represented by Cornell (1867), Johns Hopkins (1876), and Chicago (1891), and in the transformations of Yale, Harvard, Princeton, and Columbia into graduate institutions in this same period.

This transformation was extended by the rapid expansion of state universities following the passage of the Morrill Act in 1862. Some of these publicly supported institutions joined the great private research universities to dominate the shaping of both the academic disciplines and higher education generally. Surely institutions such as Cornell, Illinois, Michigan, and Berkeley were secular from the start. The resulting complex of fourteen public and private research universities, already beginning to dominate the future of higher education in the 1880s, joined together in 1900 to form the American Association of Universities. Faculty and administrators from this oligopoly organized the academic disciplines, established their professional associations, and founded their journals. In universities with religious foundations, theology tended to migrate out of the disciplines in the liberal arts and sciences to become self-contained in denominational or ecumenical divinity schools and ceased playing a major part in American academic and intellectual life at its highest and most articulate levels. Nationally unifying secular-scientific knowledge replaced divisive religious creeds, and the national universities were the beneficiaries. On this reading, and against the position argued here, universities did not supplant the leading national churches, they only separated from them and, by definition, from religion.

If further proof is needed that this institutional comparison between ecumenical church federations and nonsectarian national universities is unfair, look at the role this same complex of universities played in the professionalization and specialization of higher education, two quintessential marks of secularization and part of the same processes that toppled theology from its supremacy and denominational churchmen from university administrations and governing boards. Over 90 percent of the doctoral degrees granted in 1900 came from the fourteen universities that founded the AAU. The American Association of University Professors, founded in 1915, was a product of these same universities and the academic professional organizations that their faculties had created. This ever-increasing production of professionally trained faculty from the 1890s onward became the seed bed of secularization (and the acceptance of religious pluralism) in the larger culture. They and their students and their students' students defined collegiate education in the liberal arts, instructing generation after generation of local and national leaders in almost every sector of American life. As access to college was democratized and the tax-supported sector became increasingly dominant, the public, secular, and pluralistic values defining America became ever more powerful as they became ever more strongly institutionalized.[32]

If these brief rejoinders were as true as they are pervasively believed, one might even conclude that the rise of the national university to preeminent cultural-political status is proof that the era of religious establishment is over—the only issue remaining is to agree on when this happened. But if these rejoinders are *not* true, if they are in large part a myth to support current illusions and evasions about American national identity and about the American university, then the relationships between religion and American higher learning must be rethought, both historically and philosophically. Now that the American university is beginning to receive the same historical scrutiny that public schools had received a generation earlier, similar scales are falling from our eyes.

In the 1960s (just before the universities exploded in political and moral controversy and the beginning of the protracted culture wars began), these histories of American higher education had the same soothing message that the end of ideology story told about our politics.[33] Events quickly disabused us of both narratives, but, in the case of the American university, it has taken us much longer to discover why—perhaps because this discovery is so painful to those doing the inquiry. The first discovery is that the dating of religious disestablishment and the victory of secularization in elite universities keeps getting pushed forward, from the 1880s to the 1920s, and now, well after that late date—so far in fact that when it finally does seem to appear true (roughly the 1970s onward) the very terms used to describe the transformation have been so deconstructed by postmodernists as to seem ironic.

One must begin with a few simple facts about the secular American university and its history, starting with the Midwest, the home of the great state-supported national universities. Before the Civil War, the state universities of Indiana (1829–51, 1852–53, and 1853–59), Michigan (1852–63, 1863–69), and Missouri (1850–56) were led by ordained clergymen; these and many other state universities were also led by presidents who were not ordained clergymen but whose academic training was in theology. Moreover, a majority of professors in these early state universities were trained in theology. Lest this be thought a pre–Civil War market problem of supply, Ohio State (1893–95) and the University of Kansas (1874–83, 1883–89) were headed by Methodist clergymen, while Indiana (1875–84) and Illinois (1867–80) by Baptist clergymen. Washington Gladden (1836–1916), perhaps the most famous Social Gospel minister in America, was a candidate for the presidencies of the state universities of Wisconsin, Ohio, and Illinois in the 1890s.[34]

Moving from the Midwest to American universities generally, even when the faculty were not themselves clergymen or trained in theology, they saw their university vocation in these same national-sacred terms. Richard Ely, Simon Patten, Henry Carter Adams, John Commons, Charles Cooley, Edmund James, and many others essentially relocated American religion from denominations and religious journals to the new universities and the new professional disciplinary journals.[35] The fact that twenty-three of the fifty founders of the American Economics Association in 1885 were evangelical Protestant clergymen is less significant than the fact that the first generation of professionally trained economists were almost all trained in Germany, where political economy was framed in evangelical-Hegelian terms. The fact that four of the five major national theological journals—*Princeton Review, Unitarian Review* [Harvard], *New Englander* [Yale], and *Andover Review* [Andover Seminary]—folded in the same decade that the disciplinary journals in sociology, economics, and political and social science were founded might prove secularization were it not for the fact that the contributors to both old and new were substantially the same people and that almost all of the editors of the old religious journals, like the new secular journals, had received their advanced academic training in Germany as well.[36]

This shared German or Hegelian or historicist spirit pervaded the American university well before the Civil War and well after, binding theology, philosophy, political economy, sociology, and, later, even the study of literature, into one national-theological framework. The first center of this "new theology" was at Harvard, where a kind of romantic and evangelical Unitarianism defined national political theology and its moral philosophy in the pre–Civil War period. One product of this theology was Horace Mann, the institutional and ideological founder of common schools in America.[37] By the 1870s, five of the six faculty of Harvard's divinity school were German trained. But it was Yale and its liberal evangelical new theology that carried the day after the Civil War.[38] All three founding presidents of the new graduate universities of Cornell (Andrew Dickson White), Johns Hopkins (Daniel Coit Gilman), and Chicago (William Rainey Harper) received degrees from Yale and were taught by a largely German-trained faculty.[39]

To be sure, none of these founding figures of the new university in America became Congregational clergymen but that was because their church *was* the university, and through the university, the nation. Harper, an Old Testament scholar, founded and edited *Bible World* soon after assuming the presidency of Chicago. After serving as president of Hopkins from 1876 to 1891, Gilman assumed the presidency of both the Carnegie Institution (the key foundation that funded and encouraged the professionalization of the American higher education) *and* the American Bible Society. The reason that liberal evangelical Protestants were such active agents in the shaping of the American university (and the public schools) was precisely because, for them, it was *not a secularization but a nationalization,* a relocation of God's spirit and revelation from particular churches to a unified American people through its most educated and morally serious leadership.[40]

These institutional features might be extended and supplemented when turning to the curriculum in the national universities. To ask the seemingly simple question, When did the Bible cease to be central and secular literature supplant it?, proves difficult to answer. Like asking when secular academic journals replaced sacred academic journals, any serious answer is both disappointing and ironic. The answer is disappointing because it places the date far too *early* in our higher education history, well before universities were alleged to have become secular. The Bible taught as an authoritative and sacred text was no longer central to the curriculum as early as the 1820s and 1830s in leading national institutions such as Harvard and Yale. Christianity was already being taught nondogmatically and indirectly through its immanence in the reason of moral philosophy and natural theology. *This displacement was already necessary for any institution aspiring to instruct the whole nation.* Ironically, any dogmatic and biblically creedal core in the liberal arts curriculum would undermine its national religious role.[41]

Speaking anachronistically, liberal arts education conceived this way implicitly constituted a national-convenantal moral orientation as a social gospel and explicitly incorporated modernist elements in its theology and biblical hermeneutic. From then onward many other curricula, texts, and disciplines overlapped and succeeded each other in defining the sacred ends of liberal education as moral instruction and character formation in America. Moral philosophy was supplemented and then almost supplanted by evolutionary sociology and political economy, and was then supplemented by English letters or literature and later by the teaching of European history and still later by Western Civilization and great-books courses that began around World War I. Where in this series of courses—all explicitly shaped and defended to teach American national values, American national morality, and American national identity—can the line be drawn between sacred and secular?[42]

It should now be clear that a deeper and more perplexing issue lies behind these questions informed by church-oriented religious history. When did the American university (and our public schools) cease to be Protestant, cease to be Christian, cease to be Judeo-Christian, cease to be religious? Once one escapes the grip of denominational history and seeks to integrate our religious with our national and cultural history, these religious identity questions must be viewed through more ironic (and dialectical, pragmatic, and Hegelian) eyes, and the answers given must be somewhat paradoxical. These very paradoxes, however, are the warrant for taking the answers seriously.[43]

Let us grant that American national universities, unlike the major churches, emerged in the late nineteenth century as an interlocking, quasi-autonomous, and unified set of institutions that, through a near-monopoly of the production of college faculty and leading textbooks, came to impose their values and standards on increasing numbers of other American universities and colleges.[44] Through the separate disciplinary organizations and, later, the American Association of University Professors, universities were able to set the professional standards defining the vocation of college professor. Through ever stronger ties to the great charitable foundations that emerged in the early twentieth century, these universities defined the areas of research deemed important and provided the funds to attract the talent and organize the inquiry.[45]

Missing in this story of the ever increasing power, growth, and public prestige of national American universities, however, is the sheer energy that these institutions and their leaders devoted to discrediting and defeating *competing* educational ideals and competing definitions of the purposes of higher education. Nietzsche's imperative is an almost perfect description of this process: "If a temple is to be erected *a temple must be destroyed*: that is the law. . . ."[46] Despite later efforts to describe conflicts in higher education as that between (older) religion and (newer) science (or professionalism or objectivity or value-neutrality), this battle was, from the start, *an intra-religious one* waged on the battlefield of competing faiths and competing faith-based institutions. The standing competitor was the Protestant (and often ethnic) denominational college, and the looming competitor was the growing system of Catholic colleges and universities that came to complement the astonishing growth of the parochial school system. In this sense, the battle in higher education paralleled that within the common schools over appropriate moral and religious instruction and between the public schools and the parochial system. There was never any question that these were battles of competing faiths—first against denominational Protestantism in the 1840s and continuing against Catholic claims later in the century—and that the national religious faith embodied in the public schools was the decisive victor.[47]

Following is a list of distinctions that academics and public intellectuals variously used to distinguish between those ideas (and institutions) that shape *common* American beliefs and faiths and those ideas (and institutions) of religion that, if publicly asserted and publicly dominant, would *divide* America. Their claim was that the national universities (and the public schools) embodied the understanding of religion on the left and that their competitors represented the understandings of religion listed on the right.[48]

Experiential religion	Church religion
Religion as inward belief	Religion as outward rituals
Religion	Sectarianism
Church	Sect
Religion	Theology or dogma
Religion as conduct	Religion as creed
Practical or applied Christianity	Creedal Christianity
Morality	Religion
Moral philosophy	Theology
Natural theology	Revealed theology
Religion as Progressive Spirit	Religion as legal authority
Bible as moral literature	Bible as revealed authority

While this listing does not exhaust the ways in which these distinctions were made, it gives a clear indication of the kinds of argument used for about 150 years, both to justify public support for these universities and to describe the religious, moral, and political content of the liberal arts curriculum and its supporting research and scholarship. These same distinctions were used from the 1840s onward to justify and describe the values taught in the common schools and to defend them against those who wished directly to incorporate evangelical Protestant biblical teachings and ceremonies into the curricula and against Catholics who argued that the common schools were fronts for Protestant-sectarian churches.

Equally striking is the way in which claims of objectivity, professionalism, science, and common sense for terms on the left were matched by charges of bigotry, anti-intellectualism, reaction, and divisive self-interest against defenders of the terms on the right. The claims on the left were successfully incorporated into an historical and national framework that explicitly connected the teachings and practices of the American university (and the public schools) with the history, purposes, and destiny of the American people. This larger social-evolutionary and historical framework could then incorporate the social and natural sciences and, later, the emerging industrial and financial economy into the mission of both the university and America. This not only allied new wealth and the new managerial middle classes to the university, it even led to the creation of business schools (e.g., Wharton School at the University of Pennsylvania) that claimed to embody the same set of national-moral-religious standards claimed by the liberal arts.[49] Under this mantle, the university could justifiably claim that they were inviting and enlisting the talents and energies of *all* Americans and, by doing so, creating bonds of national loyalty and purpose that would overcome the forces and traditions that divide us.[50] Finally, the authority of this national political theology and its succession of voluntary establishments depended not on destroying or even discrediting the understandings on the right, but only in *subordinating* them as particulars to the national understanding as the universal.[51]

The conflict between this system of higher education and American Catholicism was especially bitter. Catholic higher education was, like the fundamentalist colleges, isolated and consigned to permanent secondary status. Without high accreditation, denied foundation funding, and isolated from the national academic associations and their disciplinary journals, these institutions and their faculties largely lived in their own separate worlds from the formative period in the 1880s through the 1940s.[52] This isolated status, in turn, denied them the support and connection to other national institutions that were inspirited and staffed by the new universities and their satellite colleges: the national monthlies and weeklies, national women's organizations, national professional associations, and national advisory bodies to the federal government.

Even granting this story of intellectual energy and institutional power, however, there remains the issue of whether this is, in fact, only a more complex story that ends up after all as the victory of science, secularization, and "established nonbelief." This issue is taken up in the next two chapters. A preliminary if dismissive answer would be no, because the American university has never given up its claim that its primary activities constitute the intellectual and moral ground of a liberal arts education and that this education constitutes the best basis for living a worthy life. Every American university continues to justify its existence by claiming to serve the common good and contributing to the articulation and efficacy of that good. Ask the university today, however, to articulate and justify these claims and one hears embarrassed and vague mumbling about service and democracy. But ask the university to describe values and practices that would *oppose* their claims and *subvert* their values and one hears articulate declamation against divisive religion and anti-intellectualism in the same sense that religion is listed in the right-hand column above. American universities today seem instinctively to know who and what their *enemies* are, just as Horace Mann and William James and John Dewey and the veritable army of American university faculty who variously defined the liberal arts did in their day.[53]

A more complex but still preliminary answer must begin by combining two misleading frameworks, the secularization thesis and denominational religious history, to ask again the wrong question asked earlier: When did the American university cease to be Protestant? This question, however, must now be restated:

When did the undeniable Protestantism of the American university cease to be Christian? The left-hand column in the chart above is shorthand for concepts that are at once moral and religious terms but are not distinctly Christian *in a creedal sense*. Assume that the development of their implications paved the road to an alleged secularization or "established nonbelief" in the American university (1920s) and (with a lot of help from the national courts) in the public schools starting in the 1950s. Then ask the subsidiary question: Who initiated and articulated these concepts and marched off to battle to defend them? The answer to this last question is easy: liberal evangelical and modernist Protestant churchmen, faculty, and lay intellectuals who were fighting *to keep alive the religious spirit* in an increasingly complex, materialistic, pluralistic, and stratified society. Beginning in the late nineteenth century what came to be called "modernist" Protestant Christianity was continuous with what came to define the academic disciplines and teachings in the liberal arts. Even the divinity schools and seminaries at these leading universities were organized under these same terms, adopted the same scholarly methods they mandated, recruited the same kinds of faculty they produced, and offered the same kinds of courses as these other disciplines.[54] This continuity, and the philosophical, historical, and methodological assumptions on which it rested, was maintained at least until the 1950s and arguably until the early 1970s. To be sure, over this period national university seminaries and divinity schools produced an ever smaller proportion of American clergymen even as their liberal arts graduate schools grew ever more hegemonic and oligopolistic in the staffing and direction of American higher education.

I maintained earlier, however, that this continuity had much earlier origins in America, specifically in the natural theology and moral philosophy taught first at Unitarian Harvard and then primarily at liberal evangelical Yale and at Andover Seminary. This was already a national Protestantism without creedal Christianity, already a kind of modernism and historicism that we associate with what Harold Bloom has termed "American Religion."[55] Viewed in this longer historical perspective, evidence that Protestantism was stronger than Christianity in shaping the political theology of voluntary religious establishment is found practically everywhere one looks. Whenever choices had to be made between defending specific Christian-biblical creeds and their respective church bodies and strengthening national parachurch or faith-based institutions that embodied the more embracive and democratic public religion (public schools, universities, charities, and moral, political, and religious reform movements), the latter choice was made and made decisively—even ruthlessly. Whenever a conflict arose between protecting formal-legal church and creedal practices in public schools and in public and private universities or acceding to new and more embracive ideas and spirits, the latter prevailed.[56]

How and why did this *Protestantism without Christianity* attract all this energy and talent? Why were they able successfully to enlist the support or discredit the opposition of formal church bodies? Where were its historical warrants, sources, and exemplars? Who authorized them to do what they did? Even an outline would not be possible to sketch here, but any beginning must start with "the Puritan origins of the American self,"[57] and with the ways in which we first wrote our national history and constituted our national identity within a biblical-historicist framework. Coleridgean romanticism and German historicism were implicitly known in America religious culture long before their appearance in English letters and in German scholarship.[58] As Harold Bloom has written, America has had a long tradition of "Protestantism without Christianity."[59]

Finally, a complex rejoinder might conclude, this story of the almost uninterrupted success and power of the national universities runs parallel to the story of the rise and spread of the common schools and compulsory elementary and secondary education. One need spend little time on the parallel to the public schools. Given the most superficial historical surveys, who now believes them *ever* to have been secular, nonsectarian, and religiously inclusive, including inclusive of nonbelief? From Horace Mann's first proposals in the 1840s through John Dewey's *Democracy and Education* (1915) to the strident opposition to open voucher systems today, it is clear that public schools have been the primary institutional agency to teach the reigning national political theology. Conversely, the mark of each disestablishment in the public schools has not been consensus around neutral principles, but "school wars" that are fought until a new voluntary establishment is in place.[60] This victory, encoded in philosophy, science, and common sense, *then* declares its principles neutral and fair, obligatory to all Americans of intelligence and goodwill.[61]

John Dewey's life embraced, and his writings shaped, the rise of the national university and the dominance of the public schools. For Dewey, the university was the spiritual and intellectual wellspring of the nation, whose teachings should flow through all of its institutions and practices. The medium making this a possibility is the common school, whose cause and values he spent a lifetime furthering. It is fitting to conclude this institutional analysis by recounting some of his formative ideas.

In two early essays, "My Pedagogic Creed" (1897) and "Religion and Our Schools" (1908), Dewey articulated many of the political-theological arguments made here. He begins the earlier essay by proclaiming, "I believe that all education proceeds by the participation of the individual in the social consciousness of the [human] race." He begins the later one by asserting, "A learned and self-conscious generation has fittingly discovered religion to be a universal tendency of human nature." These two rather different statements preface the same argument, because, for Dewey, participation in social consciousness is also participation in God's continuous revelation. Once this relationship is understood, Dewey's pedagogic creed is easily summarized.

I. I believe that education is a regulation of the process of coming to share in the social consciousness; and that the adjustment of individual activity on the basis of this social consciousness is the only sure method of social reconstruction.[62]

II. [A child's] powers, interests, and habits must be continually interpreted—we must know what they mean. They must be translated into terms of their social equivalents—into terms of what they are capable of in the way of social service. . . . The school is simply that form of community life in which all those agencies are concentrated that will be most effective in bringing the child to share in the inherited resources of the race, and to use his own powers for social ends.[63]

III. The progress [of the curriculum] is not in the succession of studies but in the development of new attitudes towards, and new interests in, experience . . . education must be conceived as a continuing reconstruction of experience; that the process and the goal of education are one and the same thing. . . . Our schools, in bringing together those of different nationalities, languages, traditions, and creeds, in assimilating them together upon the basis of what is common and public in endeavor and achievement, are performing an infinitely significant religious work. They are promoting the social unity out of which in the end genuine religious unity must grow.[64]

IV. I believe that the community's duty to education is, therefore, its paramount moral duty. By law and punishment, by social agitation and discussion, society can regulate and form itself in a more or less haphazard and chance way. But through education society can formulate its own purposes, can organize its own means and resources. . . . It is the business of everyone . . . to insist upon the school as the primary and most effective interest of social progress and reform in order that society may be awakened to realize what the school stands for, and aroused to the necessity of endowing the educator with sufficient equipment properly to perform his task.[65]

V. The art of thus giving shape to human powers and adapting them to social service, is the supreme art; one calling into its service the best of artists; that no insight, sympathy, tact, executive power is too great for such service. . . . I believe that in this way the teacher always is the prophet of the true God and the usherer in of the true kingdom of God.[66]

Periods of successful establishment elicit the kinds of formative social and intellectual projects for which Dewey is justly celebrated. Of course he did not speak to or for everyone, but the framework of his discourse was potentially inclusive of a corporate people because it could inform and connect almost every area of American national life from the highest reaches of academic philosophy and social science to teacher training and family life. His was a national framework not because it merely proclaimed itself such but because Americans of almost all conditions and backgrounds could participate in its productions and spirit.

As Dewey's own writings, and those of his Progressive colleagues in the 1920s attest, in periods of disestablishment and moral disorientation, this way of speaking and writing is no longer possible. Dewey continued his philosophical projects and continued to call for an American public, but the language was aesthetic and remote. A host of public intellectuals took that as a cue to become beautiful souls, standing above and outside America, as if by some national epiphany, America would come to them. Others followed Walter Lippman and took a scientific, technocratic, and ultimately manipulative path that implicitly disconnected democratic faith from their own vocations. Lacking the effective canopy of a national political theology, it seemed that they had no other choice except a kind of narcissism—unless they took up the more difficult moral and intellectual path by rethinking America and helping to reconstitute its meaning. In some ways, the 1920s are not unlike our own experience. Whether from out of our own moral and intellectual disorientation and the many alternatives that present themselves, a new consensus will result remains an open question.

NOTES

1. Hutchison 1987; and see Michaelsen 1970, 24–29; and Glenn (1988), chapter 6, on these same impulses behind the public school system.

2. See Seligman 1994. Nine years after formal disestablishment in Connecticut, Lyman Beecher concluded: "[Christianity] has survived the deadly embrace of establishments nominally Christian and now, bursting from their alliance, finds in them the most bitter opposition to evangelical doctrine and vital godliness. . . . There is no substitute but the voluntary energies of the nation itself" (in Elwyn Smith 1971b, 180–81). More than half a century later, the modernist theologian Newman Symth declared "The Passing of the Protestant Age of History," holding that Protestant churches had done their work and were now a limitation on God's continuing revelation. He saw a "coming Catholicism" in a religious consensus that would permeate the entire society and find expression in a common world church (Hutchison 1992, 175–84).

3. In the words of Jefferson, "Where then is our republicanism to be found? Not in our Constitution certainly, but merely in the spirit of our people" (Jefferson 1899, 193).

4. Even in colonial New England there was not only legal separation of church and state, but membership in the established church required evidence of inner conversion, no matter how uprightly one lived, expressed from the start in John Winthrop's distinction between the "law of love/gospel" and "mere justice." The Catholic counterpart to this was the role of self-constituted lay boards of trustees in establishing early churches and parishes in America. Dolan 1985, 110–16, 160–79, and 407–17.

5. Hofstadter 1962, part 2; Reuben (1996), especially chapters 4 and 5, on these same features in the liberal arts curriculum.

6. In contrasting European nations with America, Herbert Croly said that democracy in Europe often undermines national cohesion, whereas in America, "national cohesion is dependent, not only upon certain forms of historical association, but upon fidelity to a democratic principle" (Croly 1989, 267). Literature scholar and reform activist Vida Dutton Scudder declared in her 1898 college textbook that our chief advantage over Europe as an agent of social justice in the world is that our commitment to democracy is spontaneous because it lies at the very "foundations on which our national life is laid," requiring us "only to maintain and apply a tradition [of freedom], the chief glory of our inheritance" (Scudder 1898, 210). See also Hutchison (1992), 121–25, 132–44, and 182, on the writings of modernist theologians William Newton Clark, Newman Smyth, and Charles Augustus Briggs.

7. Seligman 1994. More generally, see O'Donovan 1996; Moltmann 1998. Part 3 of Thomas Hobbes's *Leviathan*, "Of a Christian Commonwealth," is almost entirely centered on the Hebrew Bible and not on the New Testament.

8. Reichley (1985), 230–38, 305–6, on Jews and the Republican Party during its long ascendancy, 1860–1932.

9. This is most obvious in Jewish support for the public schools and in entry into establishment universities sooner than Catholics and without paying nearly as many conversion costs. And see Levinson (1990) on different treatment of Jewish and Catholic federal judicial appointees in Senate hearings.

10. A German Jew turned down Lincoln's offer for secretary of the treasury; his son was one of the founders of the American Economics Association in 1885, in a founding group of about fifty people that included twenty-three Protestant clergymen. Eisenach 1996, 172–74.

11. Even in sociology writings that seem far removed from theology, this Hebraism continued, as it did in the "highbrow" weeklies and monthlies. See discussion in Eisenach (1994), 62–63 and 252. Cuddihy interestingly contrasts the fact that "the traditional 'authoritarian' religion-talk of Irish Catholics . . . obscured the remarkable extent of their behavioral integration with members of other groups [while] the anti-traditional and 'liberal' religion talk of many Jews obscured the persistence of de facto behavioral 'ethnocentricity'" (1978, 29).

12. In the 1903 graduating class of the University of Chicago there were 124 Protestants, 10 Jews, and 8 Catholics. Marsden 1994, 260 n.34. Half of the undergraduates were women. Fitzpatrick 1990, 84.

13. Douglas 1988; Walters 1977. In England the most notable were George Elliott and Mrs. Humphrey Ward; in America the obvious one is Harriet Beecher Stowe. For a continuation of this pattern in Progressivism and the American university, Fitzpatrick 1990.

14. Kohl 1989; Edwards 1997.

15. Lincoln was very successful in attracting a wide variety of European immigrants to the Republican Party and the antislavery cause. Gienapp 1987. This initial loyalty paid off in the realigning election of 1896. Jensen 1971.

16. Here, the best examples would be Mormons, newly formed small and independent Protestant sects, and conservative evangelicals in the South after the Civil War. And see Moore 1986.

17. Hutchison 1992, 282–87, especially the replies to Lippmann by Harry Emerson Fosdick and George Gordon. And see Conkin (1998), 158–60, on the Lippmann-Machen relationship.

18. See Silk 1988 and 1989. *First Things*, the journal founded and edited by a Lutheran convert to Catholicism, Father John Neuhaus, is a prime example.

19. Schneider 1989, 95–121.

20. Seligman (1994) argues more broadly that this difficulty goes even deeper, having its origins in the very idea of religious hyperindividualism born within the context of a charismatic community.

21. A roughly accurate listing would be: 1830–1860s, Unitarians, Congregationalists, Presbyterians, and Northern Baptists, with Universalists and Methodists as rising; 1880s–1920, Congregationalists, Presbyterians, Disciples of Christ, Methodists, Northern Baptists, Lutherans, Evangelical and Reformed, various German pietist and brethren churches, and Reformed and Conservative Jews; 1940s–1970s, all respectable Protestants, all liberal

and moderate Catholics, all non-ultra-orthodox Jews. On changing denominational demographics, see Finke and Stark 1992. For two very different and very brilliant refutations of denominational or church history as the proper focus of American religious history, see Stout and Hart (1997), and Bloom (1992). See also Elwyn Smith 1971a, especially the contributions by Smith, Michaelsen, and Mead.

22. The best example was the role of the Federal Council of Churches during World War I. But their success and flourishing was shared by Catholic and Jewish umbrella organizations as well. Schneider 1989, 116; Handy 1991, chapter 7.

23. This is the underlying dynamic of Robert Handy's argument in *Undermined Establishment* (1991), even though, I would argue, he does not fully appreciate the power and success of establishments understood as much deeper and broader than that expressed through formal ecumenical organizations—nor the successful reestablishment of the 1940s–1970s. On this later establishment, see Gaustad 1989; Marty 1996; and Silk 1988.

24. The exception, perhaps, is during wartime and for the ceremonial purposes of displaying a government-legitimating civil religion of the most uncritical sort.

25. Handy 1991; Schneider 1989.

26. "Pluralism—National Menace," *Christian Century* 68 (13 June 1951): 701–3; and see discussion in Marty 1996, 81.

27. Ernst 1974, 35–69; Eisenach 1994, 253–57.

28. Quoted in Ernst 1974, 59.

29. Marsden 1994, 343. A more correct image might be that of a massive, nonsectarian and latitudinarian established church that embraced the entire range of democratic institutions constituting American civil society, infusing them with shared purpose and value. This attempt is discussed in these terms in Eisenach 1994, 254; and Handy 1991, 184–88.

30. Mooney (1990) was just such a call and at precisely the time when heeding that call was the least likely possibility. Calls for institutionalized establishment, like calls for moderation in times of turmoil, are not heeded, just as, in periods of hegemonic calm, they are not needed. This parallels the history of Bible reading in the public schools: state-mandated institutionalization of these practices was the prelude to its death knell. At the beginning of the twentieth century, only one state required Bible reading in its schools, but by 1913, twelve more states, and by 1950, thirty-seven states "required, permitted, or condoned Bible reading in the schools" (Michaelsen 1970, 168). Few would argue from this that religion (not to speak of Protestant Christianity) in the public schools was stronger and more securely anchored in the 1950s than in the 1890s.

31. This, despite the fact that a formal church presence in their respective universities was continuous and pervasive at least through the 1920s and, in some respects, through the 1950s.

32. In 1900, five universities (Harvard, Columbia, Hopkins, Chicago, and Berkeley) produced over half of all doctorates; these and the nine other charter institutions of the American Association of Universities founded that same year granted 90 percent of the total. In the 1920s, five private and three public universities from this same group still produced more than 60 percent of all doctorates. These percentages are even more impressive in view of the rapidly growing numbers of graduate students. From fewer than 900 in 1885, in five years they increased to 2,382, ten years later to 5,832, and reached almost 10,000 by 1910. Within roughly this same period the resources of these same universities increased dramatically: endowments at Johns Hopkins from $3 million to $24

million; Yale, $ 4 million to $58 million; Columbia, $9 million to $68 million; and Harvard, $10 million to $86 million. Eisenach 1994, 12–13.

33. Vesey 1965; Hofstadter 1962. And see also Haskell (1977) on professionalism, expertise, and claims to authority.

34. Longfield 1992a, 47–49 and 64–65.

35. Eisenach 1994, 91–103; Crunden 1984; Longfield 1992a, 57–64, on Bascom, Ely, Commons, and Dewey.

36. Eisenach 1994, 92 n.25, 100, and 140; Kuklick 1985, 203–15.

37. Michaelsen 1970, 70–79 and 140–49, on Mann's ideas carried forward by John Dewey; and see Marty 1997, 50–54; and Glenn 1988, chapters 3, 5, and 6. Glenn (1988), 97–114, also traces the influence of German and north European models of common schools on Horace Mann and other American proponents of public schools.

38. Eisenach 1994, 91–103; Stevenson 1986, on Yale theology; and, more generally, Kuklick 1985.

39. Stevenson 1986, table 1, 36.

40. While the persistence of formal provisions for religion in these national universities do not, in themselves, indicate the presence of a real religious spirit, the fact that they persisted so far into the twentieth century strongly suggests an earlier religious spirit that they were loath to give up absent an equivalent replacement. In the late nineteenth century, compulsory chapel was the norm in both private and public national research universities. Remarkably, in 1940, among the most elite universities and colleges (i.e., members of the Association of American Universities), just short of half still had compulsory chapel and another 20 percent maintained voluntary chapel services. See Marsden 1994, 344–45; Reuben 1996, 118–32.

41. Glenn (1988), chapters 6 and 7, traces this same path in the public schools.

42. This is not to say that formal departments of religion and formal instruction in religion did not remain prominent features in American higher education. Only 27 percent of nationally accredited colleges in 1940 had no religious offerings in their curricula. Marsden 1994, 337. For a summary of the views of foreign observers, see Michaelsen (1970); and Mead (1975). In the common schools, formal and creedal religious elements and direct biblical teachings in the curricula were reduced almost to invisibility more than 150 years ago, but that, too, did not seem to hinder their religious or their moral mission (Glenn 1988, chs. 6 and 7; Marty 1997, 53).

43. See Bloom (1992), at the level of theory-theology; Stout and Hart (1997) and Moore (1986), at the level of historiography; and Jeffrey Stout (1998), at the level of religious ethics.

44. See Eisenach (1994), 31–37 and 138–41, for examples of authors and for dominant textbooks and their length of continuous publication.

45. Barrow (1990) is an excellent summary and is especially detailed on the role of the Carnegie Foundation for the Advancement of Teaching. See also Reuben 1996, 87.

46. Nietzsche 1969, second essay, section 24, 95.

47. Glenn 1988, chapters 7, 8, and 9. Macedo (1998), 60–62, discusses this common faith in a contemporary critique of prevailing constitutional understandings.

48. These distinctions are primarily from Hutchison (1992), but are also found in Handy 1990 and 1971; Reuben 1996, chapter 4; Michaelsen 1970, 60 and 116–17; Marsden and Longfield 1992; Herberg 1983; Mead 1975; Elwyn Smith 1971b; May 1989; King 1989b; Conkin 1995; and, for British analogues, Helmstadter and Lightman 1990.

Glenn (1988), 146 and 172–73, astutely distinguishes between the claimed religious "mission" of the public schools and their lack of specific religious content.

49. The founders and early faculty of the Wharton School, the first business college in America, are the strongest evidence of this. Simon Patten was as much a Hegelian theologian and historian of ideas as an economist. Edmund James and his prize student and young faculty appointee, Scott Nearing, were exemplars of Social Christianity. The organization and journal that James and Patten founded and edited, with Nearing on the staff, *The Annals of the American Academy of Political and Social Science,* almost perfectly embodied this combination. Eisenach 1994, chapter 5; and 1996, 176–77.

50. The head of the Department of Applied Christianity at Grinnell College in Iowa was a Jew, Edward Steiner, with a theology degree from Oberlin Seminary (Congregational), who wrote many books urging respect for the religious beliefs of immigrants, especially traditional Jews, and urged sectarian Christians not to attempt conversion of immigrants to their particular faiths. For more on Steiner, see Eisenach 1996, 174–76.

51. One should not forget that the religion built into the new university and its leading disciplines was a *fighting* faith, quite willing ruthlessly to use its energy and power to impose its will and to discipline and discredit its opponents, either directly (e.g., accreditation, rankings, AAUP sanctions, Phi Beta Kappa membership) or indirectly (e.g., Carnegie Foundation grants, General Education Board support). This parallels the struggle within the various mainline Protestant churches that resulted in the rather complete victory of the modernists, who also dominated the boards, administration, and faculty of the new universities. Hutchison 1989 and 1992; Handy 1991.

52. This is the scandal and injustice that always accompanies institutional power and arrogance. The higher education establishment in America was able to get by with and persist in this injustice to an egregious degree precisely because it represented the institution that was charged with protecting American national identity at its highest and most sacred level and, therefore, beyond serious criticism from the outside. See Marsden (1994) for the many examples of exclusion and condescension. Liberal Catholic historians too easily accept this judgment as true and deserved. Dolan 1985, 443.

53. Glenn 1988, 219–35, is especially good on how Mann and others successfully marked their enemies and the alternatives they proposed as less than completely American. Taylor (1989), 338, makes the point that contemporary liberals in the academy are "debarred by the ontology they accept from formulating and recognizing their own moral sources," making it difficult for them and others to discover their substantive moral orientations. "Their principle words of power are denunciatory. Much of what they live by has to be inferred from the rage with which their enemies are attacked and refuted" (339).

54. Cherry (1995), studying Chicago, Yale, Harvard, Vanderbilt, and Union, and six Methodist seminaries and divinity schools.

55. See note 48; Bloom 1992; and Conkin 1990.

56. On public schools Glenn 1988, chapter 6. In England, a titanic struggle took place over church and university reform in the early 1860s between modernist Broad Churchmen, on one side, and a combination of Low (biblical-evangelical) and High (creedal-ritualistic) Churchmen on the other, occasioned by the publication of *Essays and Reviews,* written by seven Broad Churchmen from Oxford. Despite overwhelming opposition by Church of England clergymen and even the bringing of heresy charges against some of the essayists, they prevailed in both university and church reform. One of them, Frederick Temple, became Archbishop of Canterbury, and two others, Benjamin Jowett and Mark

Pattison, heads of Oxford colleges. In the words of one of the essayists: "A national Church need not, historically speaking, be Christian, nor, if it be Christian, need it be tied down to particular forms which have been prevalent at certain times in Christendom [Henry Bristow Wilson]." In Eisenach 1998, 219. Wilson is extending Coleridge's distinction between the National Church and the Church of Christ.

57. Bercovitch 1975. And see Seligman 1994; and Zuckerman 1993.

58. See Bercovitch 1978, 46–47, on seventeenth-century charges by European Calvinists that American Protestantism was blasphemous in its teaching that America would be the redemptive nation. And see Bloom (1992) on Mormonism, Adventism, and other churches of distinct American origin.

59. To paraphrase a characterization of the English Unitarian Francis Newman, the brother of John Henry Newman, American national political theology had long ago ceased being (doctrinally) Christian but never ceased being (spiritually) Protestant. Evidence of this combination is found not only in the sociology and political economy texts of the 1890s and onward but also in the most widely used college textbooks on theology, such as William Newton Clarke's *Outline of Christian Theology*. This textbook ran through twenty editions between 1894 and 1914 and was published through 1927.

60. Given the intransigence of the public school establishment today in its strident defense of a principled multiculturalism without a corresponding national ideal, supporters of vouchers and of charter schools can make the plausible argument that the introduction of a deep and decentralized pluralism in public education will help build a national consensus from the ground up by creating more tolerant, competent, and public-regarding citizens than the public schools are capable of doing under their prevailing system of values.

61. This dynamic and argument are not new: see Michaelsen 1969 and 1971.

62. Dewey 1897, 93. This is prefaced by, "I believe that all reforms which rest simply upon the enactment of law, or the threatening of certain penalties, or upon changes in mechanical or outward arrangements, are transitory and futile" (Dewey 1897, 93).

63. Dewey 1897, 86 and 87.

64. Dewey 1897, 91, and 1908, 175. This latter religious argument is contrasted to the alternative that separate religious creeds be taught to their respective adherents in the public schools (released time) or that religion "be taught at special hours, times, and places by those who have properly 'got it up,' and been approved as persons of fit character and adequate professional training" (Dewey 1908, 174). Earlier in this essay he asked: "Can those who take the philosophic and historic view of religion as a flower and fruition of the human spirit in a congenial atmosphere tolerate the incongruity involved in 'teaching' such an intimate and originally vital matter by external and formal methods?" (172). Compare this to earlier public school defenders in Glenn 1988, chapters 6–9.

65. Dewey 1897, 94.

66. Dewey 1897, 95.

Chapter 5

Alternatives: Universalism, Restoration, and Nationalism

Today there appears to be a deep disjunction in political culture and values between elite national institutions and the aggregate of local cultures and values. National elites, usually called liberals, seek to ground American national identity and national policy in a highly abstract democratic Universalism. This principled liberalism denies American nationality and therefore is philosophically defenseless against any and all group-rights claims made in the name of national principles. The latter, usually called conservatives, have been mobilized nationally by dissenting intellectuals and quasi-populist political movements and given some ideological coherence through new national conservative (or neoconservative) think tanks, journals, and other media outlets. They seek to ground national identity and national policy in Restoration by bringing back to prominence and honor the value-sustaining institutions of civil society (families, churches, voluntary groups) and the shared moral understandings of vast reaches of the American middle classes.[1]

Unlike its Universalistic opponents who inherited their power from an earlier and hegemonic national liberalism, the Restorationists to this point have not been able to occupy and dominate the major redoubts of national elite power. One might put this somewhat differently by saying that conservatism, always strong locally, has increasingly won national elections, but that these electoral-political victories have not been translated into national *authority*, i.e., into intellectual and moral hegemony over the national institutions of civil society—most especially the universities—or even of the leading institutions in the national government.[2] Conversely, no matter how high and long-standing the level of liberal hegemony over these national institutions, their Universalist successors have not been able to dominate either American moral opinion or American electoral outcomes. For the past two decades they have been acting as an illusory establishment. On the basis of the inclusiveness and universality of their principles, they claim to be neutral regarding competing ways of life, neither imposing nor judging alternative conceptions of the good. Their title to rule is constitutional because their reading of the constitution is primarily driven by the Bill of Rights universalized into the fundamental source of American identity and purpose. Their judicial and bureaucratic victories have been largely offset by electoral and, increasingly, intellectual defeats.

Lying between these two sets of victors/losers is public policy. The battles waged over policy often take on the characteristics of Kulturkampf because the conflicts are in fact perceived as battles over the soul of America.[3] Make no mistake, these are battles of competing national political theologies, competing clerisies, and competing potential cultural-religious establishments. Each side's strengths in this struggle, however, also constitute its weakness—and these competing sets of strengths/weaknesses tend to be the obverse of each other. For the purpose of this essay, let us call the liberal alternative "Universalism" and its conservative counterpart "Restoration" and examine their respective strengths/ weaknesses. Only after doing this will we be in a position to assess some other political-cultural alternatives that are less prominent in the culture but have the potential for bridging both the intellectual and the social-cultural features that divide Universalism from Restoration.

LIBERAL UNIVERSALISM

The Universalists have almost all of the forms and marks of the previously successful national political, religious, and cultural liberal establishment that dominated American national life from the Progressive Era through the early 1970s. They are cosmopolitan, inclusive, mission-oriented, principled, and have extensive sources of power that are deeply institutionalized and, therefore, not directly dependent upon formal power in governments and church organizations. Having inherited from this earlier liberal-progressive establishment (certainly by birthright and often by merit) the universities, the national media, the older charitable foundations, and most national professional associations, they seemed well positioned to have continued its reign. Two major factors stood in the path to success. The first is that this group, as the major part of the dissenting left in the late 1960s and throughout the 1970s, was largely instrumental in *destroying* the moral and intellectual authority of the prevailing national liberal establishment, both in government and in the national institutions of civil society. The second factor is that this group had no political program or policy agenda (except for a time in foreign policy) that was at once significantly different from the discredited liberals and was politically feasible and electorally attractive. While it acquired a patina of populist appeal through the various victim and other marginal groups that it sponsored and claimed to represent, this sponsorship and representation alienated large sectors of the lower-middle and middle classes that previously deferred to the liberal establishment and was an honored part of the New Deal electoral coalition.

Intellectually and ideologically, "interest group liberalism," also called "pluralist democracy," was moribund. Theodore Lowi's *End of Liberalism*, published two years before John Rawls's *Theory of Justice* (1971), was both a death knell for this older liberal public philosophy and a clarion call for "juridical democracy"—that is, a formal-legal language of constitutional standards and enforceable rights.[4] This call for relimiting the federal government, however, did not reconstitute this older electoral majority on a new and invigorated basis. Democrats began to lose almost all elections contested on the basis of broad principles or national purposes. While many members of the older New Deal coalition continued to protect their interests in locally oriented legislative races by voting Democratic, they expressed their national values in executive and nationally oriented legislative races by voting Republican.

For the Universalists, ideological abandonment and electoral-political loss had its benefits as well as its temptations and dangers. The chief benefit was the explosion of "theory" in academia beginning in the 1970s, as intellectuals completed their critique of the older pluralist liberalism and sought to ground the national authority they hoped to exercise (some thought they already did) in a vocabulary adequate to their vision. *Their* liberalism as Universalism—unlike the discredited liberalism inherited from the Progressive and New Deal eras—was to be free from nationalism, racism, sexism (and every other contingent boundary they happen to reject) that stands in the way of full equality. Having inherited positions of power across a broad range of powerful national institutions, both in government and in the larger society, bearers of this new Universalistic theory not only dominated the self-understanding and purposes *inside* these locations, it seemed, for a time at least, to authorize them to define and govern the larger society—if only they could maintain a popular following. But they did not. Only when an earlier substantive liberalism lost its spiritual and cultural power did it seek to transform itself into an objective philosophy legitimating a reading of the Constitution as a neutral framework and branding opponents of that reading as ill-educated, reactionary, or extremist. In this sense, the writings of Rawls and Ronald Dworkin came just in the nick of time.

The increasing disconnection of this Universalistic rhetoric even from the practices and experiences of ordinary, popular and "operational" national institutions (churches, labor unions, businesses, school boards, legislative bodies) meant that the authoritative language of those institutions was now up for grabs, even as the language of Universalism in the 1970s and 1980s was becoming the ever more refined dogma of courts, universities, liberal religion, and the professions generally. These other national institutions were not captured by conservatives, but rather the new language of liberalism could neither describe nor offer direction to their felt needs and problems.

Another factor also fed the illusion of Universalist dominance and that was the continuing congressional electoral success in the 1980s of the old New Deal coalition. The national values and inner spirit of this electoral coalition were long dead, but its interests and alliance patterns lived on, making it difficult if not impossible to launch a successful electoral-political attack on the other institutions the Universalists dominated. This proved to be a weak reed, however, because this coalition, lacking the spiritual connections of shared national projects and purposes, was revealed for what it necessarily then became, a set of entrenched interests and privileges.

The Universalists proved incapable of articulating policies that spoke to much of this older ruling coalition and, through it, to the national community. Indeed, they became increasingly incapable of speaking to their fellow Americans. Not being able to win arguments in more democratic settings, they increasingly took positions above the battle by resorting to judicial and bureaucratic redoubts. Their rhetoric became increasingly abstract and Universalistic, while the concrete interests and groups they in fact represented appeared increasingly fragmented, particularistic, and demanding. Universalist ideology provided no standards by which to rank, sort, and judge these claims. What came to be called "multiculturalism" and "diversity" in the late 1980s was the alliance of selective and highly specific identity groupings and their interests justifying their claims and policy proposals in the name of universal rights and principles. This rhetoric was at first an amazingly powerful instrument because of its long-standing association both with a counterpart language in constitutional law, the courts, and the law schools, and with parts of the national consensual language of the civil rights movement in the 1960s and early 1970s, when it addressed legal segregation in the Southern states and some of those same overtly racist practices in public policy in the rest of the country.

The weakness of this position, however, was soon apparent. According to Judith Butler, "Whether a [universalistic / principled] claim is preposterous, provocative, or efficacious depends on the collective strength with which it is asserted, the institutional conditions of its assertion and reception, and the unpredictable political forces at work." The initially victorious Universalists, by failing to recognize that all "standards of universality are historically articulated,"[5] treated all opposition and every defeat as resulting from prejudice, ill-will, ignorance, or venality—as if anyone who opposed them was on a demonic continuum with a Southern sheriff and therefore hardly deserving of full participation in American political discourse.[6] *In short, acting as if they were already and in fact the national establishment* and guardians of its public theology, Universalists did not feel obligated to take the opposition with any intellectual or spiritual seriousness. The increasingly self-confident conservatives saw this as an arrogance beyond belief. More sophisticated critics saw the alliance between Universalism and multiculturalism as implicitly requiring an "imperial" elite or "overclass" who would define and then harmonize and adjudicate among the separate "tribes" or identity groups, but on terms set by and for the larger interests of the overclass.[7]

Increasingly, even some national elites within institutions dominated by Universalists began to desert them. Beginning in the late 1970s, many liberal public intellectuals and policy experts addressing concrete social and economic problems sought escape from their theoretical sway. Within the liberal academic community of theorists, the paradigm of "rights talk" and claims of liberal neutrality as universally valid democratic norms began to come under attack, both as the organizing narrative of liberalism and as an intellectually coherent and effective democratic political theory. Universalist claims to being above the battle were not only challenged, they were seen as attempting to constrain public discourse in ways that threatened to undermine political democracy itself. These alternatives, emerging over the past ten years or more, are examined later. We must first address the strengths/weaknesses of their outside opponent, the intellectual-moral-spiritual alternative of Restoration.

CONSERVATIVE RESTORATION

The older liberal establishment was dead and their Universalist inheritors could not win policy debates (except in some courts and many classrooms) or nationally oriented elections. The reason for this was the rise of national conservatism as a powerful popular and electoral political force. Why is it, then, that conservative Restoration, so effective in preventing Universalism from ruling, cannot itself rule? To be sure, their victories have been substantial across a range of policy issues and in setting the policy agenda—so much so that even Democratic presidential contenders now have no choice except to disavow their strongest (older) liberal and (newer) Universalist supporters. Significant conservative victories have been confined largely to the area of political economy and to some of the worst entrenched privileges having their origins in Depression-era programs. Put differently, deregulation, cost-benefit analysis, efficiency measures, and social cost measures were taking over, making untenable (and for Democratic presidential candidates, suicidal) any new policy initiatives mandated by older liberal or newer Universalistic political theory. Conversely, however, when Restorationists sought to take policy initiatives centered not in the economy and taxation but in the areas of national social values, intellectual culture, and education, they have met with little or no success. Almost every move has been challenged and often checkmated in the federal courts and in the courts of elite public opinion. Why this asymmetrical success and failure?

Most obviously, one could say that when conservative Restorationists team up with economic (often libertarian or neoclassical) conservatives, victory is theirs, not only because this is a powerful alliance in its own right but because the Universalists themselves had destroyed the moral and intellectual grounds of an earlier interest group liberalism that supported a pragmatic division of patronage and spoils to its coalitional members in the name of managed social harmony and electoral success. But this does not answer the question of why calls for deregulation, devolution, and tax cuts—often justified by neoclassical economic ideas—would gain the strong support of *moral* and *religious* conservatives, many of whom had been part of the earlier New Deal coalition and subordinate members of the national liberal establishment.

The answer, I think, is two-sided. Everywhere the national government now goes (and it has tended to go everywhere) liberal procedures and values tend to follow, threatening and even destroying the purposes and values and internally sustained moral practices of the organization or activity it has entered. Thus, local and state institutions and governments, as well as many organizations in the larger civil society, feared what they now saw as a destructive "liberal imperium" that, in the name of Universalist (and putatively neutral) principles, destroyed sources of moral cohesion in America. Whatever else they do, policies of devolution and deregulation, including federal tax cuts, have the effect of *reempowering* local or relatively autonomous moral majorities, even as they weaken the reach and power of Universalist elites. Additionally, tax cuts, devolution, and deregulation became part of a normal political process of victors seeking to defund or otherwise deprive the electoral losers of governmental resources.[8] Thus, in alliance with economic conservatives and through economic policy, Restorationists not only stopped many of their opponents' policy initiatives, they even reversed their direction.

This is decidedly not the case, however, when, through electoral victory, Restorationists seek to articulate and define the American soul—i.e., when they begin to presume the status of a national religious and cultural establishment. Even attempts to defund or destroy the bureaucratic redoubts of their opponents in the areas of national culture (NEA, NEH, PBS) and national education policy (Department of Education)—policies that could also be justified on libertarian and economic efficiency grounds—have met with resounding failure. An obvious reason for this is that economic conservatives, insofar as they adhere to neoclassical or libertarian values, do not share with moral conservatives an inner imperative to reform the culture. But even support from many moral conservatives in these cultural projects has often been halfhearted and symbolic. With the possible exception of issues of abortion and homosexual rights (especially to marriage and adoption), moral conservatives in America betray a rather weak will to power in any positive or creative sense of national projects and programs. Many of them just want to be left alone and treated as Americans in good standing by national elites.[9] Their ends are both negative and modest. Other moral conservatives fear that positive national Restorationist projects led by the national government (e.g., national school standards, media censorship or control, the funding of religiously committed academics) require the active assistance of the federal bureaucracy and other national institutions dominated by their opponents. These are wise insights.

There is a more complex reason for this weakness. Given the currently constructed identities that define the spectrum of diversity in America, the regional, racial, and religious identities of the Restorationists appear to represent a rather narrow band. The prevailing spectrum, as all identity spectra necessarily must, submerges or makes invisible many more identities than it recognizes (e.g., economic class, religion except for believer and nonbeliever). But this is the very source of the problem of political agency and power: an informal religious-cultural establishment capable of exercising national political authority *includes the authority to construct the authoritative spectrum of plurality or difference* in ways that make *its* authoritative values appear universal or national or inclusive. As long as race (largely Black or white) is the primary identity determinate and gender increasingly stresses sexual orientation, a secondary identity determinate, the Restorationists are doomed to noneconomic policy impotence and failure. Conversely, however, if race and gender/sexual orientation retreat or disperse into a host of other competing constructions of identity—become subsumed under a newly empowered national identity—many new possibilities suddenly present themselves.

A THIRD WAY? LIBERAL NATIONALISM AND PLURALIST COMMUNITARIANISM

The standoff resulting from the complementary strengths and weaknesses of these two primary political groupings in contemporary America has stimulated many third-way initiatives that seek to transcend or to bypass these divisions. The most prominent one seeks to combine an older progressive-liberal economic and social policy with a resurgent nationalism. Two noteworthy books expressing this national-liberal view are Richard Rorty's *Achieving Our Country: Leftist Thought in Twentieth-Century America* and Michael Lind's *Next American Nation*. To these must be added Lind's later *Up From Conservatism,* two by another journalist-intellectual, E. J. Dionne, Jr. (*Why Americans Hate Politics* and *They Only Look Dead: Why Progressives will Dominate the Next Political Era*), and others by political academics such as Michael Tomasky (*Left for Dead: The Life, Death, and Possible Resurrection of Progressive Politics in America*) and Kenneth Heineman (*God is a Conservative: Religion, Politics and Morality in Contemporary America*).

In these books and in others like them the message is the same: "A plague on both your houses." Almost all excoriate what I have termed the Universalists both for their alliance with a divisive and self-serving multiculturalism (and its requirement for a cosmopolitan elite or overclass) on the one hand and an evasive nationalism on the other—the refusal to honor ideals of national citizenship and patriotism until all difference (or at least those differences this overclass elite has defined as difference) has been compensated for and wiped away by affirmative action, quotas, and other forms of group rights. Almost all condemn the assumption of moral superiority and the resulting arrogance of the Universalists toward the interests and claims of ordinary working people and the churchgoing and responsible middle classes—especially if they happen to be white ethnics or

Southern—two groups critical for Democratic Party (and national liberal) dominance for most of this century.

Many Liberal Nationalist criticisms of the Restorationists hardly differ from
those of the Universalists (nativist, threatening separation of church and state, in
alliance with selfish business interests). However, they side with Restorationists
both in their national patriotism and in their defenses of institutions in civil society that seek to instill personal responsibility and family values. Very often their
nationalism takes the form of economic protectionism (tariffs, plant closure rules)
and much stricter controls over immigration. Their affirmation of nationalism and
national patriotism serves both to strengthen the force of their economic proposals
and to signal an ethic of care and responsibility for all members of the national
community. This same economic and social nationalism serves the cultural ideal
of blunting tribalism and other multiculturalist forms of group identity by affirming that their American nationalism is aggressively transracial.

This group of writers tends to stress nationalism and an activist national government. Their critique of contemporary ideological divisions share many features with Communitarian thinking that also has its intellectual and moral roots
in the national Progressive side of the New Deal.[10] This requires some initial clari-
fication. Liberal Nationalist writers such as Rorty, Lind, and Dionne seem to take
their cues from the national Progressives at the turn of the century while most
Communitarian writers are more at home with the more pluralistic liberalism of
the New Deal. Symbolically put, the former tend to respect Hamilton and Herbert
Croly and Theodore Roosevelt while the latter still prefer Jefferson and Walter
Weyl and Woodrow Wilson. More directly put, the nationalism of the former is
explicit and ruling. The nationalism of the latter is indirect and implicit, reflecting more the *residue* of national Progressivism in the New Deal and the
unarticulated consensus required for democratic pluralism to work.[11]

Communitarians have an implicit rather than an evasive nationalism, but their
understanding of our current political and spiritual condition is very close to that
of the Liberal Nationalists. Like the Liberal Nationalists, Communitarians accept
much of the conservative critique of what I have termed Universalism, especially
its willingness, in the name of rights, to demoralize and even destroy value-cre-
ating and sustaining institutions, especially families, but also neighborhood
schools and religious and other faith-based institutions in local public life and
practices. They, too, fear the disuniting effects of a rights-driven liberal-universal imperium, penetrating and destroying the "seedbeds of civic virtue" by entering areas of life and action where they were never intended to go.
Communitarians are pluralists but not principled multiculturalists, because their
pluralism—like that of the New Deal—presumes a national moral and cultural
consensus, albeit one that they feel no pressing need to make intellectually explicit or philosophically persuasive.[12]

The leading ideas and critiques of what I have termed Liberal Nationalism and
Communitarianism receive philosophical grounding and intellectual support in
contemporary philosophy and political theory, a subject taken up in the next

chapter. Here it should be noted only that Universalist defenses of the primacy of rights-based individualism and procedural neutrality have been subjected to a series of powerful critiques in contemporary political philosophy, best represented from the historicist side by Charles Taylor and Michael Sandel and from the side of a resurgent pragmatism by Richard Rorty and Stanley Fish.

A similar critique, constructed within these same philosophical perspectives, is also being made in the law schools against the claims of Universalists to be the authoritative interpreters of the U.S. Constitution.[13] Pragmatism and historicism are the two positions from which a barrage of criticism has been fired at appellate court decisions, especially those using the Fourteenth Amendment to import the values of the Bill of Rights into areas of life they were never intended to go. Without replicating the argument here, suffice it to say that this critique from the law schools complements and extends some of the noneconomic arguments of Restorationists as well as those of the Liberal Nationalists and Communitarians, especially concerning nationalism, civic virtue, and mutual responsibility.

THE PROBLEM OF FAITH

What is striking in both of these third-way literatures is the way they do and do not discuss religion and religious faith. Almost all of these writings come from the left, whether older or newer, and most seem to draw directly or through the New Deal on the spirit and social vision of the Progressive intellectuals. These Progressive intellectuals were trained in the historicism of American Protestant liberal evangelicalism and in German philosophy, theology, and social science.[14] And yet contemporary third-way writings echo the evasive nationalism of contemporary Universalists with their own evasions regarding the place of religion in national political life. This evasion might seem unavoidable given the intense religiosity and God-talk in the rhetoric of the Restorationists and the evangelical and fundamentalist church sources of their core supporters. Neither Liberal Nationalists nor pluralist Communitarians want to be associated with this rhetoric and much of the religious-cultural agenda of the Restorationists. Nevertheless, their discussion of religion is often more a tactical avoidance of the issue of religion and politics than a strategic denial of their relationship and importance.

Third-way writings are full of fruitful discussion of the relationship of the sacred to civic and political life. One such sacred source is found in their discussion of marriage, the family, and family values. Michael Lind, who argues that every successful national governing order in America has had a civil religion as part of its nationalism, makes family values the religion of his hoped-for next American republic.[15] By raising marriage and the family to *civic* prominence, he and others, often without knowing it, are restating a central theme of earlier American national political theologies in which the family is seen as the central public or civic institution in teaching and transmitting civic and moral values that underwrite our free institutions and political authority.[16] William Galston's recent article, "A Liberal-Democratic Case for the Two-Parent Family," and Michael Lind's term "civic familism" perfectly capture, but without articulating the philosophical and religious implications of, this earlier public theological ideal.[17]

Another sacred source and religious surrogate, perhaps stemming from nostalgia for the moral and cultural consensus underwriting the earlier New Deal liberal establishment, is found in calls for a heightened respect for ordinary working-class and middle-class Americans. Respecting their interests and values (and shaping economic policy to protect their local institutions and practices) would indirectly reempower their religiously based morality. Indeed, one might even explain the attraction in some of these writings to nostalgic, politically hopeless, and even irrational and destructive economic proposals (e.g., ban Wal-Marts, community purchase of steel mills, protective national industrial policies) as a kind of sublimated yearning for the restoration of some earlier sources of community solidarities—solidarities that were also centered in shared religious and moral beliefs.[18]

A third discussion of religion through the more general idea of the sacred lies in recourse to the vocabulary of political and moral romanticism when discussing community and nation.[19] Romanticism as a narrative form, and the stories in which it locates specific meanings and purposes, tends to be interwoven with larger narratives of collective destinies.[20] Thus, the discourse or scripts of romanticism have always been ways to discuss spirit and God without directly relying on biblical or church authority. Because of that translation, one could say that national political theology in America has always drawn on the vocabulary of romanticism[21]—usually, however, as part of a more explicitly religious vocabulary—to consolidate and sustain informal religious establishments. Many of today's third-way intellectuals mistakenly equate religion with church and church (or faith traditions) with increasing plurality and difference, so they must express ideas of the common faith that must underwrite both communal and national solidarity in a language of romanticism carefully constructed to distinguish it from this institutional understanding of religion. What they do not realize is that their language of romanticism—expressed as the national quest for social justice, for moral equality, for the reestablishment of community, for the common enterprise of extending freedom at home and abroad—has always been a staple of the national political theologies of informal religious establishments in America.[22]

Are these third-way writings, then, *unwittingly* reconstructing a national political theology and reconstituting the basis for a new informal religious establishment? In some ways I think they are. Only if their separate critiques and surrogates are placed within a more articulate philosophical and historical framework, however, will these efforts become manifest and coherent. What seems immediately obvious in the calls for consensual pluralism by the Communitarians and for a new nationalism by the Liberals is that both pluralism and nationalism require a common faith. Without that common faith both

Communitarians and Liberal Nationalists would be forced to act much like the Universalists they criticize as undemocratic elitists: namely, to bracket out of public discourse claims, ideas, and proposals that have their origins in specific religious commitments or other ascriptive factors that define the units that constitute both pluralism and the nation. Without a sense of shared substantive understandings and common moral sources, they, too, would be forced to disallow, in principle, public decisions "contaminated by commitment" (to use the words of a recent Supreme Court Fourteenth Amendment decision), *even if that commitment was the common product of democratic political struggle, democratic dialogue, and democratic compromise.*

Communitarians require sacred commitments of all sorts for the flourishing of their separate communities, but these communities in turn must be able to see some relationship between their particular values and those of the larger society. If they did not, if each group were seen as tightly bounded and subjectively self-standing, social harmony would require a putatively neutral and universalistic overclass whose own arguments and values would bear no philosophical or spiritual connection to those they rule. If the calls for national patriotism and civic virtue by Liberal Nationalists had no inner connection and bearing on the particular values and local identities of those they call, then nationalism itself would be a set of ideas acting as a distant, disconnected, and possibly dangerous deus ex machina.

Both Liberal Nationalists and Communitarians require a common faith, and that faith must be constructed *from within and through* the interactions and struggles of the separate commitments and experiences of the participants. Indeed, this requirement is the source of their most powerful critique of the Universalists, namely, that liberal Universalists must so constrain public discourse that democratic political life is itself undermined; that in the name of rights, public discourse (and legislation or other decisions flowing from that discourse) must be purged *from the start and before discussion begins* of all elements that are not already public in the sense of immediately accessible and belonging to all, not the particular belief or identity constituent of only a part. Public discourse as discovery and reinterpretation is ruled out.

Under these dialogic constraints, only abstract rights talk and other universalistic (and perhaps scientific) language will be permitted to be heard. As Stanley Fish and many others have so gleefully pointed out, those constrained, those not permitted to speak as equals in public deliberation, "just happen" to urge policy positions and honor collective values and have concrete interests not shared by those who would do the constraining. The universalism of the Universalists, especially in alliance with multiculturalism, is, after all, quite particular, as particular and historically contingent as those they would constrain and as those whom they would favor and sponsor.[23] Under these constraints, thick ideals of civic virtue, a deep patriotism, and nationalism itself would be disallowed in the same way that religion would.

In comparison to the Universalists, the criteria of "allowed discourse" by both the Liberal Nationalists and the Communitarians are much more democratic and open-ended. This democracy and openness, however, are made possible only *because* they, too, are constrained, but within a capacious national-spiritual horizon, a common democratic faith that presumes all within it have a right both to speak and to be listened to. Committed Universalists, in contrast (especially when they feel especially pressed by their enemies), would not hesitate (in principle and if they had the power) to constrain out great numbers of American citizens on any given policy discussion if they refuse to conform their speech to the constraints the Universalists stipulate to guarantee their meanings of equal rights and equal respect. This is another way of stating a final difference between the Universalists, on the one hand, and the Liberal Nationalists and Communitarians on the other: their differing understandings of the Constitution and its relationship to American national identity and democratic political life.

CONSTITUTIONAL FAITH

America is not only a "nation with the soul of a church," it is also a constitutional democracy. Might a shared "constitutional faith"[24] be the best third-way alternative to cut through and resolve our current ideological impasse? The answer I want to defend, already suggested in earlier chapters, is necessarily a mixture of yes and no, but now in the context of discussing current ideological alternatives. From one perspective Americans have always been united by a constitutional faith whenever we have understood the Constitution *to mean what authoritative national political orders and national political theologies say it means*. But this is only to say that constitutional interpretation is both variable and dependent. The Constitution is more a symbol of a reigning substantive consensus than itself a self-standing and self-interpreting repository of a fixed American creed. The very existence of a series of distinct political orders or regimes under the same Constitution is testament to this fact. To affirm a continuous constitutional faith on these terms is the same as denying it, and neither affirmation nor denial takes us very far. In periods of disunity and deep cultural conflict, the Constitution is always part of the problem and never an independent solution. If there is any doubt about this, one need only read the constitutional debates in the 1850s, in the 1920s and 1930s, and in today's law reviews.[25]

But even in the best of times the Constitution alone is unpromising as a source of national patriotism and purpose. Standing alone, the U.S. Constitution is a radically incomplete and partial governing document, institutionally, philosophically, and historically. Not only has it always coexisted with and depended upon scores of state constitutions and is incomprehensible both as theory and a set of practices without them,[26] it encodes in its own Bill of Rights its dependent and partial status. When one adds the ways in which wars, amendments, political party formation, realigning elections, and changing distributions of social and economic power have altered constitutional hermeneutics over time, it would be difficult to make a philosophical and substantive case for the Constitution as some fixed or comprehensive source of our national identity and purpose.[27]

Despite these factors, however, such cases have been and continue to be made. Indeed, one might say that since the breakdown of the national liberal/New Deal establishment, this case seems to be the only nationalist arrow left in the Universalists' ideological quiver, just as the federal courts and bureaucracy have been the one fairly consistent governmental source of Universalist political power. Moreover, Universalists have claimed that their reading of the Constitution has finally anchored that document on solid philosophical footings, thereby transforming it from an historically contingent and partial document to a source of sovereign national power authorized by the truth of a philosophy of justice and rights.[28]

I want briefly to examine this Universalist case for a constitutional faith, especially because it is being made at a time when there is both deep cultural conflict *and* a sort of presumptive plausibility to their position. This case is also worth examining because I think that those who are its most powerful academic critics—pragmatists, historicists, and postmodernists or antifoundationalists—are in the process of constructing a *real* alternative and a new and more credible source of national identity and common faith that place the Constitution and constitutional faith within its larger narrative.

One obvious way the Universalist position has been allied to a kind of constitutional faith has been to picture the U.S. Constitution, especially the Bill of Rights, as a neutral framework constraining and structuring political, economic, and cultural life in a diverse country. In this view, the diverse substantive ends generated by a free people in civil society must submit to one common set of coercively enforced rules and procedures. These rules serve as a thin liberal-universal imperium, while the diverse activities and purposes are the thick expressions of real communities, real identities, concrete purposes, and felt loyalties and identities. Earlier this was also the position of strong defenders of states rights in their portrait of the national government as the British Empire at its best: a necessary but dangerous and undemocratic expedient.

The Universalists' understanding of the Constitution and their understanding of the relationship of the Constitution to liberal political philosophy starts with the Bill of Rights. This is something of a paradox because the Bill of Rights comprised amendments insisted upon by antifederalist *opponents* of the Constitution as the price of their support for ratification. Federalism, states' rights, limited government, and the devolution of power were central teachings of the Bill of Rights, just as they were the ideological core of the Jeffersonian case against the Federalist Party under the Adams presidency and of the Jacksonian case against the presidency of his son, John Quincy Adams.

Far from sanctioning a universalistic and neutral framework of rights overseeing a *common* political life on the basis of a common creed, the Bill of Rights as the interpretive axis of the Constitution explicitly sanctions the power of state and local governing institutions that were neither neutral nor even particularly mindful of a clear distinction between government and the institutions of civil society.[29] Each state was presumed to be a real community, a small republic with distinct purposes, tied to other states by a limited constitutional compact. This compact created an "empire of freedom," but in the negative sense of not interfering with the internal affairs of the states and communities and conducting national affairs with a scrupulous equality or neutrality between and among conflicting state or sectional interests and values.[30] Moreover, state governments in structure and practice were much more democratic than the national government, both because they governed spheres of daily and intimate life and because their constitutions and subgovernments were driven by popular election and the dominance of legislative bodies.

In this states' rights sense of federalism, the U.S. Constitution was a limited charter of imperial liberty and not the framework for national democracy, because it protected the local liberties of states and communities to act as separate "nations"—bodies governed more by thick republican than thin liberal values and practices. Under the aegis of the Constitution, the individual was free because the national government was forbidden to regulate his speech and associations, outlaw his church, or meddle with his political institutions. Within each nation, whether acting through the state government or through local governments and voluntary organizations, however, the individual *could* be and was (and even continues to be) strictly regulated in almost all aspects of his life.[31] This is civic republicanism. The more morally and religiously homogeneous the community and the more consensual its perceived foundations, the more it could regulate behavior of all kinds because the regulation would not appear as some externally imposed coercive force but as the democratically generated formal-legal capstone of freely chosen common ends. Patriotism, the glue that held this all together, was American patriotism, but each community was like a separate nation. Patriotism in America was, in the words of Alexis de Tocqueville,

> nothing more than an aggregate or summary of the patriotic zeal of the separate provinces. Every citizen of the United States transfers, so to speak, his attachment to his little republic into the common store. . . . In defending the Union he defends the increasing prosperity of his own state or county [and] the right of conducting its affairs. . . . These are motives that are wont to stir men more than the general interests of the country and the glory of the nation.[32]

More ominously, especially in view of making a rights-based constitutional understanding the source of American identity and national authority, Tocqueville, along with Whigs and other anti-Jacksonian opponents of this constitutional understanding, also concluded that, under these conditions, Americans will become progressively *less* capable of undertaking major national purposes or of sacrificing local advantage and interests for the common good. As the memory of the Revolutionary War and the constitutional founders faded, the U.S. Constitution would become an ever more empty symbol of unity and loyalty because it *prevents* the creation of national purposes by protecting the small republics in carrying out their separately chosen and morally diverse ways of life. If the national government began to act as a small republic writ large, representing a national community with common projects, local patriotism would rise up to challenge it under the banner of freedom from oppression. Even the modest attempt to use national authority to prevent new states formed from nationally governed territory from instituting slavery precipitated a civil war and a new reading of the Constitution imposed by military victory. Before this conquest, the Constitution seemed to bestow less authority on the national government than did the Articles of Confederation, under whose aegis the Northwest Territories were organized prohibiting slave holding.

The problem I suggest here is that it is difficult to ground national identity and national patriotism in the U.S. Constitution understood as a neutral framework for protecting individual rights, then and now. The claimed virtues of neutrality and guaranteed (local or individual) freedoms are precisely the virtues that *prevent* the shaping of a common identity and national patriotism. Indeed, these virtues encourage a kind of "deep pluralism," both spatial and cultural, that may be an obstacle to a shared identity. To escape this weakness would require transforming the principles of the Bill of Rights into a national and centralizing engine of a robust liberal-democratic reform. But this in turn requires a narrative within which this transformation can be understood and justified. Historically, this was done first by Lincoln and then by the national Progressives, but the narrative was constructed transconstitutionally and with a good deal of help from a national political theology and a political party that acted as an informal religious establishment.[33]

If constitutional ratification as a nationalizing moment was blunted and diluted by the Bill of Rights, the second great nationalizing moment, the Civil War amendments, turned the Bill of Rights from liberal passivity to national civic republican action. Whether one locates this transformation in Union armies, religiously inspired antislavery movements, the hidden logic of industrial capitalism, or the covert hand of God, the formal-legal and cultural result transformed the document into a substantive representation of the American way of life.[34] But its authority and its power were *not* as a neutral framework of rights—indeed, Democratic cries against the *tyranny* of the national government reverberated in their party platforms for more than twenty years before and after the Civil War, based on this older understanding. *Their* Constitution had been taken from them by force and not by consent.

Here lies the current difficulty of combing a rights-based or thin liberal and principled understanding of the Constitution with a call for a national government with plenary power to impose those same liberal values not only on the laws and practices of all subordinate governmental bodies (through the Fourteenth Amendment) but on most of the major institutions in civil society (through a robust judicial imagination and tracing the migrations of federal tax dollars). The

Bill of Rights as a Universalist or liberal-perfectionist call to arms and as the authoritative source for legally coerced transformative moral and social projects on a national scale would require extraordinary consensus in the larger society. This consensus must be substantive and not procedural, committed and not neutral, deeply political and not above politics, and earned by democratic persuasion and the mobilization of vast amounts of intellectual and moral resources.[35] This was most obviously the case in both the Progressive and the World War II–Cold War eras. The projects underwritten at home and abroad were expressions of a *positive* liberalism, a *national* liberalism, even an *imperial-commanding-reforming* liberalism, seeking to discredit and then destroy those rights, practices, policies, and jurisdictions that stood in its way.

Historically, this discourse, both as national organic law and as national-covenantal religion, has always been an engine to nationalize rights but rarely and never exclusively *in the name of rights*—that was in fact the language of their opponents. The governing imperative of this narrative was always to establish justice, to create a more perfect union, and to fulfill a particular national destiny. Indeed, this rhetorical-theoretical-political reform engine of national civic republicanism might equally be called a great *destroyer* of all those rights whose ends do not serve the national covenant. If those barriers to the national covenant are states' rights, then states' rights must yield. If those barriers are private property rights, then property rights must yield. If those barriers are constitutional rights, then the Constitution must yield.[36] And they all did. And they will all continue to do so whenever common faith impels common projects.

It may well be that contemporary Universalists have been put in the political position where they must, to paraphrase Tocqueville, "do more honor to their philosophy than to themselves." By withholding both from themselves and from their fellow citizens their own moral sources and substantive commitments, they have severed both the Constitution and themselves from the resources and powers that an American national identity provides.

> Four score and seven years ago [1776 not 1787] our fathers brought forth on this continent, a new nation.... I am exceedingly anxious that this Union, the Constitution, and the liberties of the people shall be perpetuated in accordance with the original idea for which that struggle was made, and I shall be most happy indeed if I shall be an humble instrument in the hands of the Almighty, and of this His almost chosen people, for perpetuating the object of that great struggle.... We have grown in numbers, wealth and power, as no other nation has ever grown. But we have forgotten God. We have forgotten the gracious hand which preserved us in peace, and multiplied and enriched and strengthened us; and we have vainly imagined, in the deceitfulness of our hearts, that all these blessings were produced by some superior wisdom and virtue of our own. Intoxicated with unbroken success, we have become too self-sufficient to feel the necessity of redeeming and preserving grace, too proud to pray to the God that made us.... We here highly resolve ... that this nation, under God, shall have a new birth of freedom.[37]

Placing constitutional faith within an historical narrative, as I have just done through Lincoln's speeches, necessarily gives the Constitution two lives and two sets of meanings, an external-legal-creedal life and an internal-spiritual-national life. The outer life consists of the formal language of the document, the amendments, and legislative and court decisions (with supporting arguments and commentary) explicating the authoritative principles and rules it mandates and authorizes *at any given point in time*. But even this outer understanding is a *life*, because its principles and rules change and these external changes must be understood within a narrative that makes doctrinal sense. The U.S. Constitution has an interpretive and textual history explicated as a narrative by authoritative interpreters working within the words of the text and the cases and commentaries of constitutional law as they are at present understood.

Even this outer life, therefore, has an inner life. John Quincy Adams maintained that the Declaration of Independence was the disclosure and acknowledgment of a *prior union*, "a social compact, by which the [previously constituted] *whole people* convenanted with each citizen of the United Colonies, and each citizen with the [previously constituted] *whole people*. . . . Each was pledged to all, and all were pledged to each by a concert of souls, without limitation of time, in the presence of Almighty God, and proclaimed to all mankind." The Constitution, as the third and last stage of this national founding [the war itself was the second], represents "the formation of the Anglo-American People and Nation of North America."[38]

This two-sidedness of the Constitution is reflected in contemporary legal, moral, and political theory. The current ideological controversy between what I have termed Universalists on the one hand, and Liberal Nationalists and Communitarians on the other, is partly reflected in the current divide in academia between enlightenment modernism and (pre- or post-) enlightenment postmodernism or, in political theory and in law schools, between a principled liberalism and an historicist civic republicanism. These divides are neither merely academic nor temporary tempests in departmental or law school teapots but are in deadly earnest. They will last so long as American national identity is deeply unsettled. The claim that the U.S. Constitution is the institutional and normative source of American national identity is part of this struggle and not a solution to it.

It is perhaps no accident that the deepest and most intractable set of issues around which this debate is now conducted involves religion and religious freedom. It is certainly no accident that pragmatists, civic republicans, antifoundationalists, and postmodernists in academia (especially the law schools) are now in substantial agreement with religious evangelicals, Liberal Nationalists, and pluralist Communitarians in attacking prevailing church-state jurisprudence and, therefore, the Universalist version of American national identity.[39] The argument is simple but compelling: If the Constitution is only a minimal set of abstract liberal principles, then the national government must radically withdraw its power over most of American civil and political life. If, on the other hand, the Constitution authorizes republican virtue projects at home and abroad, then it must be read within a substantive narrative horizon that is authoritative over the American nation. The American people must both acknowledge and enforce that authority. Only democratic experience, participation, and struggle, however, will disclose that narrative, and the acknowledgment of that disclosure becomes a national covenant.

NOTES

1. Wolfe 1998.

2. There are many discussions of the mobilization of religious conservatives in national politics. Two, however, stress the fact that religious fundamentalism and moral conservatism have always tended to be powerful forces locally and that it was in response to invasion by aggressively liberal national political majorities and federal court decisions that they became politically mobilized. Ribuffo (1993) is an excellent survey of the persistence of fundamentalism in American culture since its proclaimed demise in the 1920s, and Lowi (1995) reformulates the earlier Jacksonian model of small republics to speak of local moral majorities who, under Reagan, became a national political force in alliance with classical or laissez-faire liberals.

3. The suddenness and stridency of support for Clinton from left intellectuals is proof enough—as if to call for Clinton's impeachment is in fact to denigrate the moral commitments and ways of life of a whole sector of America's boomer generation—a potential "coup d'culture."

4. Lowi 1969; Rawls 1971. In a later book, Lowi (1995), chapter 6, is even more despairing of the possibility of restoring a limited liberal regime based on the rule of law.

5. In Nussbaum 1996, 46.

6. Fish (1997), 2,283, calls this an attempt by liberals to create "an epistemological criminal class."

7. Especially Lind 1995 and 1996; and see Tomasky 1996; Dionne 1996; and Heineman 1998. I call these writings Liberal Nationalist and discuss them later in this chapter.

8. Lowi 1995, chapter 4; Frum 1994.

9. This ambivalence between national restoration and group recognition is nicely captured in Watson 1997.

10. See three wide-ranging collections of Communitarian writings: Etzioni 1995 and 1998; and Glendon and Blankenhorn 1995.

11. Marty (1997) 80, aptly calls this consensus pluralism: "Pluralism as it emerged in discourse around 1950 was an effort by those who had generally represented sameness before but were now in teamwork with some of those who had not been included." See Plotke (1996), on the national progressive elements in the New Deal political order. Stettner (1993) wants to make the entire spirit of the New Deal much more national-Progressive than it in fact was by seeing its origins in Herbert Croly. Morone (1998) traces the roots of this difference by distinguishing between the centrality of the national mobilizing efforts of the Progressives and the less nationalistic and more bureaucratic-administrative mobilizing efforts of the New Deal.

12. The almost perfect statement of this formulation is Daniel Boorstin, *Genius of American Politics* (1953), especially if read in conjunction with Louis Hartz, *Liberal Tradition in America* (1955), and David Truman, *Governmental Process* (1951). Many of the critiques of Sandel's *Democracy's Discontent* (1996) in Allen and Regan (1998) raise this same nationalist issue.

13. Communitarians can also draw on the legacy of consensus pluralism represented by Robert Dahl, who stressed in all of his writings the limited role that the federal courts and constitutionalism can play in the protection of rights. "Insofar as there is any general protection in human society against the deprivation by one group of the freedom desired by another it is probably not to be found in constitutional forms. It is to be discovered, if any at all, in extra-constitutional factors." Dahl 1956, 134.

14. Eisenach 1994, chapters 2 and 3.

15. "Civic familism" is Lind's functional equivalent of earlier informal religious establishments. And see the Galston, Doherty, and Waite articles in Etzioni 1998; and Selznick 1992. The title of a recent book by Abshire and Brower (1996), *Putting America's House in Order: The Nation as a Family*, nicely expresses this pattern of thinking. Compare to Jane Addams (1902 [1964]) on the family as a democratic institution.

16. This "doctrine of free institutions" articulated by the Whig Party and appropriated by the Republican Party also includes schools and churches as well as other publicly oriented institutions in civil society. See Howe 1979, 1990, 1997b; Handy 1971 and 1990; Eisenach 1994.

17. Galston 1998; Lind 1995, 277–85; and see the essay by Joan Williams in Allen and Regan 1998. More generally on the sacredness of civil institutions, see Sullivan 1995a and 1995b.

18. Sandel 1996; and see discussions and critiques in Allen and Regan 1998.

19. Edward Shils (1997) put it this way: "Legitimacy is not a rational deduction from first principles of natural or divine law or of the sovereignty of the people. It is certainly not habit; it is not a mechanical or a condition reflex. The acknowledgment of legitimacy is an act of belief; it is an act of belief in sacred, i.e., charismatic, things. An individual who accepts the legitimacy of the law and of authority acknowledges the sacred by participation in its objectivated symbolic form which is an emanation from its source. The source is the highest authority in a collectivity constituted by residence in a bounded national territory. The sacred source is the national collective self-consciousness" (218).

20. Abrams 1973.

21. See the collection of Communitarian writings in Etzioni 1995 and 1998; and Glendon and Blankenhorn 1995; and see Sandel 1996; and Taylor 1985a and 1991. An exception to this pattern is Fowler 1989; and, less directly, Glendon 1991.

22. Compare Michael Lind's imagined "museum" of the projected coming American republic to the churches, temples, and cathedrals that symbolized earlier national faiths. Lind 1995, chapter 9.

23. Fish 1997 and 1998. "Liberalism cannot claim as a ground for excluding religion from public policy questions a superior or even a different epistemology from that of religion. . . . The truth of liberalism (and falsity of illiberal religions) cannot rest on an epistemology that is different and, for public policy issues, better epistemology—because it is fairer, more reasonable, more respectful of autonomy, more consistent with our being free and equal, etc.—than the epistemology employed to support religious claims, including the claim of illiberal religions" (Alexander 1993, 764–65).

24. Levinson 1988. This was the first book from the academic left that seriously asked questions about national (constitutional) loyalty and the profession of law, and took oaths seriously.

25. See Posner (1995), chapter 2, on why "doctrinal" law review articles cannot be either central or definitive in periods of intellectual dissensus. See also Sunstein 1993 and Williams 1998. All seem to argue that constitutional jurisprudence must be justified within the framework of a larger philosophy and political theory. Most antifoundationalists turn to pragmatism as the only theory that links political democracy with rule of law.

26. Elazar 1998; Lowi 1995.

27. Ackerman 1993 and 1996; Sunstein 1993.

28. Dworkin 1996; Raz 1988; Rawls 1971. For the best discussion and critique of these three writers as a group, see Neal (1997), chapters 4–8.

29. The pervasively used term in the nineteenth century, "free institutions," embraced not only governments, but juries, schools, churches, libraries, local militias, fire companies, political parties, and the whole panoply of charitable, reform, and service organizations. See note 16. Federalism before the Civil War could plausibly be understood this way.

30. Thus, slavery could be local, but freedom would be national. Thus, states could have legally established churches, but the nation would be godless in the sense of having nothing to do with issues of religion. Thus, states and localities could rigorously regulate morals and speech but the national Congress was forbidden to do so. This view is biased toward Jefferson rather than Hamilton, but it has a deep historical source in British imperial policy toward the separate colonies prior to the 1760s and the events leading to the War of Independence. The U.S. Constitution replaced the Articles of Confederation because the central authority it established more effectively carried out the functions long and successfully performed by British imperial authority.

31. Lowi (1969 and 1995) is especially good on this idea of federalism as warranting extensive state "police power." Under state governance, husbands were given extensive powers over their wives; some people were permitted to own others; and economic and social life was often strictly regulated.

32. Tocqueville, 1981, Vol. 1, ch. 7, 83.

33. As usual, Herbert Croly (1909) put the issue succinctly. Bewailing the "monarchy of the Constitution," he declared that "impartiality is the duty of the judge rather than the statesman, of the courts rather than the government." A national democratic state "must on the whole make the rules in its own interest. It must help those men who are most capable of using their winnings for the benefit of society" (192).

34. Ackerman 1996; McPherson 1991. For cultural, philosophical, and social-cultural transformations, McClay 1994; Greenstone 1993; Gienapp 1987.

35. This is the premise of Morone 1998. This mobilization and consensus were largely achieved from World War II through the Cold War and into the 1970s. Marty 1996; King 1989a; Silk 1988; Voskuil 1989.

36. Here I refer variously to the overthrow of the Articles of Confederation; the northern imposition of the Civil War Amendments; the Progressive critique of "the monarchy of the Constitution" and its subsequent radical reinterpretation by pragmatists and legal realists; and the long-standing extra-constitutional practices of the national security state in both world wars and throughout the Cold War period.

37. Gettysburg Address, 1863; speech, 1861; national fast day proclamation, 1863; in Elazar 1998, 67 and 128–29.

38. Adams 1831, 17–18, and 1839, 5. A less global statement of this kind of constitutional understanding would counsel appellate courts and court intellectuals to see constitutional adjudication as participating inside these larger narratives and experiences and not standing above them. This is the message of the antifoundationalists and civic republicans and is the feature that connects them with many writers considered on the right, such as Posner, and many evangelical critics of contemporary church-state jurisprudence. See Witte (2000) and collection in Lugo (1994).

39. See, for example, Tushnet 1985; Williams 1998; and Fish 1997. They do not agree with many of the policy positions of the religious right, but they accord their views equal epistemological status in a tolerant and democratic community. Democratic discourse and self-understandings must be within interconnected narrative frameworks, but this can only take place as a practice and cannot be guaranteed by a universal umpire with a rule book. Democratic politics is never only a game. Two recent books, Feldman 1996, and Craycraft 1999, employ the same intellectual methods to reach entirely opposite conclusions. Feldman concludes that American church-state jurisprudence has always legitimated Christian hegemony over our public life and culture; Craycraft argues that this same jurisprudence has consistently subverted Christian beliefs. And see Neuhaus 1998.

Chapter 6

Signs: The Past and Future Establishment

Is voluntary religious establishment any longer a possibility? Is a reconstituted politically and morally authoritative American national identity any longer a possibility? In terms of the argument of this book, this is the same as asking, in the title of a recent book forecasting a new national political identity and order, Will there be a "next American nation?"[1] Because the Constitution alone is an insufficient source of national political authority and national identity and because Americans will never adhere together for long through state worship or presidential charisma, the more appropriate question might be, From what intellectual and moral sources and from what institutions will an intellectual framework be constructed to serve as the basis for the next national political order? My answer is that the only possible institution is the American university and that the intellectual and spiritual sources for this task remain the same as they have always been, namely, the master narratives in the human sciences and the humanities that serve to interpret and integrate our social and self-knowledge.

Given the politicization of knowledge and the conditions of intellectual disarray (some call it nihilism) that now prevail in the universities, this proposal might appear laughable and even perverse. I think it important to be reminded, however, that the American university, from its origins more than a century ago, has almost continuously served as the seminary and even the church of American political theology. Its moral-political foundations *and the source of its contemporary legitimacy and power* still rest on fulfilling this function. In periods of successful informal religious establishment and coherent national political orders, the university seems almost automatically to fulfill this function. And in times of crisis, the university can play an almost prophetic role in calling the nation to the highest aspirations of its reigning values. This call, however, is often not heeded, and the logic of events and national elections dissolve the reigning consensus. In the period of disestablishment that results, the university is first isolated and then rent with inner conflict. The isolation occurs because it continues to speak as if it represented political and moral consensus of the nation even when that consensus is no longer there—this is a situation of illusory establishment.

One result of this loss of moral voice and political relevance is simple careerism and the cynicism and hypocrisy that necessarily follow in its train of demoralization. As the university seeks to reclaim its higher function, however, it confronts formidable obstacles because it is seeking to speak to a nationally authoritative constituency in the larger society that has yet to be created. Moreover, within the university, there now exist many competing visions of the future of the country and therefore of the kinds of moral and intellectual ligaments that would bind this envisioned constituency. All of these responses were evident in the American university in the 1918–1940s period, and all of these responses are occurring today.

The bad faith, bad manners, and false positions that often accompany culture wars in the university are not to be simply disparaged and condemned as some character defect of academics. In one sense, they are the salutary result of taking the university's national mission seriously; in another sense, they are testament to the real political and moral passion that should be a part of all serious scholarship in the human sciences and the humanities. That one's own commitments are best revealed by the enemies one condemns is unfortunate but hardly to be avoided when it is not yet clear who and where one's friends in the larger society might be. This is the very meaning of disestablishment and the very reason that the American university almost instinctively tries to get out from under its sway. It can only reclaim inner coherence and civility by creating the framework for a new voluntary religious establishment and national political consensus.

In spite of this turmoil and inner conflict, the major American universities as an institutional complex and an institutional culture have been remarkably coherent and single-minded in the exercise of their authority over higher intellectual culture. For more than a century this authority has enforced a strict uniformity on all other American colleges and universities or subordinated them under the values of their ideals. In marked contrast to churches, they have brooked little deviation from a unified norm and have been energetically—even ruthlessly—efficient in punishing deviations.[2] When the core complex is in disarray, so is the entire higher educational periphery.

On the eve of the last century, when the University of Chicago's president, William Rainey Harper, speaking at the University of California at Berkeley, equated the spirit of the new research university with a "religion of democracy," this idea was perfectly understood by his audience. The university, he said, is the "prophet," "priest," "philosopher," and "Messiah" of the mission to democratize both America and the world. *If free from interference by church and state*, the American university can fulfill this sacred national role because it can then explore, reveal and inculcate man's best possibilities undistorted by sectarian, economic, and political interests and powers. Intellectual freedom is the precondition for higher political, moral, and religious freedom. The American university must be an evangelical church, participating in a continuous and progressive revelation and instilling this vision and knowledge into the nation so that the nation might bring brotherhood and justice into the world.

The university carries God's spirit into the nation not through coerced doctrine but through voluntary, dedicated, and selfless study, teaching, and service. Here Harper echoed the ideas of his most famous faculty recruit, John Dewey, who saw in the achievement of democracy a prophetic fulfillment, "in which the distinction between the spiritual and the secular has ceased, and as in Greek theory, as in the Christian theory of the Kingdom of God, the church and the state, the divine and the human organization of society are one."[3] In the language of one of our national anthems, "freedom's holy light" can shine only when knowledge is pursued freely under the protective authority of "Great God, our King."[4]

One might want to reduce Harper's (and Dewey's) call to a mainline masculine Protestant power play—but this discounts the fact that this ideal (with some of its religious metaphors changed and its gender references altered) remains the only worthy moral and political source of legitimacy for the American university that is on offer.[5] This is especially true today because the spirit of the contemporary university was born in the rebellions of the late 1960s, when the university was charged with having *betrayed* this birthright and lost its soul, reduced to serving whatever self-serving economic and political power commanded. Indeed, it was the defenders of the status quo in the 1960s who wanted to discredit the spiritual vision of Harper and Dewey in order to anchor their own claim that the modern "multiversity" was the disinterested and value-free servant of all interests and values in America. Their reduction fed the saving myth that the university was purged of religion and became secular in the 1920s. This was also the standard reading in disciplinary and university histories written in the 1950s and 1960s in seeking to explain the social, intellectual, and ideological changes in the university between World War I and the Cold War.[6] But this understanding is false, first, because it mistakes the *translation* of spirit into common sense (and science and humanist values) with the *repudiation* of spirit and, second, because it cannot account for the crucial spiritual role played by the university in legitimating both domestic liberalism, especially civil rights, and liberal antifascism and anticommunism in the 1940s through the 1960s—a role so central that the university soon became the primary site where the battle for disestablishment was fought by the antiwar movement in the 1970s.

The truth is that in both Harper's university and in ours, the search for truth is, first and foremost, free and for its own sake in order that its teachings enter and inform our personal and our common life. Without this high and even sacred democratic purpose, the fate of the university would come to rest on how well it serves whatever customers, for whatever reasons, happen to purchase its goods and services (and many other kinds of institutions might perform these services more efficiently and in a more consumer-friendly way). Spirit would move elsewhere or disappear into sectarian redoubts. If our current condition, as a nation and as a university, flows from the turmoil beginning in the late 1960s, we must examine this period with some care before deciding whether the American university as American Church can and will reclaim its originating purpose and whether a new consensus and a new informal religious establishment are in the making.

SOME COSTS OF DISESTABLISHMENT

Like establishment history generally, the most recent disestablishment of the American university is heavy with irony. The first irony is that in the 1960s the establishment defense of the university against New Left disestablishmentarians was that the American university had no soul of its own. It was the very embodiment of fairness, objectivity, and neutrality. The modern research university was explicitly defended as a multiversity whose creed was service to all of the various values and interests of a pluralist democracy.[7] Berkeley's Clark Kerr, lecturing at Harvard, proclaimed that the university was value-free and morally neutral because it embodied and served all of American society in all of its diversity. Here enters the second irony: the university, without a claimed soul of its own, defended its authority because it was the veritable dynamo of America's moral, economic, political, and spiritual virtue-power in the world, shaping and channeling the energies of America into the defense of freedom at home and abroad. The university did not need a distinct soul because America was the soul. What Kerr called secularization was in fact successful establishment: its political theology became the larger society's universal principles and common sense. But could this consensus be maintained if it were defended on principles above the battle and in the face of energetic and talented people inside the university who could unmask this defense with narratives of injustice, moral incoherence, and hypocrisy?

In this same period the virtue and power of the national political establishment were defended in exactly the same value-free terms as the national university. Social scientists and historians declared our national rulers transideological and the national political system beyond ideology. A new and value-free pluralist democracy had been created in which all values become interests, all interests get a hearing, and no single interest is permitted to dominate. The constitution of freedom is procedural fairness and neutrality.[8] In retrospect these twin defenses appear almost as parodies of intellectual-spiritual complacency and moral-political hypocrisy. Even worse, they do not begin to do justice to the operative religious values and the admirable moral and political accomplishments of the liberal establishment that ruled America in the 1940s through 1960s.[9]

The ironies of this establishment denial are mirrored in the ironies of disestablishment desire. The first irony is that, from the start, the New Left desperately wanted the university *to regain its soul*, to become reborn as a democratic and confessional church in order to witness against an imperialist American state and a racist and materialist society. Their jeremiad was a call to conversion and higher service, a call that requires opposition and sacrifice and suffering.[10] Regarding the Vietnam War and racial segregation, they were singularly successful in this call. Indeed, university administrators and older faculty quickly capitulated to demands for university reform made in the name of combating imperialism and racism in the same way that an earlier generation had capitulated in the name of fighting fascism and communism.[11] Regarding the internal issues of ecclesiology—university governance, curricula reform, and the reconstruction of the disciplines—the critics were much less successful. In these areas many changes occurred—again and again—but the putative victors markedly failed to instill shared ideas and values on which to reconstitute the university as a common enterprise. What resulted instead was twenty-five years of incessant struggle and intense scholarship (the two go together) in the human sciences and the humanities. This is our present condition: an intellectual and spiritual disestablishment that has persisted not by design but by default.[12] During this same period, again mostly by default, the term administrative nihilism became an apt description of university policy-making, and internecine warfare seemed a fair characterization of disputes in and between the disciplines.

SOME BENEFITS OF DISESTABLISHMENT

A quarter of a century of bureaucratic and intellectual power struggles in the university, however, has *not* ended in mutual destruction. Here we need Hegel and the logic of agonistic spirits to understand what has happened. Toward the end of the day, there have been clear winners and losers in precisely those areas of intellectual life that are the intellectual and spiritual sources of what Whitman had earlier termed "a sublime and serious Religious Democracy sternly taking command, dissolving the old, sloughing off surfaces, and from its own interior and vital principles, reconstructing, democratizing society."[13]

What are the signs of this emergent spirit and what has it dissolved? Dissolved was the exhausted liberal establishment theology that equated existing American society and practices with the achievement of social justice and democracy. At its least self-conscious extreme, this theology ended by excluding any traces of divisive church religion (their gospels might be a rebuke to establishment self-satisfaction) from a serious place in the university and its disciplines, resulting in a kind of complacent established nonbelief.[14]

This bland and value-free secularism in the human sciences and the humanities that identified objectivity and scientific method with American practice and American practice with democratic values was soon subjected to withering intellectual *and spiritual* attack. All of these disciplines are now much more self-conscious, deeper, and more interesting because they were opened up to new values and orientations drawn from cultural, religious, and philosophic traditions long ignored or forgotten. Struggles over matters of the soul and of intellectual

vocation demand a critical spirit and, for all the resulting querulousness and oc-
casional dogmatism, require recourse to and recovery of historical and moral
sources to make coherent arguments. This, in itself, signals a new receptivity for
the life of the spirit in the disciplines and in the university. The most overt result
is that religion—even some church religion—and matters of the spirit now have
a much more overt and obvious presence in all of these disciplines, in the humanities generally and in the life of the university, than they did in the 1970s.[15]

Like it or not—and many traditional liberal academics do not—both
"innerness" and "enchantment" are back in the disciplines and in the university.
I would point first to critiques starting in the 1960s in the social sciences and
humanities that have now transformed the moral and political orientations of these
disciplines. Not only have many areas of the social sciences long ago jettisoned
behaviorism and other superficial claims of objectivity and value neutrality, they
have come together under the rubric of the human sciences that draw upon the
moral sources and resources of philosophy, cultural history, religion, and ethics.
This shift has often resulted in ignoring older departmental and disciplinary
boundaries and creating new communities of scholarship based on the "experiential foundationalism" of shared moral orientations.[16] The orientations that are
driving these fields are precisely those that take seriously the role of personal
identity and moral commitment in human agency and in human history. Even
academic philosophy—at least the academic philosophy that other intellectuals
and academics now read—had begun to rediscover phenomenology and pragmatism. This, too, is a source of religious depth, for both phenomenology and pragmatism place spirit, experience, and purpose *inside* thought and therefore inside
the history of thought. Social history generally and women's studies in particular—despite their postures of *ressentiment*—have rediscovered spirit as a guide
to understanding, infusing history, the humanities, and the social sciences with
issues of identity and directing reflection on and research into the moral and religious sources of the self.

My own field of moral and political philosophy has attained an energy, reach,
and attractive power outside of political science departments, even as it has drawn
on resources and ideas far outside its earlier narrative boundaries. With these
resources, political theorists have launched a many-sided reconsideration of the
foundations of liberalism, individualism, and rights. Entailed in this reconsideration is a rediscovery of civic republicanism either as an alternative to or as a
deeper understanding of liberalism. In seeking to recover more civically oriented
ideas of individuality and citizenship, this enterprise has necessarily drawn upon
narratives and ideas excluded from the dominant story of liberalism and modernity that ended in the ahistorical and procedural ideal of the unencumbered bearer
of rights and maker of choices. Put differently, moral and political philosophy
rediscovered its relationship to history and power—to life—enabling it to rewrite
its own history and chart a future for political theory that includes religious spirit
and moral purpose. Here again, the writings of Charles Taylor are both exem-
plary and causal.[17]

Beyond the intellectual fruits of these new enterprises, it must be stressed that all this flowering of spirit takes place in a university that now includes racial, religious, and ethnic mixes and spirits quite inconceivable only twenty years ago. Whether all this intellectual creativity in these conditions will come to constitute the basis of a shared and authoritative political theology remains to be seen. The case is that there is now a lot more serious dialogue and much less shouting between and among these communities of scholarship than at any time in the past two decades. This is illustrated by the ways in which we now routinely borrow from across disciplinary boundaries and integrate their various racial, moral, or religious orientations in our teaching and research.[18] This process, in turn, calls for the construction of common historical narratives to anchor the exchange. As more scholars envision common projects of scholarship and study, so they construct common pasts to shape that future. These narratives, moreover, are primarily *national* constructs addressed both to American universities and to *national* audiences of political intellectuals and other opinion leaders.

Alasdair MacIntyre's *After Virtue*—a book that crosses over and through many disciplinary and ideological boundaries—has reminded us to pay attention to stories: it is through personal, professional, institutional, and political narratives that we orient ourselves to the world. By examining and reflecting on those stories of which we are already a part, one can interpret the growth and decay of spirit in the world.[19] From the 1960s onward, every deep critique of an academic discipline and every creation of new scholarly communities required at some point a story, both to unmask and to show new directions. In America, this is commonly referred to as our attachment to the jeremiad, and many of our unmaskings take precisely this moralistic and dialectical form. Is there any doubt that these critiques are political-theological? Disciplinary jeremiads proclaim what *national* covenants have been broken, what *national* commitments have not been kept, what *national* errands have gone unfulfilled in our scholarship and our teaching. These proclamations, in turn, become invitations both to reform one's own scholarly calling and to reclaim the covenant on a higher level. What these narrators and narratives have *not* done is to ask where these covenants, commitments, and errands originated, how they might be justified as binding, and *who is authorized to speak in their name*. To address fully any one of these questions is to address them all.

Even absent this last step, the stories now being written can be seen as preparation for and signs of answers and thus for a new national political theology to underwrite a new intellectual and spiritual consensus. Evidence for this is the fact that these narratives recall and replicate the very values and practices from which establishment theology in America had been constructed in the past. Histories of American academic thought and disciplinary fields written today, for example, mirror much more closely those written in the 1930s and 1940s (i.e., national and reformist) than those written in the 1950s and 1960s (i.e., pluralist and methodological) in that they openly acknowledge the religious and political values and purposes of the founders and practitioners.[20] Because the disciplines of philosophy and the social sciences were so central to the founding values of the modern university at the turn of the century, the histories written today are recovering some of these same values for the American university. Histories of American political thought and of liberalism have undergone parallel transformations, not only in highlighting the importance of religion, citizenship, and civic virtue in their initial articulations, but in complicating earlier individualist and constitutionalist understandings of the identity of liberalism itself.[21]

Within the larger context of the history of political thought, older narratives of progressive secularization have increasingly been supplanted by histories of the continuous interplay of religion and spirit in the history of ideas of freedom. The increasing attention paid to civic republicanism and its religious dimensions in early modern British thought and in early American thought has been complemented by rediscovery of the religious elements in leading liberal theorists such as Hobbes, Locke, and Mill. The new social history, with its stress on how social movements come into being, has had the paradoxical effect of stressing the importance of ideas—but these ideas combine the sacred and secular, the philosophically sophisticated and the passionately profane. Even the law schools have contributed to and benefited from these new histories, especially in discussing the historical dimensions of the constitutional adjudication of religious freedom and church-state separation.

In the academy, as in the larger society, one might say that spiritually dead establishmentarians are routinely and rightly hoisted on their own petards because those petards were constructed from real spiritual experiences, moral choices, and political commitments now most vividly remembered by their critics. This was as true at the time of the First Great Awakening in the 1740s as it was in the 1960s.[22] At these moments it is the critics who seek to reclaim history because they claim the duty to call America back to its covenantal obligations. It remains an open question whether all of the resulting spiritual and intellectual *agon* in the university today will ultimately produce a reconstituted political theology for the nation. It is, I think, rapidly producing one in microcosm and for itself, however, that effectively includes participants who in the larger political and cultural world are neither conversing with nor understanding each other. Whether these emerging master narratives uniting distinct moral orientations and scholarly communities in the humanities and the human sciences will achieve spiritual mastery of—and reconstitute the soul of—the university is the first question. Whether this newly inspirited university can or will reclaim its spiritual role in the larger society is the next one. The best we can do for now is to look for the signs and help call them forth.

In what follows, I raise as examples some topics around which I think consensus is being shaped. The substantive basis for this consensus is agreement about what should be done now and in the future; the procedural basis for this consensus is increasing agreement about the past. These common stories contain and are continuous with the prophecy; together they constitute the narrative framework for a newly emerging American political theology.

LIBERAL ARTS EDUCATION

In 1997 the College Entrance Examination Board published a collection of essays under the title, *Education and Democracy: Re-imagining Liberal Learning in America.* The next year, the Woodrow Wilson Center with Cambridge University Press published a collection of essays under the title, *In Face of the Facts: Moral Inquiry in American Scholarship.* Both enterprises look to pragmatism as a way of recentering liberal learning and shaping a new moral and political consensus. Two quotes from John Dewey introduce the editor's prologue in the former collection. The first asserts that "in this country" democracy is the "unified frame" within which education finds its purpose and direction. The second asks whether America should be seen as an offshoot of Europe or as "a New World." That Dewey opts for the latter view "is neither brash patriotic nationalism nor yet a brand of isolationism. It is an acknowledgement of [national] work to be done." The afterword also recalls Dewey, this time through a 1931 conference he chaired entitled "The Curriculum for the Liberal Arts College," and calls now for "anchoring the future in the past." The fifteen essays that lie in between are testaments not only to the re-enchantment of scholarship in the liberal arts disciplines but are calls to translate this re-enchantment of scholarship into a "unified frame" both for liberal arts education and for a reclaimed American national identity: "the ways of scholarship should become the ways of democracy."[23]

The lead essay in the second collection, "Pragmatism, Science, and Moral Inquiry," explores the writings of neopragmatists in American philosophy that might restore "the importance of evidence and experience to the justification of ethical principles,"[24] providing, thereby, a unified grounding for the social [human] sciences and the humanities. Contrasting this framework with both foundationalist (Kantian, utilitarian) and narrow coherentist theory (moral intuitions about particular cases of ethical choice), this essay links pragmatism to historical narrative and to American experience. This essay and others that follow link contemporary trends in academic scholarship with a more ethically and nationally oriented ideal of a liberal arts education.

The dominant term used in the College Board collection is "pragmatic liberal education." This idea of pragmatism is not abstract and methodological, but substantive and national, historically grounded in our culture ("the *legacy* of American pragmatism") and representing "the democratic aspirations of the nation."[25] Two features stand out here: first is the unabashed *nationalism* built into the very meaning of pragmatic liberal education. "Finding merit in pragmatism presupposes that U.S. academics would be willing to see value in American intellectual traditions and resources."[26] This call for the rediscovery of America is also a critique of the European-centered liberal arts education represented in the 1950s by both Harvard's General Education program and Columbia's Literature, Humanities, and Contemporary Civilization curricula. Louis Menand put it perfectly: "General education was a *benign substitute* for a national ideology in the Cold War era."[27] By the end of the 1960s, academic culture began to reject this core

model for a variety of good and bad reasons, but it became increasingly irrelevant in any case, given the kinds and variety of students now seeking higher
education in America.[28] Future canons in the liberal arts will be increasingly
American or, at the least, canons received on American terms. This, too, has been
one of the (perhaps unintended) fruits of gender, ethnic, and race studies—all of
them thoroughly Americanist in origin, subject, and audience. As the canon has
become more inclusive it has also become less cosmopolitan and more national.[29]

A second feature in both collections is the unabashed *civic moralism* built into
the call for liberal arts scholarship and education to embody a life of democratic
citizenship.[30] As one essayist put it: "Like it or not, we are publicly on record as
committing ourselves and our institutions to promoting leadership and citizenship." In the other collection, three essays address the elements of moral responsibility, moral inquiry, and moral discourse in the fields, respectively, of political
theory (Jean Elshtain), political science (Marion Smiley), and law (Joan Williams).[31]

The virtue of pragmatism is that it necessarily combines learning and doing,
reflection and struggle, principles and narrative. Because of its grounding in history and experience, pragmatism is "relational (it never exists in the abstract or
in isolation from a world containing both other persons and concrete realities . . .),
creative (it never merely registers sense data passively . . .), and imbued with
historically specific cultural values (it is never 'human' or universal but always
personal and particular)."[32] Our personal identities and our collective experience
are scripted within a democratic society, and we would be incapable of both coherent thought and morally coherent actions outside that society. Thus, social
inquiry and social action are as interdependent as American liberal arts education should be inseparable from "passionate justice-seeking."[33] If we are true to
pragmatism's founders and to our American legacy, these essays argue, liberal
education must be "inseparable from [a] commitment to democracy as an ethical ideal."[34]

Explicitly, these writings call for the recovery of a distinctly American national
"experiential foundationalism"[35] in both liberal arts education and in scholarship
in the liberal arts disciplines. Implicitly, they call for a regrouping of
experientialism in scholarship (what I have called re-enchantment) around shared
visions of social justice.[36] Historically, pragmatism was part of the Progressive
revolution in philosophy and the social sciences at the turn of the century, and
together they were the intellectual underpinnings of a liberal arts discipline and
of a democratic social gospel. The language used in these essays is not that different. One essay remarks on the ways that gender and ethnic studies are implicitly
pragmatist in their connections "between learning and life" and that this kind of
pragmatism is "now being seriously recommended as high-priority and even *sal-
vational* directions for the praxis of liberal education." By transforming this spirit
into "a pedagogy of engagement and service," liberal arts scholarship and
education can again be what they always were at their best in America: an
"aspirational democracy" through "justice seeking . . . the expectation that a

liberally educated individual, by definition, seeks and works to expand justice and equity in a world lived in common with others."[37]

We must underline the fact that this program for liberal arts education and scholarship explicitly rejects both the Universalist (left) and the Restorationist (right) alternatives discussed earlier, even as it complements recent Liberal Nationalist and Communitarian writings. What is partly hidden in this call, however, is what is also hidden in the alternatives it complements. In the collection just examined, the Dewey in evidence is the one writing in the 1920s and after. This highlights works written after the collapse of Progressivism as a national and democratically supported political force and has the effect of isolating Dewey (and us) from the larger intellectual, religious, and ethical communities of which he was a part and from which he drew his ideas in the 1890s through World War I. To draw on that larger legacy of pragmatism for liberal arts education and to explore the historicist and philosophical foundations of their scholarship would be to uncover both an America and an intellectual founding generation (including Dewey) that was much more vigorously Hegelian and national-evangelical in its scholarship and teachings than in the demoralized and disestablished period of the 1920s and 1930s.[38]

Hiding that larger and richer background also has the potential of turning the legacy of pragmatism into a complacent ratification of a kind of intolerant and unreflective liberal political correctness that dominates the academy today. In effect, one risks reimporting some of the bad faith and bad air of 1920s Progressive liberalism with its little coteries of beautiful souls too good for engagement and struggle in democratic politics.[39] Purging pragmatism of its earlier history and connections in the founding period of the American university and its disciplines deprives it *today* of connections to the religious experiences and commitments of increasing numbers of the students it wants to educate in the liberal arts. The result might then be a pragmatic liberal education as aloof and isolated from the experiences of those it teaches as those more elitist and isolating calls today for restructuring the liberal arts on a purely cosmopolitan philosophical ideal.[40] This is not the intent—precisely the opposite—but without a richer and deeper national narrative of our intellectual and cultural legacy, neither teacher nor student will quite know what is being called for and what is at stake.

NATIONAL CITIZENSHIP

A second and related sign of an emerging national political theology is the rather sudden resurgence of writings on ideas of American nationality and citizenship. These writings now span almost the entire range of academic disciplines in the liberal arts, from political philosophy through American intellectual and political history, culture studies, and literature to constitutional history and law. While disputes over immigration and anxiety about the effects of economic globalization might have been the immediate causes of this inquiry, there are deeper reasons which range from struggles over American identity encoded in disputes in political philosophy and theories of law to the emergence of gender and racial studies. What is important to note here, however, is that the very introduction of ideas of nationality, citizenship, and the obligations they might entail was highly controversial.[41] Given the dominance of an ahistorical and universalistic language of rights combined with narratives of passive and self-contained victim groups, it was a hard-won achievement even to get a hearing for ideas of collective agency and purpose. Once on the table, moreover, this nationalist discussion forced a series of major retreats by those for whom national citizenship and patriotism were a philosophical and an ideological embarrassment.

To uphold a purely cosmopolitan or deracinated ideal of American citizenship now requires that its defenders enter the narrative fray rather than pretend to stand over and above it. An interesting précis of this shift is a recent collection of essays, *For Love of Country: Debating the Limits of Patriotism,* in which Martha Nussbaum's defense of cosmopolitan patriotism is subjected to a withering attack from a wide variety of ideological and philosophical positions.[42] Another is the collection of papers and responses in *Immigration and Citizenship in the Twenty-First Century,* originally part of a workshop on that topic. These essays demonstrate both the resistance to and the increasing power of ideas of American national identity among academics and public intellectuals. Indeed, the title of their report, *Becoming American/America Becoming,* itself indicates how the attempt to address issues of immigration and naturalization requires addressing the larger issue of American national identity.

Another sign that discussion of national citizenship and American identity is becoming a significant organizing category of public intellectual discourse is that this discussion is becoming increasingly removed from the narrow discourse of constitutional law and rights. Because the U.S. Constitution barely mentions citizenship and because the separate states historically controlled almost all sites in which formal political participation was exercised, federal court decisions regarding citizenship have necessarily diluted its meaning and import. Because citizenship is such a thin and insubstantial idea in the Constitution, a purely constitutional understanding severs its relationship to a shared nationality. The courts and their theoreticians had ignored the fundamental fact that citizenship is a derivative, not a constitutive, of nationality.[43] Confirming Herbert Croly's argument ninety years ago, a purely constitutional reading of citizenship is a barrier to democratic nationality. The salutary result is that discussion of national citizenship and American identity now increasingly incorporates the broader range of perspectives from the liberal arts, especially political theory, cultural studies, and American social, literary, and intellectual history. The removal of this discussion from out of *official and coercive sites of state discourse* and into the more voluntary arenas of civil society through cultural and historical interpretation not only reflects more clearly our national experience, it makes possible the construction of a *narrative* of national citizenship that draws on the rich fund of scholarly resources in history, the humanities, and the social sciences built up during the past decades. One hopes that this narrative will now increasingly set the terms by which constitutional principles and doctrines will be formulated and understood, and not vice versa.[44]

RACE

The reopening of discussions of nationality and citizenship has also been made possible by the retreat of race as the central category of inclusion and exclusion. While the constitutional and institutional issues of legal segregation were in fact addressed and decisively resolved more than twenty years ago, the continued use of this discourse to extract deference, obedience, and resources from the rest of the society proved too tempting to give up. To continue to equate race with caste even as America has increasingly become transracial in its everyday culture and practices (and as the assimilation of new immigrants has proceeded at almost breakneck speed) only advantages older entrenched power holders in America. While state-bureaucratic and university-bureaucratic structures continue to encode racial categories, public and academic practices (not to speak of popular culture, marriage, sports, religion, and business) are increasingly free of its categories. Within the university, moreover, the free life of inquiry and scholarship has clearly begun its integrative work: there is no field in the humanities or the social sciences (with the possible exception of analytic philosophy) that has not been transformed by having confronted and contended with the issue of race and the new scholarship produced by students of race.

The ever smaller remnant that uses "the great Black exception" as proof of racist exclusion no longer commands and constrains academic discourse and therefore can no longer demand assent as proof of intelligence and virtue.[45] Indeed, this great exception argument has had the paradoxical effect of enlarging the category of the privileged-as-racist to include all colors and ethnic traditions—including large sectors of the Black middle classes. As categories within this "we" group increasingly enlarge and multiply, the boundaries separating them are more easily crossed because the only category to include them all is American.[46] As the universalist-multicultural explanatory framework has lost its dominance, more historicist, pragmatist, and ironic readings of racial and ethnic-immigrant experiences take its place. These histories are written more from inside the group experience and explain much more frankly and fully the role that leaders from within these groups played in shaping American understandings of its shared values and principles. In contrast to universalist writings of racial and immigrant history, ones which make each group something of a passive victim of American oppression, these new histories necessarily place group experience within a common national story because these groups are seen as coauthors of that story and coactors within its script.

CHURCH AND STATE / RELIGION AND NATION

The recent retreats and backtracking by those whose universalistic discourse constitutes a barrier to the construction of a common American narrative in the areas of citizenship and race are even more evident in the area of religion and public life. I want to chart this retreat in historical and constitutional discourse on church-state separation as another opening for a new national self-understanding regarding religion and American identity. One important lesson from the recent scholarship of the critical legal theorists is to treat skeptically claims of neutrality.[47] A corollary of this advice is to pay less attention to principles and more attention to the history within which principles are voiced. Very often, this argument goes, the application of neutral principles or neutral procedures coercively privileges status quo interests, practices, and powers. By treating status quo distributions of power, property, voice, and status as natural or given, the application of neutral principles often serves to keep out new claimants, new voices, and new values.

These critical legal theorists, along with other pragmatists and deconstructionists, have subjected both the discourse and the court decisions on church-state relationships to withering attack. One result has been a steady intellectual retreat by strict separationists, especially now that the constitutional and political history of church-state relationships is now more clearly written and understood.[48] Another and more general result has been a call for courts to pay more attention to the internal norms and facts at issue in the cases before them. This call urges the courts to withdraw from many areas of deep normative disagreement and to provide room for other democratic institutions and modes of discourse to have their say so that, together, we can seek to compose or reconcile diverse viewpoints.[49]

This retreat from strict separation is paralleled by retreats in the liberal political philosophy that sanctioned those older constitutional doctrines, notably in the writings of John Rawls.[50] Church-state separation based on neutral principles rests philosophically on a kind of principled and ahistorical liberalism that posits a realm of procedural agreement on principles that can be established *before democratic discussion and disagreement can properly begin.* Archetypically, to keep religion and even religious motivations out of the discussion from the start would create conditions of discourse within which rational discussion ensues and rational agreement can be reached. It did not take too much reflection to notice that the major difficulty lies in defining the boundaries of religion, the rational, and politics. In a democratic society with many different arenas of decision making, the added difficulty is how to decide *who is to be authorized to do the defining.*[51]

Historically, and under the series of consensual canopies of voluntary establishment, this was a relatively easy task because the authorized definers were also the commonly recognized public theologians and philosophers who define both American national identity and the appropriate boundaries of religion and public life. These canopies not only sanctioned multiple centers of decision making, they encouraged local solutions, mutual forbearance, and toleration. Even after effective cultural and intellectual disestablishment, as in the case today, these older definers, definitions, and boundaries often continue to dominate coercive public institutions by default. As is also the case today, however, new spirits, new energies, and new values can now vie for expression and recognition, and the superceded establishment can hardly put them down for long by court fiat.[52] Cryptically put (but in ways that students of church-state jurisprudence will immediately recognize), the free speech clause of the First Amendment has been forced into service to protect religious expression because the free exercise and no establishment religious clauses have been misused by the courts to prevent new religious expressions in public life.[53]

Within the field of liberal political theory the salutary result of backtracking is that defenders of universalist values must now defend those values as a politically chosen national way of life against competing ways of life and within a narrative construction of American identity in competition with other historical understandings of American identity.[54] While the institutions of church and state rightly remain separated, religious spirit and public life cannot be. Under the previous dispensation, bracketing out religion from public discourse also bracketed out discussions of nationality and American identity.

Lying behind both church-state discourse and the larger philosophical and constitutional issues this discourse entails is whether religious freedom should be seen as a *principle* that can be justified on abstract philosophical grounds or whether religious freedom is a *practice* that is located in historical settings and must receive justifications—even abstract-universal justifications—from within a shared narrative understanding. One can put this another way: do the principles of religious freedom stand above and outside history and experience or does the shared interpretation of our history and experience provide the framework within which principles of religious freedom are understood? This is the great divide in constitutional hermeneutics: whether the document (especially the Bill of Rights and Fourteenth Amendment) should be read as logically and directly mandating larger universal philosophical foundations (Dworkin, Raz, sometimes Rawls) for interpretation in overruling political majorities or whether the document should be read within a narrative structure (but *not* original intent) that incorporates political, religious, cultural, and institutional history.

The universally recognized incoherence in contemporary church-state jurisprudence is witness to the unmasking and discrediting power of the historicist and pragmatic argument. In effect, these critics assert that whenever a *state* of religious freedom is declared achieved by the courts by applying a universal principle, what has actually resulted is only a temporary settlement concerning the prevailing limits of toleration. Toleration is not a principled and equal freedom for all religions under an endless horizon of neutrality but a particular and historical legitimation of particular practices and patterns of toleration. The settlement at any time follows real struggles among conflicting groups and purposes and is never final, either philosophically or historically.[55] This is, perhaps, another way of saying that a living Constitution can only achieve different kinds and degrees of toleration and never a fully achieved state of freedom. A living Constitution requires what Stanley Fish and others have called "ad hoccery," because only a more case-by-case address and determination keeps the discourse open, allows for other institutions of government to play a role, and permits new and different purposes, voices, and people to be heard—and, increasingly, they are.

AMERICAN RELIGIOUS HISTORY

When Gordon Wood's classic, *The Creation of the American Republic, 1776–1787,* was published in 1969, historians of the American founding, including Wood, practically ignored religion and religious ideas as major constitutive elements. In a recent essay, "Religion and the American Revolution" (1997), Wood charts the revolutionary revisions in our understanding of early American history. Thanks to social and women's history, to culture studies, and to the politicization of literature departments—as well as to the normal processes of scholarship among American political historians—religion and religious ideas are now central and even defining categories in understanding the creation of America in the founding period. Wood both describes and explains this new historiography this way:

> The notion that Americans suffered a religious recession during the Revolution is an optical illusion, a consequence of historians looking for religion in the wrong places. One kind of American religion may have declined during the Revolution, but it was more than replaced by another kind. Religion was not displaced by the Revolution; instead, like other central elements of American life, it was radically transformed.[56]

Drawing on J. C. D. Clark's *Language of Liberty* (1994), Wood explains that the American Revolution was also the victory of one kind of religious understanding over another because the war for independence was also a "civil war of religion." America was founded in a war that "released more religious energy and fragmented Christendom to a greater degree than had been seen since the upheavals of seventeenth-century England or perhaps since the Reformation."[57] Wood's recent essay is important because, more than any other contemporary historian, his earlier writings kept alive and extended the tradition of Progressive historiography we associate with Charles Beard, namely, that American national history must be understood as democratic conflict and struggle over nation building and national identity.[58] Significant also is the relationship between this historiography and the shaping of national Progressive and pragmatic intellectual culture by academics at the turn of the century.[59] As if repeating this earlier moment in intellectual and cultural integration, the editors of a collection on this new historiography note the recent scholarly reintegration of American religious history into American national history. This integration required the displacement of church-oriented religious history and the help of racial, gender, cultural, and social historians. Indeed, one could put this relationship another way: without this new religious history, *the writing of a new and shared national narrative would not be possible.*

This conclusion is also suggested in Harold Bloom's *American Religion* (1992), another innovative example of a new nationalist and experiential understanding of American identity. Bloom, too, bypasses a denominational understanding of American religion to focus on religious ideas and impulses that cut across and through all American religions but especially those more marginal movements and groupings that were "made in America." By so doing, he places religion at the very center of American culture and raises some of the issues of religious and national identity entailed by informal religious establishment under conditions of political democracy and religious freedom.

> If we are Americans, then to some degree we share in the American Religion, however unknowingly or unwillingly. The religious critic sets forth to appreciate the varieties of the American religious experience, following in this the founders of our religious criticism: Emerson and William James.[60]

While neither "a Christian by faith, nor a Protestant by sensibility," Bloom is an American and therefore shares a common religion with other Americans. His attempt to characterize this common religion requires an initial series of moves that places his analysis squarely inside the new religious historiography. He first asks us to distinguish the imported from the domestic forms of religion in America. The former divides religion by creed, church, and doctrine, while the latter unifies it by nation and shared experience. Next, we must concentrate on the common features of the domestic forms and then look for the penetration and appearance of these common features in the more particular expressions and practices of American religion as differentially received from Europe. This is another way of saying that "so creedless is the American Religion that it needs to be tracked by particles rather than by principles." Finally, if we are to discover and understand our common religion, the approach must first be experiential and not theological or philosophical. Like the place of the aesthetic in literary criticism, "There must be a similarly irreducible element when we study religion; our experience is prior to analysis, whether we call what we experience 'the divine' or 'the transcendental' or simply 'the spiritual.'"[61]

This analysis concludes with the argument that American Religion is at once gnostic, because it presumes an identity-solitude with God/Christ before all time and against all time, and American because only through that identity and history is this presupposition made.[62] Perhaps Paul Tillich put it more clearly: "Religion cannot come to an end, and a particular religion will be lasting to the degree in which it negates itself as a religion. Thus Christianity will be a bearer of the religious answer as long as it breaks through its own particularity." Sidney Mead then adds: "Tillich's view seems to me implicit in the whole American experience with religious pluralism."[63]

What Bloom has done through religious criticism, historians have done by writing religious history in new ways. Laurence Moore's *Selling God: American Religion in the Marketplace of Culture* (1994) traces the myriad ways in which American religions have shaped, penetrated, and appropriated popular culture and, in so doing, created common moral and religious self-understandings in the face of deep church religious differences. Thus, even those people and practices relatively immune to the moral and religious teachings of the churches imbibe them nonetheless through popular culture. When that avenue is foreclosed to members of churches and ethnic traditions whose identity is forged in the conscious *rejection* of both elite and popular moral and religious values, the religious energies released into the culture by their rejection of it (e.g., early Mormons, early Catholics, Black churches, Jehovah's witnesses) often turn round to help shape that common culture. As Moore's *Religious Outsiders* (1986) argued, rejection was often another way of asking for respect and acceptance, and the path to this respect and acceptance was largely through the avenues of popular culture. In this way, alienated and opposing leaders often become the most effective agents for assimilation into a common American faith and identity. Many of Moore's outsiders are Bloom's "fountains."[64] Multicultural and race theorists have a lot to learn from both Moore and Bloom.

A NEW AMERICAN NARRATIVE

Is voluntary establishment any longer a possibility? Is a reconstituted politically and morally authoritative American national identity any longer a possibility? To these initial questions must now be added a third: Is it any longer possible to write a common American history? One could write a long essay simply summarizing the recent calls, denials, and mediations addressed to this very question. I think, however, that the question posed this way is wrongly put—as if one might simply will or call for or deny the possibility of a new Bancroft or a new Beard. American history is as American historians do, and the way history is done is to address felt issues and felt problems and felt experiences within received and revised historiographical models. The writing of American national history is both creature and creator of American cultural identity, so the writing of history is an inseparable part of the process of the destruction and creation of cultural understandings, symbols, and artifacts. Perhaps the best answer to the historical question, then, is to ask the cultural one. Granting that the prevailing common culture was undermined beyond restoration in the 1970s and 1980s, do we have a culture in common now? One ironic response was provided recently by Robert Bellah.

I might begin my talk this morning somewhat facetiously by asking the question, not whether there is a common American culture, but how is it that a plenary session of the American Academy of Religion is devoted to this question in a society with so powerful and monolithic a common culture as ours? The answer, however, is obvious: it has become part of the common culture to ask whether there is a common culture in America.[65]

He goes on to recount Anthony Appiah's review of Nathan Glazer's *We Are All Multiculturalists Now*, in which Appiah notes the exponential increase in a database list of the use of the term multicultural in major newspapers (0 items in 1988; 33 items in 1989; 600 in 1991; 1,500 in 1994) and then concludes, "When it comes to diversity it seems we all march to the beat of a single drummer."[66] Bellah concludes that America is uniquely receptive to multiculturalism as a common culture because it was singularly without a legally established church. Just as a common national religion has been a changing but persistent feature of our common culture, so has and will a common national ethnos become a changing but persistent feature of that same culture. Indeed, says another writer on multiculturalism, David Hollinger, "I urge more attention to religiously defined cultures and suggest some of the consequences of looking upon religious groups as 'ethnic' and upon ethnic groups as 'religious.'"[67]

What I take these arguments to mean is that a reconstituted common culture—what Richard Rorty calls ethnocentrism—is already substantially in formation in the academy. What this culture lacks is a deep philosophical and convincing narrative structure. To be sure, this multicultural culture initially claimed a *philosophical* grounding as the source of commonality, but its philosophical universalism was a *rejection in principle* of a common nationality because it claimed to stand above all ascriptive and historically contingent narratives. This philosophical source is neither substantive nor national and has too limited and abstract a vocabulary for citizens to adapt for use in democratic discourse. Indeed, this vocabulary discourages democratic voices and democratic struggle because it claims to be only procedural and value-free and thus intentionally divorced from the experiences and commitments of those participating in public discourse. Its ontology and its authority seem only to legitimate the power of courts to overrule decisions reached by more democratic and less imperial procedures.

Fortunately, this Universalist foundation for American public life has been so effectively critiqued and undermined that it is now in retreat. But this retreat has also been the occasion for counterattack. The good news is that the only effective form this counterattack can now take is *as a counter-narrative* in the form of an *ethnocentric, historical, and national* liberalism. Symbolically put, Richard Rorty can now claim both John Rawls and Michael Sandel as potential allies, even while other Universalists rush to revise their principles to accord with this increasingly shared narrative identity. It is a very hopeful sign that both American history and liberal political theory are increasingly written to get heard rather than to get even or to rule imperiously. Getting heard requires some narrative connection—some affiliation and sympathy—between and among the stories we are separately part of and the stories we tell in common. This suggests that the stridency and separateness of identity discourse and identity politics will increasingly give way to more accommodating discourses and identities because the participants now increasingly possess and are possessed by narratives that connect them.[68]

NOTES

1. Lind 1995.

2. Marsden 1994, 429–40; and see Longfield 1992a and 1992b; Hart 1992. On the central role of enforcement by the Carnegie Foundation and its subsidiary organs, Reuben 1996, 87; Barrow 1990, chapter 3.

3. Quoted in Marsden 1994, 249–50. Both Dewey and Harper were termed democratic Fichte's, and rightly so, for both had been steeped in Fichtean and Hegelian ideas of the university by their many German-trained teachers.

4. "My Country, 'Tis of Thee," fourth stanza, Samuel F. Smith (1808–1895).

5. For a recent discussion of liberal arts and the American university that picks up some of these earlier progressive and democratic and pragmatic themes, see the essays in Orrill 1997, discussed below.

6. Also, by reading religion as meaning church or sectarian religion, this account could explain the relatively smooth entry of Jews, Catholics, and nonbelievers into the major national universities, especially toward the end of this period.

7. Kerr 1963.

8. Dahl 1967; and see Neustadt 1976, on the modern presidency as a morally neutral integrator of all major social interests. For a powerful critique of claimed neutral principles as legitimating court decisions, Sunstein 1993. This latter critique mirrors in constitutional jurisprudence the many critiques of interest-group pluralism by political scientists two decades earlier.

9. King in Hutchison 1989a; Lacy 1989; Handy 1971; Silk 1988.

10. A nice description from his Berkeley experience of this religious element of the 1960s radicals and its relationship to earlier religious movements in America is by May (1989), 17, who credits his Berkeley colleague Robert Bellah with this insight. Harvey Cox, *The Secular City* (1965), was an early attempt (too early, as it happened) to make this connection theologically explicit.

11. While the most obvious was the abolition of ROTC programs and the banning of CIA recruiters and other government officials from campus, the most important was permitting the mobilization of scholarship, classrooms, and university resources for distinctly partisan political purposes. This obviously led (and still does) to some rather egregious violations of liberal and academic freedom principles. Ellis 1998.

12. It is only natural, then, that from the late 1960s onward, the dominant rhetoric in both university and public life has been a rights and power discourse. In the university, the demand for equal opportunity for all methods and values within the traditional disciplines and the right to establish new disciplines and programs on demand were singularly successful as long as the money held out and standing interests were met. Not all

identity groups were treated equally or given recognition, but only those declared by those now in power to have been unfairly excluded by the previous establishment.

13. Walt Whitman 1955, 531. Hegel's writings are now being read precisely in terms of his political theology; see Ward 1999 and Ware 1999.

14. Marsden 1994.

15. Perhaps the most interesting and daring articulation of this shift is Connolly 1999.

16. An excellent history of these effects over the past thirty years is the introduction by Fox and Westbrook in Fox and Westbrook 1998, 1–9. This introduction touches on themes of the replacement of disciplines by interdisciplinary studies, a focus on American experience, and the role of narrative in the human sciences. A good discussion of this dynamic is Green 1996, 24–28.

17. Taylor 1985a, 1985b, 1989, 1990. Earlier and much more significantly for the narrative of early modern political thought was the sudden rise to prominence of the Cambridge School of historians, represented by Quentin Skinner, John Dunn, John Pocock, and many others who strongly influenced the next generation of scholars. This body of scholarship reintroduced both civic republicanism and, to a lesser extent, religion, into the narrative of liberal political thought.

18. This phenomenon recalls the crossed boundaries and shared orientations of the social sciences and humanities in American universities in the 1890s and early 1900s, especially in sociology, political economy, philosophy, and theology. See Reuben 1996, chapters 4 and 5; Eisenach 1994, chapters 1–3; Livingston 1994; Feffer 1993; Ross 1990; Fitzpatrick 1990.

19. MacIntyre 1984. Like Charles Taylor's *Sources of the Self*, this book has an audience and influence that cut across the ideological divides discussed in the previous chapter. And see Booth (1999) and the collection of writings on this theme in Hinchman and Hinchman (1997).

20. Herbert Schneider 1946; Dorfman 1949; Gabriel 1940; and, even earlier, Dombrowski 1936.

21. Some prominent examples, Bercovitch 1975; Howe 1970, 1979 and 1997a; Greenstone 1993; Major Wilson 1974; Gienapp 1987; Gerring 1997 and 1998. On constitutional and legal history, see Horwitz 1992; Ackerman 1993 and 1996; Sunstein 1993.

22. Contrast, for example, the tone and spirit of Clark Kerr's *The Uses of the University* (1963) to Robert Paul Wolff's rejoinder, *The Ideal of the University* (1969).

23. Charles Anderson 1997, 127.

24. Elizabeth Anderson 1998, 15.

25. Orrill 1997, xxii–xxiii, emphasis added; and see Kimball 1997, 45–69.

26. Kimball 1997, 57.

27. Menand 1997, 5, emphasis added.

28. Nationalist themes are also found in the articles by Elizabeth Minnich, Alexander Astin, and Charles Anderson in this collection.

29. See Rorty 1998, 80–83.

30. Astin 1997, 213.

31. Elshtain 1998; Smiley 1998; Williams 1998. See also essays by Taylor 1985a and 1985b; and Posner 1995, chapters 5, 6, and 19.

32. Kloppenberg 1997, 75.

33. Minnich 1997, 194.

34. Kloppenberg 1997, 89.

35. Green 1996, 26. Karen Brown in Fox and Westbrook (1998) calls this the anchoring of moral inquiry in "rigorous, dense [stories] that give sustained attention to morality as a key component of culture" (quoted in intro., 7). Elizabeth Anderson (1998), 20, distinguishes between historically concrete "thick evaluative concepts and judgements" and philosophically abstract "thin ethical concepts," arguing that both moral philosophy and the human sciences should be located within the former. See also Festenstein (1997), chapter 5, for a discussion of Richard Rorty's national meaning of ethnocentrism as the starting point for social knowledge.

36. This call for pragmatic liberal education is complemented by calls for a pragmatic liberal political theory as a way to escape the conundrums and contradictions of rights discourse. Festenstein 1997; Charles Anderson 1990; Menand, 1997b; Gutting, 1999; David L. Hall 1993; Hoopes 1998; Stuhr 1993 and 1997; and the studies showing the relationship between pragmatism and earlier progressive and social democratic values, Kloppenberg 1986; Westbrook 1991; Feffer 1993; Eisenach 1994; Livingston 1994.

37. Knefelkamp and Schneider 1997, 335, 337, and 343, emphasis added. They add: "Service is the implicit social contract between each profession and the larger society" (338).

38. Kuklick 1985 and 1989; Rockefeller 1991; Eisenach 1994; Feffer 1993; Livingston 1994; Herbert Schneider 1946; Dorfman 1949; Gabriel 1940; Dombrowski 1936. Two recent papers on Hegel, Ward 1999 and Ware 1999, nicely capture the intellectual and political-theological framework of these early Progressives.

39. Here I refer to the splitting of the Progressive intellectuals into elite technocrats, Marxists of all varieties, withdrawn aesthetes, and nostalgic but lost reformers.

40. The best example is Dewey himself (1922), 303–5. And see Nussbaum 1997. This study would encode in American liberal arts education a sort of "adversarial cosmopolitanism" and thus an experiential disconnection from, and a needless mystification for, the vast majority of American students.

41. An indication of this is the chary language used in a pamphlet issued through Duke's public policy school in 1997, representing the views of a workshop of prominent academics and public intellectuals on immigration and citizenship. Pickus 1997. The very issue of an American identity was controversial (8–10). America's political and social history (11–14), the meaning and practices of naturalization (14–21), and dual citizenship (22–25) carried that original controversy into these topics as well. Suggested revisions of the naturalization oath (31–32) were all in the direction away from the nationalist affirmations in the current oath and away even from the diluted version proposed by the Commission on Immigration Reform. The most diffident version of these suggested oaths is: "I swear to support and defend the Constitution and laws of the United States of America against all enemies, foreign and domestic. I hereby affirm that as of today I owe primary allegiance to the United States; that I renounce any political allegiance to any other state or sovereignty that is inconsistent with this primary loyalty"(31–32). For the collection of articles and responses written by participants in this workshop, Pickus 1998. And see Beiner 1995.

42. Nussbaum 1996. See especially responses by Hilary Putnam, Judith Butler, and Charles Taylor, who use pragmatic and phenomenological critiques. Another collection of articles and responses is in Pickus 1998; see especially the article by David Hollinger and responses by Kwame Anthony Appiah and John J. Miller to other articles.

43. In the words of the sociologist Edward Shils (1997): "The readiness to acknowledge the rights of other individuals within one's own society and the disposition to fulfil

obligations to other individuals, to the institutions and authorities of one's own society, are functions of the strength of the nationality and the national collective self-consciousness. . . . This national self-consciousness is the matrix of citizenship; it is the self-consciousness of the civil society" (207).

44. Rogers Smith's highly praised *Civic Ideals* attempts to combine both perspectives. For critiques of this attempt, see Rosen 1998; Morone 1999; Eisenach 1999a; McWilliams 1999. For the author's rejoinder to the latter three essays, see Smith 1999. Recent histories of women's citizenship without the right to vote extend and deepen this argument. Parker, 1997; Isenborg, 1998.

45. The most impassioned and convincing recent work taking this position is Hochschild (1996), but even new nationalists like Michael Lind sometimes rely on this great exception argument and its implied charge of racism to extort support for entrenched liberal social programs and to maintain ties with the remaining parts of the traditional liberal electoral coalition.

46. This is especially troubling to those who worry about Jewish identity, expressed best in the title of a recent book, *How Jews Became White Folks and What That Says about Race in America* (Brodkin 1998).

47. Sunstein 1993. A good example of this backtracking is Thieman 1996; a good summary of this development is Joan Williams 1998.

48. There is such an abundance of literature on this that I will only provide a sample here: Steven Smith 1995; Fish 1997; and Miller 1988, are three very different but all excellent critiques. See also Tushnet 1985; Morrissey 1997; Witte 2000; and the collection in *DePaul Law Review* 39 (1990). For broader historical and cultural analysis with less emphasis on court decisions and legal writings, see collections in Lugo 1994; Noll 1990; James Wood 1989; and Hunter and Guiness 1990.

49. Sunstein 1999; Posner 1990, chapters 7 and 15.

50. Contrast *Theory of Justice* with *Political Liberalism* and later writings on the issue of constraining religious and religiously motivated discourse in politics. And see Sandel 1996; Neal 1997; and Andrew Murphy 1998.

51. Just a sample: Steven Smith 1995; Macedo 1995; Andrew Murphy 1998 and forthcoming; Tushnet 1985; Neal 1997; Fish 1997, Lugo 1994. Contrast Alexander 1993: "Liberalism cannot claim as a ground for excluding religion from public policy questions a superior or even a different epistemology from that of religion. . . . The truth of liberalism (and falsity of illiberal religions) cannot rest on an epistemology that is different and, for public policy issues, better epistemology—because it is fairer, more reasonable, more respectful of autonomy, more consistent with our being free and equal, etc.—than an epistemology employed to support religious claims, including the claim of illiberal religion" (764–65) to Greenawalt 1990: "Only direct naturalist claims seem likely to be a fruitful subject of exchange in political debates over legislation and public policy" (1,033). See also the discussion between Audi and Wolterstorff 1996. Three recent doctrinal discussions based on some of these newer pragmatic and historical understandings are Witte 2000; Morrissey 1997; and Perry 1997.

52. Indicative of this is the collection of essays addressing the role of religion in the university published by *Academe* (1996), the bulletin of the American Association of University Professors, containing arguments and perspectives that, in all probability, would not have been published by the AAUP only a decade ago. See especially essays by William Scott Green, David A. Hoekema, Martin E. Marty, and Joshua Mitchell.

53. The issue is, of course, much more complex than this. Tushnet (1985) is an excellent guide through this discourse.

54. See Rogers Smith's (1997) epilogue calling for a "Party of America" as an implicit acknowledgment of this; and see McWilliams 1999; and Eisenach 1999a. The phenomenon of liberal perfectionism as a political and cultural reform project and not a series of timeless and neutral principles above the battle is also evidenced in Kernohan 1998, a sort of gloves-off universalism, concluding that "a liberal state committed to the moral equality of persons must accept a strong role in reforming our cultural environment." These moves are strong confirmations of Fish (1997) and elsewhere, who not only charged that the foundational claims of the Universalists were disguised ideology ("'mutual respect' should be renamed 'mutual self-congratulation,'" 2,291) but objected to the insistence that nonliberals play the liberal theory game (2,312–13) or be consigned to "an epistemological criminal class" (2,283). Also implicit in this recent backtracking is the need for toleration to replace the now discredited claims of neutrality. This is discussed in the conclusion below.

55. See Andrew Murphy 1997 and forthcoming.

56. Wood 1997, 177.

57. Wood 1997, 179 and 185. This new historiography has now been consolidated and popularized in Phillips 1999 and Paul Johnson 1995.

58. One cannot go into the confusions and misunderstandings occasioned by Hofstadter (1955 and 1968) on this issue (conflating national Progressives and Populists), but see McCorkle 1984; Barrow 1988; and Eisenach (1994) for discussion of the national republicanism and antipopulism of Beard.

59. Livingston 1994; Feffer 1993; Eisenach 1994. And see Barrow (1988), on Beard to show what a firm opponent he was of antifederalism, Jeffersonianism (especially the Virginia and Kentucky Resolutions), and Populism generally. Hofstadter just got it wrong, as did historians writing on the professionalization of the social sciences such as Haskell 1977, and Ross 1990. A good corrective is Reuben 1996, chapters 3–5.

60. Bloom 1992, 28.

61. Bloom 1992, 28. All this said, Bloom then gives us both the history and the development of a national political theology and, implicitly, the theological underpinnings for the series of informal but authoritative religious establishments that have constituted our national identity. When he attempts to characterize that theology in the language of imported religion (i.e., doctrinal, sectarian, philosophical), he meets with the same order of difficulties that any church or denominational understanding of American religious establishment confronts. He is at pains to untangle the formal categories to account for the result. "I am not a Christian by faith, nor a Protestant by sensibility, and so I am hardly disconcerted to discover that the American Religion is post-Christian, despite its protestations, and even that it has begun to abandon Protestant modes of thought and feeling. I argue in this book that the American Religion, which is so prevalent among us, masks itself as Protestant Christianity yet has ceased to be Christian. Religion, in the ostensibly Protestant United States, is something subtly other than Christianity, though to say that we are a post-Christian country is misleading. Rather, we are post-Protestant, and we live a persuasive redefinition of Christianity" (28, 32, 45).

62. Bloom's analysis is nicely complemented by the writings of the historian Paul Conkin. His study of the Cane Ridge revival (1990) stresses its national inclusive and not denominational church features, and his study of reformed Protestant Christianity in

America (1995) concludes that creedal and doctrinal coherence in the "Reformed mainstream" was lost by the early post–Civil War period, suggesting that the theology of "American" religion was, as it were, starting to become modernist and national and historicist from the early nineteenth century onward. And see Ribuffo (1993) for an analysis of recent books that show the overlapping and crosscutting features of evangelical, fundamentalist, charismatic, Pentecostal, and New Age religious impulses that have now penetrated into almost all church bodies. Walsh (1990 and 1997) is an integration of historicist and Hegelian readings of spirit within a Catholic theological framework.

63. Tillich quoted in Mead 1975, 63. This argument parallels that of modernist theologians at the turn of this century, summarized in Hutchison 1992, 175–84.

64. This same, somewhat ironic, reading of our religious past is evident in two major collections of essays: Noll 1990 and Lacy 1989. In Lacy, see especially essays by Bruce Kuklick on Dewey and American theology; William McGuire King on the Social Gospel as a form of religious accommodation in Protestant theology; and Henry May on how social history recovers the centrality of religion in rewriting contemporary American intellectual history.

65. Bellah 1998, 613.

66. Bellah 1998, 613.

67. Hollinger 1995, 14.

68. Martin Marty, one of America's foremost church historians—and critic—of the role of religion in American public life, begins a recent book on the need for retrieving a common good with a call for just such a narrative foundation. "If the stories of any substantial groups are untold or if and when groups turn exclusive about their histories and talk only among themselves, the nation will be impoverished. It is such impoverishment that has helped induce the shock that I am calling the American trauma." Marty 1997, 6.

Conclusion

Pragmatic Nationalism and the Rebirth of Toleration

Are all these signs a kind of whistling in the dark? Yes, because that is unavoidable when attempting a kind of prophecy. Moreover, this whistling is a way of asking of my sign bearers a kind of disciplined self-awareness and knowledge of our country that they may be incapable of achieving. Like Mark Twain's description of what a Mississippi river boat pilot must know to pilot up and down the rivers and tributaries that connect America, it is a daunting task in social and self-understanding. On the other hand, the humanistic disciplines in American academic culture (including a saving measure of what Richard Hofstadter called our "anti-intellectualism") are uniquely able to undertake this task. Professional, bureaucratic, political, and personal imperatives all point in this direction. Professional, because we are duty-bound to read, assess, and assimilate the varieties of new scholarship produced by our colleagues; bureaucratic, to preserve (or reclaim) the dominant voice of the liberal arts in the definition and direction of higher learning; political, because the ends of the university in America must continue to embrace and extend democratic civic purposes in order to flourish; and personal, because, in democratic and fluid America, personal identity, professional identity, and civic identity must be continuously mediated and integrated if one is to think and act consciously and effectively, as a person and as a citizen.

Against this prophetic hope lies the possibility of failure. Individually, American intellectuals are not all that bold, and American academic culture since the 1960s has often encouraged retreat into the safe harbors of defensive personal, professional, and civic identities. Pick your phobia: if a Jew, it's Christian America; if Catholic, a Protestant America; if liberal Protestant, a fundamentalist America; if an evangelical Christian, a secular-humanist America; if female, a male America; if Black, a White America; if gay, a heterosexual America; if White, a multicultural America. From each of these redoubts, attacks on our fellow citizens are easy to launch. Academia now often appears dominated by a somewhat cramped coalition of authorized identities, and its faculty is well positioned to do the launching. It is often difficult to resist these temptations: they give us a certain self-righteous pleasure while permitting release from the more demanding obligations and disciplines of both civility and citizenship.

But we must not give in. We must remember that each of these sites and identities is also an American site and an American identity and that each of us would be culturally and intellectually deprived and politically and socially doomed were we displaced from that common ground. Indeed, outside of an American experience and an American struggle within which our identities are shaped, none of these particular identities *as such* has much of a script or a story—a recognizable identity or a meaningful history. Identities forged in American experience provide the interpretive language and symbol system through which we attain our particular self-understandings. Each phobia against which we think we define ourselves is, by that very reason, incorporated into our own identity. That is the curse and that is the hope of democratic political and cultural life in America. If we are to know ourselves we must know our country and countrymen.

TOLERATION AND INTELLECTUAL COURAGE

The twinned possibility of multicultural tribalism and universalism is as great a barrier to self- and social understanding as attempts to restore an earlier America, and both paths open to intolerance, incivility, and bad citizenship. Under a universalism without national horizons, each and every way of life, and each and every tribal claim, has in principle an equal status. Toleration is not required because no judgments need be made (except those required to maintain the universalistic framework of freedom).[1] Toleration, in contrast, requires both judgment and courage because it is always forged in history, through concrete struggle among particular groups and ways of life, and within a national framework. Judgment is required because not every claim can be tolerated: every regime of toleration is a *regime*, built by the concrete struggles and mediations that went into its constitution.[2] Courage is required because every struggle and negotiation and mediation occasioned by new claimants for recognition requires self- and national reinterpretation and new self- and national understandings by all participants in the struggle. This is only another way of saying that every new achievement of toleration results from the kind of pragmatic and dialectical process described in Dewey's philosophy[3] and is the spiritual and experiential ground of what Harold Bloom called American Religion.

It is easy enough to reject calls for restoring the virtues and practices of toleration and civility because they can be read as a step back from more principled and universalistic notions of citizenship and freedom. Toleration and civility never start and never end on a procedurally neutral playing field. But that is the historicist and pragmatic point: in democratic and national political life toleration and civility never were, never are, and never will be completely neutral. This can be stated succinctly in juridical terms: "To distinguish between policies and principles and to link rights with the latter but not the former is arbitrary. There is no basis for excluding collective goals in determining the scope of legal rights."[4] That is why democratic discourse as reflection upon and mediations of differences is required to create the shared experiences that become foundational as common ground and collective goals. That is why our national story is both tragic and comedic and can be told in the dialectical manner of a jeremiad. That is why the virtues of civility and toleration are so central, why judgment and courage are required, and why voluntary religious establishments—sacred forms of our national narrative—have been constitutive of American national identity and a national culture "where mutual forbearance prevails."[5]

Recent writings urging the democratic virtues of toleration and civility remind us that these virtues require coherent boundaries and shared purposes.[6] The alternatives of Restoration and Universalism are each incapable of sustaining a people with enough ties and trust for these virtues to be practiced. Restoration under contemporary conditions is sanctioning mass retreat into self-enclosed ethno-religious enclaves. Universalism under contemporary conditions is an elitist retreat into narcissistic cosmopolitanism, leaving a mean spirited tribalism in its wake. Academia has too many beautiful souls as it is, and not enough tolerant and engaged scholars and citizens.

PRAGMATISM AND NATIONAL IDENTITY

This conclusion is, finally, another way of saying that pragmatic nationalism is the only nationalism worthy of framing a *democratic* American self-understanding, philosophically, constitutionally, and historically. Over the last decade and more, historians, philosophers, and political and legal theorists have begun to reshape the American legacy of pragmatism into the beginnings of what I have termed a political theology for the next American establishment.[7] A less controversial term for this might be a shared moral orientation or a national narrative held sacred. While these recent writings by no means speak in one voice, they all seem to carry a common message. Only a pragmatic nationalism is grounded in democratic experiences and democratic stories. These stories have never been the creation or monopoly of coercive power and law, even though coercive power and constitutional law have always been annexed to the dominant ones. Only a pragmatic nationalism has room for tragedy as well as comedy and, most of all, for irony and the humility, civility, and tolerant spirit that irony brings in its train. Only a pragmatic nationalism encourages us to see spirit and transcendence and principles in and through our shared experiences and struggles, and encourages us to see our own experiences as bound up with the experiences of others. Only a pragmatic nationalism honors democratic political life and experience as the first ground of freedom and, because it does, requires ever wider affiliations and connections of those who would claim to be free.

NOTES

1. Fish 1987, 1997, and 1998; Steven Smith 1990; and see Kingwell (1995) on civility and toleration.

2. Macedo (1998), following from his earlier critique of Rawls in 1995; and see Walzer 1997 and Andrew Murphy 1997.

3. Westbrook 1991, especially chapter 10, a brilliant analysis of Dewey's discussion of the relationship of philosophy to democracy.

4. Posner 1990, 239.

5. Tushnet 1985, 738.

6. Some important examples are Macedo 1998; Steven Smith 1990; Taylor 1990; Sandel 1990; Kingwell 1995; Sinopoli 1993 and 1995; Strike 1996; and Andrew Murphy 1997. The corresponding call for courts to "decouple judicial legitimacy from objectivity" by substituting a view of adjudication as part of, rather than standing above, the political community is also an endorsement of the virtue of toleration. Williams 1998, 267; and see Posner (1990 and 1995), chapter 6, calling for a more fact- and experience-based jurisprudence.

7. Appropriately for the construction of a new cultural-intellectual consensus, the disciplinary categories overlap, so the classifications here are somewhat arbitrary and the writings cited only a sample. Historians: Kloppenberg 1986 and 1998; Kuklick 1985 and 1989; Westbrook 1991; Feffer 1993; Livingston 1994. Philosophers and political theorists: Rorty 1989 and 1992; Bernstein 1978; Elizabeth Anderson 1998; David L. Hall 1993; Festenstein 1997; Kingwell 1995; Charles Anderson 1990; Hoopes 1998. Legal theorists: Fish 1987, 1997, and 1998; Sunstein 1993 and 1999; Ackerman 1993 and 1996; Joan Williams 1998; Tushnet 1985; Posner 1990 and 1995.

Bibliography

Abbott, Lyman. 1918. *The Twentieth Century Crusade.* New York: Macmillan.
———. 1901. *The Rights of Man.* New York: Houghton Mifflin.
Abrams, M. H. 1973. *Natural Supernaturalism: Tradition and Revolution in Romantic Literature.* New York: Norton.
Abshire, David, and Brock Brower. 1996. *Putting America's House in Order: The Nation as a Family.* Westport, Conn.: Praeger.
Academe. Bulletin of the American Association of University Professors, vol. 82, no. 6 (November–December 1996).
Ackerman, Bruce A. 1996. *We the People,* Volume 2. *Transformations.* Cambridge: Harvard University Press.
———. 1993. *We the People,* Volume 1. *Foundations.* Cambridge: Harvard University Press.
———. 1980. *Social Justice in the Liberal State.* New Haven: Yale University Press.
Adams, John Quincy. 1839. *The Jubilee of the Constitution: A Discourse.* New York: Samuel Colman.
———. 1831. *An Oration Addressed to the Citizens of the Town of Quincy.* Boston: Richardson, Lord and Holbrook.
Ahlstrom, Sydney E. 1972. *A Religious History of the American People.* New Haven: Yale University Press.
Alexander, Larry. "Liberalism, Religion, and the Unity of Epistemology." *San Diego Law Review* 30, no. 4 (Fall 1993): 763–797.
Allen, Anita L., and Milton C. Regan, Jr., eds. 1998. *Debating Democracy's Discontent: Essays on American Politics, Law, and Public Philosophy.* New York: Oxford University Press.
Anderson, Charles W. 1997. "Pragmatism, Idealism, and the Aims of Liberal Education." In *Education and Democracy: Re-imagining Liberal Learning in America*, edited by Robert Orrill, 111–130. New York: College Entrance Examination Board.
———. 1990. *Pragmatic Liberalism.* Chicago: University of Chicago Press.
Anderson, Elizabeth. 1998. "Pragmatism, Science, and Moral Inquiry." In *In Face of the Facts: Moral Inquiry in American Scholarship,* edited by Richard W. Fox and Robert E. Westbrook, 10–39. Washington D.C.: Woodrow Wilson Center Press; New York: Cambridge University Press.

Astin, Alexander. 1997. "Liberal Education and Democracy: The Case for Pragmatism." In Orrill, *Education and Democracy.*

Audi, Robert, and Nicholas Wolterstorff. 1996. *Religion in the Public Square: The Place of Religious Convictions in Political Debate.* Lanham, Md.: Rowman & Littlefield.

Barrow, Clyde. 1990. *Universities and the Capitalist State: Corporate Liberalism and the Reconstruction of American Higher Education.* Madison: University of Wisconsin Press.

———. "Charles A. Beard's Social Democracy: A Critique of the Populist-Progressive Style in American Political Thought." *Polity* 21 (1988): 253–276.

Bascom, John. 1898. *Sociology.* New York: G. P. Putnam's Sons.

Bass, Dorothy C. 1989. "Ministry on the Margin: Protestants and Education." In *Between the Times: The Travail of the Protestant Establishment in America, 1900–1960,* edited by William R. Hutchison, 48–71. Cambridge: Cambridge University Press.

Batten, Samuel Zane. 1911. *The Social Task of Christianity: A Summons to the New Crusade.* New York: Flemming H. Revell.

———. 1898. *The New Citizenship: Christian Character in Its Biblical Ideals, Sources, and Relations.* Philadelphia: Union Press.

Beiner, Ronald, ed. 1995. *Theorizing Citizenship.* Albany: SUNY Press.

✓ Bellah, Robert N. "Is There a Common American Culture." *Journal of the American Academy of Religion* 66, no. 3 (Fall 1998): 613–625.

———. 1968. "Civil Religion in America." In *Religion in America,* edited by William G. McLoughlin and Robert N. Bellah, 3–23. Boston: Beacon Press.

Benson, Lee. 1961. *The Concept of Jacksonian Democracy.* Princeton: Princeton University Press.

Bercovitch, Sacvan. 1978. *The American Jeremiad.* Madison: University of Wisconsin Press.

———. "How the Puritans Won the American Revolution." *The Massachusetts Review* (Winter 1976): 597–630.

———. 1975. *The Puritan Origins of the American Self.* New Haven: Yale University Press.

Bernstein, Richard. 1978. *The Restructuring of Social and Political Theory.* Philadelphia: University of Pennsylvania Press.

Billington, Ray. 1964. *Protestant Crusade, 1800–1860: A Study of the Origins of American Nativism.* New York: Times Books.

Bloch, Ruth. 1990. "Religion and Ideological Change in the American Revolution." In *Religion and American Politics,* edited by Mark Noll, 44–61. New York: Oxford University Press.

Bloom, Harold. 1992. *The American Religion: The Emergence of a Post-Christian Nation.* New York: Simon and Schuster.

✓ Boorstin, Daniel. 1953. *The Genius of American Politics.* Chicago: University of Chicago Press.

Booth, W. James. "Communities of Memory: On Identity, Memory, and Debt." *American Political Science Review* 93, no. 2 (June 1999): 249–262.

Brodkin, Karen. 1998. *How Jews Became White Folks and What That Says about Race in America.* New Brunswick: Rutgers University Press.

Brown, Samuel Windsor. 1967 (1912). *The Secularization of American Education as Shown by State Legislation, State Constitutional Provisions and State Supreme Court Decisions.* New York: Russell and Russell.

Burnham, Walter Dean. 1970. *Critical Elections and the Mainsprings of American Politics.* New York: Norton.

Burtchaell, James T. 1998. *The Dying of the Light: The Disengagement of Colleges and Universities from Their Christian Churches.* Grand Rapids, Mich.: Eerdmans.

Butler, Judith. 1996. "Universality in Culture." In *For Love of Country: Debating the Limits of Patriotism,* Martha Nussbaum, edited by Joshua Cohen, 45–52. Boston: Beacon Press.

Butler, Jon, and Harry S. Stout, eds. 1998. *Religion in American History.* New York: Oxford University Press.

Carlisle, Janice. 1991. *John Stuart Mill and the Writing of Character.* Athens: University of Georgia Press.

Carter, Stephen L. 1993. *The Culture of Disbelief: How American Law and Politics Trivialize Religious Devotion.* New York: Anchor Books.

———. "Evolutionism, Creationism, and Treating Religion as a Hobby." *Duke Law Journal* 1987, no. 6 (1987): 977–996.

Carwardine, Richard J. 1993. *Evangelicals and Politics in Antebellum America.* New Haven: Yale University Press.

Cherry, Conrad. 1995. *Hurrying toward Zion: Universities, Divinity Schools, and American Protestantism.* Bloomington: Indiana University Press.

———. 1989. "Nation, Church, and Private Religion: The Emergence of an American Pattern." In *Readings on Church and State,* edited by James E. Wood. Waco, Tex.: J. M. Dawson Institute of Church-State Relations, Baylor University.

Clark, J. C. D. 1994. *The Language of Liberty, 1660–1832: Political Discourse and Social Dynamics in the Anglo-American World.* New York: Cambridge University Press.

Cohen, Naomi. 1992. *Jews in Christian America: The Pursuit of Religious Equality.* New York: Oxford University Press.

Conkin, Paul K. 1998. *When All the Gods Trembled: Darwinism, Scopes, and American Intellectuals.* Lanham, Md.: Rowman & Littlefield.

———. 1995. *The Uneasy Center: Reformed Christianity in Antebellum America.* Chapel Hill: University of North Carolina Press.

———. 1990. *Cane Ridge: America's Pentecost.* Madison: University of Wisconsin Press.

Connolly, William E. 1999. *Why I Am Not a Secularist.* Minneapolis: University of Minnesota Press.

Cooley, Charles. 1909. *Social Organization: A Study of the Larger Mind.* New York: Scribner.

Cox, Harvey. 1965. *The Secular City.* New York: Macmillan.

Craycraft, Kenneth R. 1999. *The American Myth of Religious Freedom.* Dallas: Spence Publishing Company.

Croly, Herbert. 1989 (1909). *The Promise of American Life.* Boston: Northeastern University Press.

———. 1914. *Progressive Democracy.* New York: Macmillan.

Cross, Whitney. 1950. *The Burned-Over District: The Social and Intellectual History of Enthusiastic Religion in Western New York, 1800–1850.* Ithaca: Cornell University Press.

Crunden, Robert M. 1984. *Ministers of Reform: The Progressives' Achievement in American Civilization, 1889–1920.* Urbana: University of Illinois Press.

Cuddihy, John M. 1978. *No Offense: Civil Religion and Protestant Taste.* New York: Seabury Press.

Curtis, Susan. 1991. *A Consuming Faith: The Social Gospel and Modern American Culture.* Baltimore: Johns Hopkins University Press.

Dahl, Robert. 1967. *Pluralist Democracy in the United States.* Chicago: Rand McNally.

———. 1956. *Preface to Democratic Theory.* Chicago: University of Chicago Press.

Dewey, John. 1977. "Religion and Our Schools." *The Middle Works, 1899–1909,* vol. 4: 1907–1909. Carbondale: Southern Illinois University Press. First published in 1908, then republished in 1929, 1939, and 1940).

———. 1976. "The School and Social Progress." *The Middle Works, 1899–1924,* vol. 1: 1899–1901. Carbondale: Southern Illinois University Press. First published in 1899.

———. 1972. "My Pedagogic Creed." *The Early Works, 1882–1898,* vol. 5: 1895–1898. Carbondale: Southern Illinois University Press. First published in 1897.

———. 1934. *A Common Faith.* Terry Lectures, New Haven: Yale University Press.

———. "An American Intellectual Frontier." *The New Republic* (10 May 1922): 303–305.

Dewey, John, and James Tufts. 1908. *Ethics.* New York: Henry Holt.

Dionne, E. J., Jr. 1996. *They Only Look Dead: Why Progressives Will Dominate the Next Political Era.* New York: Simon and Schuster.

———. *Why Americans Hate Politics.* New York: Simon and Schuster.

Dohen, Dorothy. 1967. *Nationalism and American Catholicism.* New York: Sheed and Ward.

Dolan, Jay P. 1985. *The American Catholic Experience: A History from Colonial Times to the Present.* New York: Doubleday.

Dombrowski, James. 1966 (1936). *The Early Days of Christian Socialism in America.* New York: Octagon Books.

Dorfman, Joseph. 1949. *The Economic Mind of American Civilization,* vol. 3: 1865–1880. New York: Viking Press.

Douglas, Ann. 1988. *The Feminization of American Culture.* New York: Doubleday.

Dudziak, Mary L. "The Little Rock Crisis and Foreign Affairs: Race, Resistance, and the Image of American Democracy." *Southern California Law Review* 70, no. 6 (1997): 1641–1716.

———. "Desegregation as a Cold War Imperative." *Stanford Law Review* 41 (November 1988): 61–120.

Dworkin, Ronald. 1996. *Freedom's Law: The Moral Reading of the American Constitution.* Cambridge: Harvard University Press.

Edwards, Rebecca. 1997. *Angels in the Machinery: Gender in American Party Politics from the Civil War to the Progressive Era.* New York: Oxford University Press.

Eisenach, Eldon. 1999a. "Liberal Citizenship and American National Identity." In *Studies in American Political Development,* vol. 13, edited by Karen Orren and Stephen Skowronek. New York: Cambridge University Press.

———. 1999b. "Progressive Internationalism." In *Progressivism and the New Democracy,* edited by Jerome Mileur and Sidney Milkis. Amherst: University of Massachusetts Press.

———. 1998. "Mill and Liberal Christianity." In *Mill and the Moral Character of Liberalism,* edited by Eldon Eisenach. University Park: Penn State Press.

————. 1996. "Bookends: Seven Stories Excised from the *Lost Promise of Progressivism.* In *Studies in American Political Development,* edited by Karen Orren and Stephen Skowronek. Vol. 10. New York: Cambridge University Press.

————. 1995. "Pragmatic Democracy and Constitutional Government." In *Studies in American Political Development,* edited by Karen Orren and Stephen Skowronek. Vol. 9. New York: Cambridge University Press.

————. 1994. *The Lost Promise of Progressivism.* Lawrence: University Press of Kansas.

————. 1990. "Reconstituting the Study of American Political Thought in a Regime Change Perspective." In *Studies in American Political Development,* edited by Karen Orren and Stephen Skowronek. Vol. 4, 169–228. New Haven: Yale University Press.

————. "Mill's *Autobiography* as Political Theory." *History of Political Thought,* vol. 8 (1987): 111–129.

————. "Cultural Politics and Political Thought: The American Revolution Made and Remembered." *American Studies* 20 (1979): 71–98.

Ellis, Richard J. 1998. *The Dark Side of the Left: Illiberal Egalitarianism in America.* Lawrence: University Press of Kansas.

Elazar, Daniel J. 1998. *Covenant and Constitutionalism.* Vol. 3, *The Covenant Tradition in Politics.* New Brunswick, N.J.: Transaction.

Elshtain, Jean Bethke. 1998. "Political Theory and Moral Responsibility." In Fox and Westbrook, *In Face of the Facts,* 40–56.

————. 1994. *Democracy on Trial.* New York: Basic Books.

Ely, Richard. 1903. *Studies in the Evolution of Industrial Society.* Chautauqua, N.Y.: Chautauqua Press.

————. 1893. *Outlines of Economics.* Chautauqua, N.Y.: Chautauqua Press.

Ernst, Eldon G. 1974. *Moment of Truth of Protestant America: Interchurch Campaigns Following World War I.* Missoula, Mont.: Scholars' Press.

Essays and Reviews. 1860. London: John W. Parker and Son.

Etzioni, Amitai, ed. 1998. *The Essential Communitarian Reader.* Lanham, Md.: Rowman & Littlefield.

————. ed. 1995. *New Communitarian Thinking: Persons, Virtues, Institutions, and Communities.* Charlottesville, Va.: University of Virginia Press.

Feffer, Andrew. 1993. *The Chicago Pragmatists and American Progressivism.* Ithaca: Cornell University Press.

Feldman, Stephen M. "Principle, History, and Power: The Limits of the First Amendment Religion Clauses." *Iowa Law Review* 81 (March 1996): 833–882.

————. 1996. *Please Don't Wish Me a Merry Christmas.* New York: New York University Press.

Ferguson, Robert A. 1996. *The American Enlightenment, 1750–1820.* Cambridge: Harvard University Press.

Festenstein, Matthew. 1997. *Pragmatism and Political Theory: From Dewey to Rorty.* Chicago: University of Chicago Press.

Finke, Roger, and Rodney Stark. 1992. *The Churching of America, 1776–1990: Winners and Losers in Our Religious Economy.* New Brunswick: Rutgers University Press.

Fish, Stanley. 1998. "Boutique Multiculturalism." In *Multiculturalism and American Democracy,* edited by Arthur M. Melzer, Jerry Weinberger, and M. Richard Zinman. Lawrence: University Press of Kansas.

——. "Mission Impossible: Settling the Just Bounds between Church and State." *Columbia Law Review* 97 (December 1997): 2255–2333.

——. "Liberalism Doesn't Exist." *Duke Law Journal* 1987, no. 6 (1987): 997–1001.

Fitzpatrick, Ellen. 1990. *Endless Crusade: Women Social Scientists and Progressive Reform.* New York: Oxford University Press.

Follett, Mary Parker. 1934 (1918). *The New State.* London and New York: Longmans, Green.

Fowler, Robert Booth. 1989. *Unconventional Partners: Religion and Liberal Culture in the United States.* Grand Rapids, Mich.: Eerdmans.

Fox, Richard W. 1997. "Experience and Explanation in Twentieth-Century American History." In *New Directions in American Religious History,* edited by Harry S. Stout and P. G. Hart, New York: Oxford University Press.

Fox, Richard W., and Robert B. Westbrook, eds. 1998. *In Face of the Facts: Moral Inquiry in American Scholarship.* Washington, D.C.: Woodrow Wilson Center Press; New York: Cambridge University Press.

Franklin, Nancy. "1776." *The New Yorker* (8 September 1997): 93–94.

Frum, David. 1994. *Dead Right: The End of the Conservatism of Hope and the Rise of the Conservatism of Fear.* New York: Basic Books.

Gabriel, Ralph H. 1956 (1940). *The Course of American Democratic Thought.* New York: Roland Press.

Galston, William. 1998. "A Liberal-Democratic Case for the Two-Parent Family." In Etzioni, *Essential Communitarian Reader.*

Gaustad, Edwin S. 1989. "The Pulpit and the Pews." In *Between the Times,* edited by William R. Hutchison, Cambridge: Cambridge University Press.

——. 1987. *Faith of Our Fathers: Religion and the New Nation.* San Francisco: Harper and Row.

Gerring, John. "Culture versus Economics: An American Dilemma." *Social Science History* 23 (1999): 129–172.

——. 1998. *Party Ideologies in America, 1828–1996.* New York: Cambridge University Press.

——. 1997. "Party Ideology in America: The National Republican Chapter, 1829–1924." In *Studies in American Political Development,* edited by Karen Orren and Stephen Skowronek. Vol. 11. New York: Cambridge University Press.

Giankos, Perry E., and Albert Karson, eds. 1966. *American Diplomacy and the Sense of National Destiny.* Vol. 1. Belmont, Calif.: Wadsworth.

Gienapp, William E. 1987. *The Origins of the Republican Party, 1852–1856.* New York: Oxford University Press.

Ginsberg, Benjamin. 1993. *The Fatal Embrace: Jews and the State.* Chicago: University of Chicago Press.

Glazer, Nathan, and Daniel Patrick Moynihan. 1970. *Beyond the Melting Pot.* 2d rev. ed. Cambridge: MIT Press.

Glendon, Mary Ann. 1991. *Rights Talk: The Impoverishment of American Political Discourse.* New York: Free Press.

Glendon, Mary Ann, and David Blankenhorn, eds. 1995. *Seedbeds of Virtue: Sources of Competence, Character, and Citizenship in American Society.* Lanham, Md.: Madison Books.

Glenn, Charles Leslie, Jr. 1988. *The Myth of the Common School.* Amherst: University of Massachusetts Press.

Green, William Scott. "Religion within the Limits." In *Academe* 82, no. 6. Bulletin of AAUP (1996): 24–28.

Greenawalt, Kent. "Religious Convictions and Political Choice: Some Further Thoughts." *DePaul Law Review* 39, no. 4 (Summer 1990): 1019–1046.

Greenstone, David. 1993. *The Lincoln Persuasion: Remaking American Liberalism.* Princeton: Princeton University Press.

Gutting, Gary. 1999. *Pragmatic Liberalism and the Critique of Modernity.* Cambridge: Cambridge University Press.

Hall, David L. 1993. *Richard Rorty: Prophet and Poet of the New Pragmatism.* Albany: State University of New York Press.

Handy, Robert. 1991. *Undermined Establishment: Church-State Relations in America, 1880–1920.* Princeton: Princeton University Press.

———. 1990 "Protestant Theological Tensions and Political Styles in the Progressive Period." In Noll, *Religion and American Politics,* 281–301.

———. 1971. *A Christian America: Protestant Hopes and Historical Realities.* 2d ed. New York: Oxford University Press.

———. "The American Religious Depression, 1925–1935." *Church History* 29 (1960): 3–16.

Hart, D. G. 1992. "Faith and Learning in the Age of the University: The Academic Ministry of Daniel Coit Gilman." In *The Secularization of the Academy,* edited by George Marsden and Bradley J. Longfield, 107–145. New York: Oxford University Press.

———. 1992. "American Learning and the Problem of Religious Studies." In Marsden and Longfield, *Secularization of the Academy,* 195–233.

Hartz, Louis. 1955. *The Liberal Tradition in America.* New York: Harcourt, Brace and World.

Haskell, Thomas. 1977. *The Emergence of Professional Social Science in America.* Urbana: University of Illinois Press.

Heineman, Kenneth. 1998. *God Is a Conservative: Religion, Politics and Morality in Contemporary America.* New York: New York University Press.

Helmstadter, Richard, and Bernard Lightman, eds. 1990. *Victorian Faith in Crisis: Essays on Continuity and Change in Nineteenth-Century Religious Belief.* Stanford: Stanford University Press.

Herberg, Will. 1983 (1955). *Protestant, Catholic, Jew.* Chicago: University of Chicago Press.

Hill, Geoffrey. "Clarendon and the opposition to Hobbes's 'monstrous Soveraign.'" *Times Literary Supplement,* (11 June 1999): 11.

Hinchman, Lewis P., and Sandra K. Hinchman, eds. 1997. *Memory, Identity, Community: The Idea of Narrative in the Human Sciences.* Albany: State University of New York Press.

Hittinger, Russell. "The Catholic Theology of John Courtney Murray." *The Weekly Standard* (4 and 11 January 1999): 32–35.

Hobbes, Thomas. 1982. *De Cive.* Westport, Conn.: Greenwood Press.

Hochschild, Jennifer L. 1996. *Facing Up to the American Dream: Race, Class, and the Soul of the Nation.* Princeton: Princeton University Press.

Hoekema, David A. "Politics, Religion, and Other Crimes against Civility." In *Academe* 82, no. 6 (1996): 33–37.

Hofstadter, Richard. 1968. *The Progressive Historians.* New York: Alfred A. Knopf.

———. 1962. *Anti-intellectualism in American Life.* New York: Vintage Books.

———. 1955. *Age of Reform: From Bryan to FDR.* New York: Alfred A. Knopf.

Hollinger, David A. 1995. *Postethnic America: Beyond Multiculturalism.* New York: Basic Books.

———. "How Wide the Circle of the We? American Intellectuals and the Problem of the Ethnos since World War II." *American Historical Review* 98 (1993): 317–337.

Hoopes, James. 1998. *Community Denied: The Wrong Turn of Pragmatic Liberalism.* Ithaca, N.Y.: Cornell University Press.

Hoover, Kenneth. 1997. *The Power of Identity: Politics in a New Key.* Chatham, N.J.: Chatham House Publishers.

Horwitz, Morton J. 1992. *The Transformation of American Law, 1870–1970: The Crisis of Legal Orthodoxy.* New York: Oxford University Press.

Howe, Daniel Walker. 1997a. *Making the American Self: Jonathan Edwards to Abraham Lincoln.* Cambridge: Harvard University Press.

———. 1997b. "Protestantism, Voluntarism, and Personal Identity in Antebellum America." In Stout and Hart, *New Directions in American Religious History.*

———. 1990. "Religion and Politics in the Antebellum North." In Noll, *Religion and American Politics.*

———. 1979. *The Political Culture of the American Whigs.* Chicago: University of Chicago Press.

———. 1970. *The Unitarian Conscience: Harvard Moral Philosophy, 1805–1861.* Cambridge: Harvard University Press.

Hudson, Winthrop S., ed. 1970. *Nationalism and Religion in America: Concepts of American Identity and Mission.* New York: Peter Smith.

Hunt, Robert P., and Kenneth Grasso, eds. 1992. *John Courtney Murray and the American Civil Conversation.* Grand Rapids, Mich.: Eerdmans.

Hunter, James Davison, and Os Guiness, eds. 1990. *Articles of Faith, Articles of Peace: The Religious Liberty Clauses and the American Public Philosophy.* Washington, D.C.: The Brookings Institution.

Hutchison, William R., ed. 1992. *The Modernist Impulse in American Protestantism.* Durham: Duke University Press.

———. 1989a. *Between the Times: The Travail of the Protestant Establishment in America, 1900–1960.* Cambridge: Cambridge University Press.

———. 1989b. "Protestantism as Establishment." In Hutchison, *Between the Times.*

———. 1987. *Errand to the World: American Protestant Thought and Foreign Missions.* Chicago: University of Chicago Press.

Isenberg, Nancy. 1998. *Sex and Citizenship in Antebellum America.* Chapel Hill: University of North Carolina Press.

Jaenicke, Douglas W. "The Jacksonian Integration of Parties into the Constitutional System." *Political Science Quarterly* 101 (1986): 85–107.

Jefferson, Thomas. 1899. *The Writings of Thomas Jefferson.* Edited by Paul Leicester Ford. Vol. 10. New York.

Jensen, Richard. 1971. *The Winning of the Mid-West: Social and Political Conflict, 1888–1896.* Chicago: University of Chicago Press.

Johnson, Donald B., and Kirk H. Porter, eds. 1975. *National Party Platforms, 1840–1972.* Urbana: University of Illinois Press.

Johnson, Paul. "God and the Americans." *Commentary* 99, no. 1 (January 1995): 25–45.

Kann, Mark E. 1990. "Individualism, Civic Virtue, and Gender in America." In *Studies in American Political Development,* edited by Karen Orren and Stephen Skowronek. Vol. 4. New Haven: Yale University Press.

Keller, Morton. 1977. *Affairs of State: Public Life in Late Nineteenth Century America.* Cambridge: Harvard University Press.

Kelley, Robert L. 1979. *The Cultural Pattern in American Politics: The First Century.* New York: Alfred A. Knopf.

Kennedy, David M. 1980. *Over Here: The First World War and American Society.* New York: Oxford University Press.

Kernohan, Andrew. 1998. *Liberalism, Equality, and Cultural Oppression.* New York: Cambridge University Press.

Kerr, Clark. 1963. *The Uses of the University.* Cambridge: Harvard University Press.

Kimball, Bruce. 1997. "Naming Pragmatic Liberal Education." In Orrill, *Education and Democracy.*

King, William McGuire. 1989a. "The Reform Establishment and the Ambiguities of Influence." In Hutchison, *Between the Times.*

———. 1989b. "An Enthusiasm for Humanity: The Social Emphasis in Religion and Its Accommodation in Protestant Theology." In *Religion and Twentieth-Century American Intellectual Life,* edited by Michael J. Lacy. New York: Cambridge University Press.

Kingwell, Mark. 1995. *A Civil Tongue: Justice, Dialogue, and the Politics of Pluralism.* University Park: Penn State Press.

Kleppner, Paul. 1987. *Continuity and Change in Electoral Politics, 1893–1928.* Westport, Conn.: Greenwood Press.

———. 1970. *The Cross of Culture: A Social Analysis of Midwestern Politics, 1850–1900.* New York: Free Press.

Kloppenberg, James T. 1998. *The Virtues of Liberalism.* New York: Oxford University Press.

———. 1997. "Cosmopolitan Pragmatism: Deliberative Democracy and Higher Education. In Orrill, *Education and Democracy.*

———. 1986. *Uncertain Victory: Social Democracy and Progressivism in European and American Thought.* New York: Oxford University Press.

Knefelkamp, Lee, and Carol Schneider. 1997. "Education for a World Lived in Common with Others." In Orrill, *Education and Democracy.*

Kohl, Lawrence F. 1989. *The Politics of Individualism: Parties and the American Character in the Jacksonian Era.* New York: Oxford University Press.

Kraut, Benny. 1989. "A Wary Collaboration: Jew, Catholics, and the Protestant Goodwill Movement." In Hutchison, *Between the Times.*

Kuklick, Bruce. 1985. *Churchmen and Philosophers: From Jonathan Edwards to John Dewey.* New Haven: Yale University Press.

———. 1989. "John Dewey, American Theology, and Scientific Politics." In Lacy, *Religion and Twentieth-Century American Intellectual Life.*

Lacy, Michael J., ed. 1989. *Religion and Twentieth-Century American Intellectual Life.* New York: Cambridge University Press.

Levinson, Sanford. "The Confrontation of Religious Faith and Civil Religion: Catholics Becoming Justices." *DePaul Law Review* 39 (1990): 1047–1081.

———. 1988. *Constitutional Faith.* Princeton: Princeton University Press.

Bibliography

Lincoln, Abraham. 1967. *The Political Thought of Abraham Lincoln,* ed. Richard N. Current. Indianapolis: Bobbs-Merrill.

Lind, Michael. 1996. *Up From Conservatism: Why the Right Is Wrong for America.* New York: Free Press.

———. 1995. *The Next American Nation: The New Nationalism and the Fourth American Revolution.* New York: Free Press.

Livingston, James. 1994. *Pragmatism and the Political Economy of Cultural Revolution, 1850–1940.* Chapel Hill: University of North Carolina Press.

Longfield, Bradley J. 1992a. "From Evangelicalism to Liberalism: Public Midwestern Universities in Nineteenth-Century America." In Marsden and Longfield, *Secularization of the Academy.*

———. 1992b. " 'For God, for Country, and for Yale': Yale, Religion, and Higher Education between the World Wars." In Marsden and Longfield, *Secularization of the Academy.*

Lowi, Theodore. 1995. *The End of the Republican Era.* Norman: University of Oklahoma Press.

———. 1969. *The End of Liberalism.* New York: W. W. Norton.

Lugo, Luis E., ed. 1994. *Religion, Public Life, and the American Polity.* Knoxville: University of Tennessee Press.

Macedo, Stephen. "Transformative Constitutionalism and the Case of Religion: Defending the Moderate Hegemony of Liberalism." *Political Theory* 26 (1998): 56–80.

———. "Liberal Civic Education and Religious Fundamentalism: The Case of God v. John Rawls." *Ethics* 105 (1995): 468–496.

MacIntyre, Alasdair. 1984. *After Virtue.* South Bend: University of Notre Dame Press.

McClay, Wilfred. 1994. *The Masterless: Self and Society in Modern America.* Chapel Hill: University of North Carolina Press.

Maclear, J. F. 1971. "The Republic and the Millennium." In *The Religion of the Republic,* edited by Elwyn Smith. Philadelphia: Fortress Press.

McClymer, John F. 1980. *War and Welfare: Social Engineering in America, 1890–1925.* Westport, Conn.: Greenwood Press.

McCorkle, Pope. "The Historian as Intellectual: Charles Beard and the Constitution Reconsidered." *American Journal of Legal History* 28 (1984): 314–363.

McCormick, Richard. 1986. *The Party Period and Public Policy: American Politics from the Age of Jackson to the Progressive Era.* New York: Oxford University Press.

McGerr, Michael E. 1986. *The Decline of Popular Politics: The American North, 1865–1928.* New York: Oxford University Press.

McPherson, James M. 1991. *Abraham Lincoln and the Second American Revolution.* New York: Oxford University Press.

McWilliams, Wilson Carey. 1999. "On Rogers Smith's *Civic Ideals.*" In *Studies in American Political Development,* edited by Karen Orren and Stephen Skowronek. Vol. 13. New York: Cambridge University Press.

Marsden, George. 1994. *The Soul of the American University: From Protestant Establishment to Established Nonbelief.* New York: Oxford University Press.

———. 1980. *Fundamentalism and American Culture.* New York: Oxford University Press.

Marsden, George, and Bradley J. Longfield, eds. 1992. *The Secularization of the Academy.* New York: Oxford University Press.

Marty, Martin. 1997. *The One and the Many: America's Struggle for the Common Good.* Cambridge: Harvard University Press.

————. 1996. *Modern American Religion. Vol. III: Under God, Indivisible, 1940–1960.* Chicago: University of Chicago Press.

————. 1990 "The Twentieth Century: Protestants and Others." In Noll, *Religion and American Politics.*

————. 1989. "Living with Establishment and Disestablishment in Nineteenth-Century Anglo-America." In Wood, *Readings on Church and State.*

————. 1986. *Modern American Religion. Vol. I: The Irony of It All, 1893–1919.* Chicago: University of Chicago Press.

————. 1981. *The Public Church.* New York: Crossroad.

May, Henry F. 1989. "Religion and American Intellectual History, 1945–1985: Reflections on an Uneasy Relationship." In Lacy, *Religion and Twentieth-Century American Intellectual Life.*

Mead, Sidney E. 1975. *The Nation with the Soul of a Church.* New York: Harper and Row.

————. 1971. "The Fact of Pluralism and the Persistence of Sectarianism." In E. Smith, *The Religion of the Republic.*

Melzer, Arthur M., Jerry Weinberger, and M. Richard Zinman, ed. 1998. *Multiculturalism and American Democracy.* Lawrence: University Press of Kansas.

Menand, Louis. 1997a. "Re-imagining Liberal Education." In Orrill, *Education and Democracy.*

————, ed. 1997b. *Pragmatism: A Reader.* New York: Random House.

Michaelsen, Robert. 1971. "Is the Public School Religious or Secular?" In E. Smith, *Religion of the Republic.*

————. 1970. *Piety in the Public School.* New York: Macmillan.

————. "Common School, Common Religion? A Case Study in Church-State Relations, Cincinnati, 1869–70." *Church History* 38 (1969): 201–217.

Miller, William Lee. 1990. "The Moral Project of the American Founders." In Hunter and Guiness, *Articles of Faith.*

————. 1988. *The First Liberty: Religion and the American Republic.* New York: Paragon House.

Mills, C. Wright. 1988. *Sociology and Pragmatism.* New York: Paine Publishers.

Minnich, Elizabeth Kamarck. 1997. "The American Tradition of Aspirational Democracy." In Orrill, *Education and Democracy.*

Mitchell, Joshua. "Of Answers Ruled Out: Religion in Academic Life." In *Academe* 82, no. 6 (1996): 29–32.

Moltmann, Jürgen, 1998. *A Passion for God's Reign: Theology, Christian Learning and the Christian Self.* Edited by Miroslav Volf, with responses by Nicholas Wolterstorff and Ellen T. Charry. Grand Rapids, Mich.: William B. Eerdmans Publishing Company.

Monsma, Stephen V. 1996. *When Sacred and Secular Mix: Religious Nonprofit Organizations and Public Money.* Lanham, Md.: Rowman & Littlefield.

Mooney, Christopher F. 1990. *Boundaries Dimly Perceived: Law, Religion, Education, and the Common Good.* Notre Dame: University of Notre Dame Press.

Moore, R. Laurence. 1994. *Selling God: American Religion in the Marketplace of Culture.* New York: Oxford University Press.

————. 1989. "Secularization: Religion and the Social Sciences." In Hutchison, *Between the Times.*

——. 1986. *Religious Outsiders and the Making of Americans*. New York: Oxford University Press.

Morone, James A. 1999. "The Other's America: Notes on Rogers Smith's *Civic Ideals.*" In *Studies in American Political Development*, edited by Karen Orren and Stephen Skowronek. Vol. 13. New York: Cambridge University Press.

——. 1998. *The Democratic Wish: Popular Participation and the Limits of American Government*. New Haven: Yale University Press.

Morris, Charles R. 1997. *American Catholic*. New York: Times Books, Random House.

Morris, John N. 1966. *Versions of the Self: English Autobiography from John Bunyon to John Stuart Mill*. New York: Basic Books.

Morrissey, Daniel J. "The Separation of Church and State: An American Catholic Perspective." *Catholic University Law Review* 47 (1997): 1–50.

Murphy, Andrew. Forthcoming. *Conscience and Community: Revisiting Toleration and Religious Dissent in Early Modern England and America*. University Park: Penn State Press.

——. "Rawls and a Shrinking Liberty of Conscience." *Review of Politics* 60 (1998): 247–276.

——. "Tolerance, Toleration, and the Liberal Tradition." *Polity* 29 (1997): 593–623.

Murphy, Howard. "The Ethical Revolt against Christian Orthodoxy in Early Victorian England." *American Historical Review* 60 (1955): 800–817.

Murray, Robert K. 1964. *Red Scare: A Study in National Hysteria, 1919–1920*. New York: McGraw.

Neal, Patrick. 1997. *Liberalism and Its Discontents*. New York: New York University Press.

Neuhaus, Richard John. "On Not Permitting the Other to Be Other." *First Things* 79 (January 1998): 62–79. Review of Stephen Feldman, 1996.

Neustadt, Richard. 1976. *Presidential Power: The Politics of Leadership with Reflections on Johnson and Nixon*. New York: Wiley.

Nietzsche, Friedrich. 1969. *The Genealogy of Morals*. Translated by W. Kaufmann and R. J. Hollingdale. New York: Vintage.

Noll, Mark, ed. 1990. *Religion and American Politics*. New York: Oxford University Press.

Norton, Anne. 1998. "The Virtues of Multiculturalism." In Melzer, *Multiculturalism and American Democracy*.

Novak, Michael. 1972. *The Rise of the Unmeltable Ethnics*. New York: Macmillan.

Nussbaum, Martha. 1997. *Cultivating Humanity: A Classical Defense of Reform in Liberal Education*. Cambridge: Harvard University Press.

——. 1996. *For Love of Country: Debating the Limits of Patriotism*. Edited by Joshua Cohen. Boston: Beacon Press.

O'Donovan, Oliver. 1996. *The Desire of the Nations: Rediscovering the Roots of Political Theology*. New York: Cambridge University Press.

Orrill, Robert, ed. 1997. *Education and Democracy: Re-imagining Liberal Learning in America*. New York: College Entrance Examination Board.

Ortega y Gasset, Jose. 1932. *The Revolt of the Masses*. New York: Norton.

Parker, Alison. 1997. *Purifying America: Women, Cultural Reform, and Pro-Censorship Activism, 1873–1933*. Urbana: University of Illinois Press.

Parrington, Vernon. 1927. *Main Currents in American Thought*. Vol. 1. New York: Harcourt, Brace and Company.

Patten, Simon. 1907. *The New Basis of Civilization*. New York: Macmillan.

Perry, Michael J. 1997. *Religion in Politics: Constitutional and Moral Perspectives*. New York: Oxford University Press.

Peterson, H. C., and G. C. Fite. 1957. *Opponents of War, 1917–1918*. Madison: University of Wisconsin Press.

Peterson, Linda. 1986. *Victorian Autobiography: The Tradition of Self-Interpretation*. New Haven: Yale University Press.

Phillips, Kevin. 1999. *The Cousins' Wars: Religion, Politics, and the Triumph of Anglo-America*. New York: Basic Books.

Pickus, Noah M. J. 1997. *Becoming American / America Becoming*. Durham, N.C.: Terry Sanford Institute of Public Policy, Duke University. Final Report of the Duke University Workshop on Immigration and Citizenship.

———, ed. 1998. *Immigration and Citizenship in the Twenty-First Century*. Lanham, Md.: Rowman & Littlefield.

Plotke, David. 1996. *Building a New Democratic Political Order: Reshaping American Liberalism in the 1930s and 1940s*. New York: Cambridge University Press.

"Pluralism—National Menace." *Christian Century* 68 (13 June 1951): 701–703.

Posner, Richard. 1995. *Overcoming Law*. Cambridge: Harvard University Press.

———. 1990. *The Problems of Jurisprudence*. Cambridge: Harvard University Press.

Putnam, Hilary. 1996. "Must We Choose between Patriotism and Universal Reason?" In Nussbaum, *For Love of Country*.

Rawls, John. 1993. *Political Liberalism*. New York: Columbia University Press.

———. 1971. *Theory of Justice*. Cambridge: Harvard University Press.

Raz, Joseph. 1988. *The Morality of Freedom*. New York: Oxford University Press.

Reed, James Eldin. "American Foreign Policy: The Politics of Missions and Josiah Strong, 1890–1900." *Church History* 41 (1972): 230–245.

Reichley, James. 1985. *Religion in American Public Life*. Washington, D.C.: Brookings Institution.

Reuben, Julie. 1996. *The Making of the Modern University: Intellectual Transformation and the Marginalization of Morality*. Chicago: University of Chicago Press.

Ribuffo, Leo. "God and Contemporary Politics." *Journal of American History* 79 (March 1993): 1515–1553.

Rockefeller, Steven C. 1991. *John Dewey: Religious Faith and Democratic Humanism*. New York: Columbia University Press.

Roof, Wade Clark, and William McKinney. 1987. *American Mainline Religion*. New Brunswick: Rutgers University Press.

Rorty, Richard. 1998. *Achieving Our Country: Leftist Thought in Twentieth-Century America*. Cambridge: Harvard University Press.

———. 1992. *Consequences of Pragmatism: Essays*. Minneapolis: University of Minnesota Press.

———. 1989. *Contingency, Irony and Solidarity*. New York: Cambridge University Press.

Rosen, Jeffrey. "America in Thick and Thin." *The New Republic* (5 and 12 January 1998).

Ross, Dorothy. 1990. *The Origins of American Social Science*. New York: Cambridge University Press.

Sandel, Michael. 1996. *Democracy's Discontent*. Cambridge: Harvard University Press.

———. 1990. "Freedom of Conscience or Freedom of Choice?" In Hunter and Guiness, *Articles of Faith*.

Schaffer, Ronald. 1991. *America in the Great War: The Rise of the War Welfare State.* New York: Oxford University Press.

Schmidt, Alvin J. 1997. *The Menace of Multiculturalism.* Westport, Conn.: Praeger.

Schneider, Herbert W. 1946. *A History of American Philosophy.* New York: Columbia University Press.

Schneider, Robert A. 1989. "Voice of Many Waters: Church Federation in the Twentieth Century." In Hutchison, *Between the Times.*

Scudder, Vida Dutton. 1898. *Social Ideals in English Letters.* Boston and New York: Houghton Mifflin.

Seligman, Adam B. 1994. *Innerworldly Individualism: Charismatic Community and Its Institutionalization.* New Brunswick, N.J.: Transaction Publishers.

Selznick, Philip. 1992. *The Moral Commonwealth: Social Theory and the Promise of Community.* Berkeley: University of California Press.

Shefter, Martin. 1978. "Party, Bureaucracy, and Political Change in the United States." In *Political Parties: Development and Decay,* edited by Louis Maisel and Joseph Cooper. Beverly Hills: Sage Publications.

Shils, Edward. 1997. *The Virtue of Civility: Selected Essays on Liberalism, Tradition, and Civil Society.* Edited by Steven Grosby. Indianapolis: Liberty Fund.

Silbey, Joel H. 1991. *The American Political Nation, 1838–1893.* Stanford: Stanford University Press.

Silk, Mark. 1989. "The Rise of the 'New Evangelicalism': Shock and Adjustment." In Hutchison, *Between the Times.*

———. 1988. *Spiritual Politics: Religion and America since World War II.* New York: Simon and Schuster.

Sinopoli, Richard. "Thick-Skinned Liberalism: Redefining Civility." *American Political Science Review* 89 (1995): 612–620.

———. "Liberalism and Contested Conceptions of the Good: The Limits of Neutrality." *Journal of Politics* 55 (1993): 644–663.

Skowronek, Stephen. 1993. *The Politics Presidents Make.* Cambridge: Harvard University Press.

———. 1982. *Building a New American State: The Expansion of National Administrative Capacities, 1877–1920.* New York: Cambridge University Press.

Smiley, Marion. 1998. "Moral Inquiry within the Bounds of Politics; or, A Question of Victimhood." In Fox and Westbrook, *In Face of the Facts.*

Smith, Elwyn, ed. 1971a. *The Religion of the Republic.* Philadelphia: Fortress Press.

———. 1971b. "The Voluntary Establishment of Religion." In Smith, *Religion of the Republic.*

Smith, Rogers M. 1999. "Beyond Morone, McWilliams and Eisenach? The Multiple Responses to *Civic Ideals.*" In *Studies in American Political Development,* edited by Karen Orren and Stephen Skowronek. Vol. 13. New York: Cambridge University Press.

———. 1997. *Civic Ideals: Conflicting Ideals of Citizenship in U.S. History.* New Haven: Yale University Press.

Smith, Samuel F. "My Country, 'Tis of Thee," fourth stanza.

Smith, Steven D. 1995. *Foreordained Failure: The Quest for a Constitutional Principle of Religious Freedom.* New York: Oxford University Press.

———. "The Restoration of Tolerance." *California Law Review* 78 (1990): 305–356.

Smylie, John E. "National Ethos and the Church." *Theology Today* 20 (1963): 313–321.

Stettner, Edward A. 1993. *Shaping Modern Liberalism: Herbert Croly and Progressive Thought*. Lawrence: University Press of Kansas.

Stevenson, Louise L. 1986. *Scholarly Means to Evangelical Ends: The New Haven Scholars and the Transformation of Higher Learning in America, 1830–1890*. Baltimore: Johns Hopkins University Press.

Stout, Harry S., and P. G. Hart, eds. 1997. *New Directions in American Religious History*. New York: Oxford University Press.

Stout, Jeffrey. "Commitments and Traditions in the Study of Religious Ethics." *Journal of Religious Ethics* 25, no. 3 (1998): 23–56.

Strike, Kenneth. "Must Liberal Citizens be Reasonable?" *Review of Politics* 58 (1996), 41–51.

Strong, Josiah. 1915. *The New World Religion*. New York: Doubleday, Page, and Company.

Stuhr, John J. 1997. *Genealogical Pragmatism: Philosophy, Experience, and Community*. Albany: State University of New York Press.

———. 1993. *Philosophy and the Reconstruction of Culture: Pragmatic Essays after Dewey*. Albany: State University of New York Press.

Sullivan, William M. 1995a. "Reinstitutionalizing Virtue in Civil Society." In Glendon and Blankenhorn, *Seedbeds of Virtue*.

———. 1995b. "Institutions as the Infrastructure of Democracy." In Etzioni, *Essential Communitarian Reader*.

Sunstein, Cass. 1999. *One Case at a Time: Judicial Minimalism on the Supreme Court*. Cambridge: Harvard University Press.

———. 1993. *The Partial Constitution*. Cambridge: Harvard University Press.

Swierenga, Robert P. 1990. "Ethnoreligious Political Behavior in the Mid–Nineteenth Century: Voting, Values, Cultures." In Noll, *Religion and American Politics*.

Taylor, Charles. 1991. *The Ethics of Authenticity*. Cambridge: Harvard University Press.

———. 1990. "Religion in a Free Society." In Hunter and Guinness, *Articles of Faith*.

———. 1989. *Sources of the Self*. Cambridge: Harvard University Press.

———. 1985a. "What Is Human Agency?" In *Human Agency and Language: Philosophical Papers I*. Cambridge: Cambridge University Press.

———. 1985b. "Neutrality in Political Science." In *Philosophy and the Human Sciences: Philosophical Papers II*. Cambridge: Cambridge University Press.

Thieman, Ronald F. 1996. *Religion in Public Life: A Dilemma for Democracy*. Washington: Georgetown University Press for the Twentieth Century Fund.

Tocqueville, Alexis de. 1981. *Democracy in America*. New York: Random House.

Tomasky, Michael. 1996. *Left for Dead: The Life, Death, and Possible Resurrection of Progressive Politics in America*. New York: Free Press.

Truman, David. 1951. *The Governmental Process*. New York: Knopf.

Turner, James. 1992. "Secularization and Sacralization: Speculations on Some Religious Origins of the Secular Humanities Curriculum." In Marsden and Longfield, *Secularization of the Academy*.

Tushnet, Mark. "The Constitution of Religion." *Connecticut Law Review* 18 (1985): 701–738.

Tuveson, Ernest. 1968. *Redeemer Nation: The Idea of America's Millennial Role*. Chicago: University of Chicago Press.

Vesey, Lawrence. 1965. *The Emergence of the American University*. Chicago: University of Chicago Press.

Voskuil, Dennis N. 1989. "Reaching Out: Mainline Protestantism and the Media." In Hutchison, *Between the Times.*

Walsh, David. 1997. *The Growth of the Liberal Soul.* Columbia: University of Missouri Press.

———. 1990. *After Ideology: Recovering the Spiritual Foundations of Freedom.* New York: HarperCollins Publishers.

Walters, Ronald G. 1977. *The Antislavery Appeal: American Abolitionism after 1830.* Baltimore: Johns Hopkins University Press.

Walzer, Michael. 1997. *On Toleration.* New Haven: Yale University Press.

Ward, James. "Hegel's Resolution of the Theological-Political Problem." Paper presented at the annual meeting of the American Political Science Association, Atlanta, September 1999.

Ware, Robert Bruce. "Hegel's Politics of Spiritual Expression." Paper presented at the annual meeting of the American Political Science Association, Atlanta, September 1999.

Watson, Justin. 1997. *The Christian Coalition: Dreams of Restoration, Demands for Recognition.* New York: St. Martin's Press.

Weinstein, James. 1984. *The Decline of Socialism in America, 1912–1925.* Rev. ed. New Brunswick: Rutgers University Press.

Westbrook, Robert B. 1991. *John Dewey and American Democracy.* Ithaca, N.Y.: Cornell University Press.

Whitman, Walt. 1955. *Leaves of Grass.* New York: Holt, Rinehart and Winston.

Williams, Joan C. 1998. "Religion, Morality, and Other Unmentionables: The Revival of Moral Discourse in the Law." In Fox and Westbrook, *In Face of the Facts.*

Wilson, John F. "Religion, Political Culture, and the Law." *DePaul Law Review* 41 (1992): 821–840.

———. 1990. "Religion, Government, and Power in the New American Nation." In Noll, *Religion and American Politics.*

Wilson, Major. 1974. *Space, Time and Freedom: The Quest for Nationality and the Irrepressible Conflict, 1815–1851.* Westport, Conn.: Greenwood Press.

Wilson, Woodrow. 1908. *Constitutional Government.* New York: Columbia University Press.

Witte, John, Jr. 2000. *Religion and the American Constitutional Experiment: Essential Rights and Liberties.* Boulder: Westview Press.

Wolfe, Alan. 1998. *One Nation, After All.* New York: Viking.

Wolff, Robert Paul. 1969. *The Ideal of the University.* Boston: Beacon Press.

Wood, Gordon. 1997. "Religion and the American Revolution." In Stout and Hart, *New Directions in American Religious History.*

———. 1969. *The Creation of the American Republic, 1776–1787.* Chapel Hill: University of North Carolina Press.

Wood, James E., ed. 1989. *Readings on Church and State.* Waco: J. M. Dawson Institute of Church-State Relations, Baylor University.

Wuthnow, Robert. 1994. *Producing the Sacred: An Essay on Public Religion.* Urbana: University of Illinois Press.

———. 1990. "*Quid Obscurum*: The Changing Terrain of Church-State Relations." In Noll, *Religion and American Politics.*

———. 1988 *The Restructuring of American Religion*. Princeton: Princeton University Press.

Wynn, Neil A. 1986. *From Progressivism to Prosperity: World War I and American Society*. New York: Holmes and Meier.

Young, Iris Marion. 1995. "Polity and Group Difference: A Critique of the Ideal of Universal Citizenship." In Beiner, *Theorizing Citizenship*.

———. 1990. *Justice and the Politics of Difference*. Princeton: Princeton University Press.

Zuckerman, Michael. 1993. *Almost Chosen People: Oblique Biographies in the American Grain*. Berkeley: University of California Press.

Index

Abbott, Lyman, 41, 42, 48n47
Adams, John, 25, 45n6, 111
Adams, John Quincy, 8, 35, 45n6, 52,
    111, 115
Addams, Jane, xi, 8, 24, 60, 117n15
American Association of Universities
    (AAU), 84, 95n32. *See also*
    universities / higher education
American Association of University
    Professors (AAUP), 84, 97n51,
    145n52. *See also* universities /
    higher education
American Economic Association (AEA),
    85, 94n10
anticommunism, xi, 123; and the Red
    Scare, 43. *See also* wars
Articles of Confederation, 113, 118n30

Backus, Isaac, 29
Bancroft, George, xi, 67, 70n19, 138
Bascom, John, 65, 72n43
Beard, Charles, 136, 138, 144nn58–59
Beecher, Lyman, 65, 69n6, 93n2
Bellah, Robert, 44n2, 56–57, 138–39
biblical hermeneutics, 70n22, 77, 87; and
    political theology, 70n20. *See also*
    Social Gospel / Social Christianity
Blaine amendment, 3
Bloom, Harold, 90–91, 137–38, 144nn61–
    62, 148
British Empire, 26, 111, 118n30
Butler, Judith, 27n5, 102

Carter, Stephen, 27n14
church history, 38–39, 83, 94n21; and
    political history, 2, 38–39, 134; and
    religious history, xi, 38–39, 71n32,
    94n21, 136–138; and secularization
    thesis, 30, 38–41, 61, 63, 83–86, 89–
    90, 124, 128
churches / religions: Amish, 14–16, 19–21;
    Baptist, 15, 17, 20, 28n26, 29, 60, 82,
    85, 94n21; Catholic, 3, 17–21, 24–25,
    36, 59, 62–63, 71n36, 77–81, 87–89,
    147; Church of England, 46n24, 79,
    97n56; Congregational, 23, 28n24, 38,
    48n47, 82–83, 86, 94n21, 97n50; Dis-
    ciples of Christ, 94n21; Episcopal, 36,
    46n24, 79; Federal Council of Churches,
    81, 95n22; fundamentalist, 24, 36, 40,
    43–44, 79, 81, 89, 107, 116n2, 144n62,
    147; Hutterite, 14–16, 19; Interchurch,
    82; Irish-Catholic, 18–19, 23, 36, 62, 79;
    Jewish, 13, 15, 19–21, 24, 38–41, 45n9,
    58, 62–64, 77, 147; liberal-evangelical,
    94nn9–10, 21, 97n50, 143n46; Method-
    ist, 28n26, 82, 85, 94n21, 97n54; Mor-
    mon, 18, 20, 27n18, 36, 39, 41, 79,
    94n16, 98n58, 138; National Council of
    Churches, 81–82; parachurches, 17, 24–
    25, 38, 64, 77–78, 90; Presbyterian, 16,
    38, 82–83, 94n21; Promise Keepers, 16–
    17; Unitarian, 23, 29, 36, 48n47, 67, 83,
    85–86, 90, 94n21, 98n59. *See also*
    church history

Acknowledgments

I want to thank my fellow participants at the 1996 and 1997 conferences at Georgetown University, "One Nation Under God? A Scholarly Project on the Fate of Religion in American Public Life," directed by H. Bruce Douglass and Joshua Mitchell, for helping me get this project started. I also thank Wilfred McClay and Ted McAllister, two of the editors of Rowman & Littlefield's "American Intellectual Culture" series, both for encouraging the project and for their incisive critiques and suggestions. For the same reasons I thank James Block. Over many years and through countless conversations with Russell Hittinger, Tom Horne, Michael Mosher, Paul Rahe, Nicholas Capaldi, Jacob Howland, and John Bowlin, all colleagues at the University of Tulsa, I have been fortunate to participate in a continuing informal seminar on political and moral philosophy. I hope that this book will help the conversation continue. Finally, I thank Hank Knight, University Chaplain, for making possible five glorious weeks of writing two summers ago at Wroxton College, England.

About the Author

Eldon Eisenach received his undergraduate degree from Harvard and his graduate degrees from Berkeley. His research interests center on the relationship between religion and liberal political thought in England and America, represented by *Two Worlds of Liberalism: Religion and Politics in Hobbes, Locke and Mill* (Chicago, 1981) and *The Lost Promise of Progressivism* (Kansas, 1994). He recently edited and contributed to *Mill and the Moral Character of Liberalism* (Penn State, 1998). Next year he plans to have published eleven earlier articles and essays under the title *Sacred Narrative Power and Liberal Political Truth: Essays on Hobbes, Locke, Bentham and Mill*. His next book-length project, *The Inner Light of Liberalism*, will examine the writings of a group of close followers of John Stuart Mill. Except for a year as a visiting professor (1991-1992) at Cornell University, where he had taught earlier (1970-1979), he has been chair of the Political Science Department at the University of Tulsa since 1985.